Charts: Major Skills and Tools (continued)

Skill	Tool	Page
Changing the order of series	SERIES function	194
Controlling series and categories	Paste Special command	201
Creating a chart	New command	136
Creating a chart from multiple ranges	Mouse, New command	151
Creating a combination chart	Combination command	179
Editing series names	SERIES function	194
Editing the SERIES functions	Formula bar	194
Exploding a pie chart wedge	Mouse	165
Opening a chart from disk	Open command	214
Printing a chart	Print command	156
Saving the chart	Save As, Save commands	149
Selecting a chart type	Gallery menu	141
Selecting patterns for a chart	Patterns command	169

Databases: Major Skills and Tools

Skill	Tool	Page
Built-in database functions	Paste Function command	265
Computing statistics from a database	Built-in database functions	264
Defining a criteria range	Set Criteria command	234
Defining a database range	Set Database command	229
Deleting records	Delete command	256
Extracting records	Extract command	247
Finding records	Find command	237
Formulating comparison criteria	Formula bar	235
Formulating computed criteria	Formula bar	257
Inserting records	Insert command	232
Matching data in criterion expressions	Formula bar	270
Organizing a database	Worksheet	221
Sorting a database	Sort command	221

Macros: Major Skills and Tools

Skill	Tool	Page
Choosing Relative/Absolute recording mode	Absolute/Relative Record commands	297
Controlling a recording session	Start/Stop Recorder commands	289
Naming a macro	Record command	284
Performing a macro	Run command, keyboard	292
Recording a macro	Record command	282
Running a macro	Run command, keyboard	303
Saving a macro sheet	Save As command	303
Testing a macro	Worksheet, macro sheet	292

The ABC's of Excel
on the Macintosh

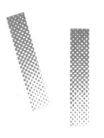

The ABC's of Excel
on the Macintosh™

Douglas Hergert

San Francisco • Paris • Düsseldorf • London

Cover design by Thomas Ingalls + Associates
Cover photography by Casey Cartwright
Series design by Jeffrey James Giese
Chapter art design by Suzanne Albertson

Library of Congress Card Number: 88-61913
ISBN 0-89588-562-X
Manufactured in the United States of America
10 9 8 7 6 5 4 3 2 1

Acknowledgments

My first thanks go to editor Jon Strickland for his graceful yet efficient work on the manuscript. In addition, I wish to thank Rudolph Langer, Dianne King, and Barbara Gordon for their ideas and help at the outset; and the following individuals at SYBEX for their work on the book: Jason Roberts, technical review; Robert Myren, word processing; Aidan Wylde, typesetting; Eddie Lin, proofreading; Suzanne Albertson, design and paste-up; Sonja Schenk and Jeff Green, screen reproductions; and Paula Alston, indexing.

Contents at a Glance

Introduction   xvi

Part I: Welcome to Excel   xx

Chapter 1: Your First Look at Excel   3

Part II: Organizing Your Data with Worksheets   29

Chapter 2: Managing Worksheet Windows   31

Chapter 3: Building a Worksheet   55

Chapter 4: Working with Formulas and Functions   83

Chapter 5: Learning More about Formulas
and Functions   109

Part III: Enhancing Your Presentations with Charts   131

Chapter 6: Creating Charts from Your Worksheet Data   133

Chapter 7: Customizing Your Charts   159

Chapter 8: Understanding the SERIES Function   185

Chapter 9: Changing the Orientation of Charts   199

Part IV: Managing Data with Excel Databases   219

Chapter 10: Working with Databases in Excel   220

Chapter 11: Performing Database Operations   245

Chapter 12: Using the Built-in Database Functions   261

Part V: Streamlining Your Work with Macros   275

Chapter 13: Recording Macros in Excel   277

Index   306

Table of Contents

Introduction   *xvi*

Part I: Welcome to Excel   *xx*

1 Your First Look at Excel   *3*

What Excel Can Do for You   4
Managing Your Personal Finances on Excel   8
Producing Scientific Worksheets   14
Using Excel in Business   16
Beginning Your Work in Excel   20
Getting On-Line Help in Excel   23
A First Look at Excel Menus   25

Part II: Organizing Your Data with Worksheets   *29*

2 Managing Worksheet Windows   *31*

The Elements of a Window   32
Scrolling a Worksheet Window   34
Using the Scroll Boxes for Localized Scrolling   34
Scrolling over the Entire Worksheet   37
Scrolling Back to the Beginning of the Worksheet   38
Using the Show Active Cell Command   39

Selecting a Single Cell   40

  Using the Mouse to Activate a Cell   40

  Using the Keyboard to Activate Cells   42

  Using the Goto Command   43

Selecting a Range of Cells   44

  Changing the Active Cell in a Range   45

  Selecting Entire Rows and Columns   46

Sizing and Moving a Window   48

Opening a New Window and Closing a Window   50

3   *Building a Worksheet*

3   *Building a Worksheet*   *55*

Entering Data into a Worksheet   56

  Entering a Column of Numbers with the Formula Bar   57

  Editing an Entry   60

  Saving the Worksheet for the First Time   62

  Inserting a Column and Entering Labels   65

  Adjusting Column Widths   67

  Formatting Numbers   70

Creating Formulas in a Worksheet   74

  Creating a Formula by Pointing   75

  Copying the Formula down a Column   77

Completing the Worksheet   78

  Inserting Rows at the Top of the Worksheet   79

  Changing Text Styles   80

  Printing the Worksheet   81

4   *Working with Formulas and Functions*   *83*

Creating the Sales Data Worksheet   84

  Opening a Worksheet File from Disk   84

Reviewing the Basic Worksheet Skills 85
More about Entering Formulas 89
Relative and Absolute References 89
Calculating with Built-in Functions 95
Testing What-if Scenarios 99
Controlling the Printing Process 102
Using the Page Setup Command 102
Using the Print Command 104
Closing the Worksheet 106

5 Learning More about Formulas and Functions 109
Continuing the Sales Data Worksheet 110
Performing a Cut-and-Paste Operation 112
Naming a Worksheet Range 114
Using a Lookup Function 117
Entering the Bonus Formula on the Worksheet 117
Copying Two Formulas at Once 120
Working with Date Values 120
Dividing the Window into Panes 121
Entering Dates from the Keyboard 122
Understanding Serial Numbers 124
Performing Date Arithmetic 127

Part III: Enhancing Your Presentations with Charts 131

6 Creating Charts from Your Worksheet Data 133
Preparing the Seasonal Precipitation Worksheet 134
Creating Your First Chart 136

Using the Gallery Menu   139

Adding New Elements to the Chart   142

Saving the Chart   149

Creating a Chart from Multiple Worksheet Selections   151

Selecting More than One Range on the Worksheet   152

Creating a Chart from the Selected Ranges   154

Printing a Chart   156

7 *Customizing Your Charts* *159*

Adding New Graphic Elements to a Chart   160

Adding Unattached Text   161

Adding an Arrow   162

Pulling Out a Wedge of the Pie   165

Modifying the Existing Format of a Chart   167

Using the Format Menu   168

Changing the Text Background   169

Adding Gridlines   171

Changing the Background of the Entire Chart   175

Changing Individual Patterns in the Chart   177

Modifying Entries on the Supporting Worksheet   178

Producing a Combination Chart   179

8 *Understanding the SERIES Function* *185*

How Excel Organizes a Chart   186

Understanding Series and Categories   188

Predicting the Orientation of a Chart   189

The SERIES Function   190

Modifying the SERIES Function   193

Changing the Series Names and the Order of the Series   194

9 *Changing the Orientation of Charts* *199*

Using the Paste Special Command 201

    Creating the Chart 202

    Completing the Chart 206

Making Multiple Selections to Control Chart Orientation 209

Using the Page Setup Command 211

Opening a Chart onto the Desktop 213

Part IV: Managing Data with Excel Databases *219*

10 *Working with Databases in Excel* *220*

Organizing a Database 221

Sorting Database Records 223

    Sorting by One Key 224

    Sorting by More than One Key 225

Defining a Database 229

    Using the Set Database Command 230

    Inserting New Records in the Database 232

    Defining Selection Criteria 234

Performing a Find Operation 237

    Multiple Comparison Criteria 240

11 *Performing Database Operations* *245*

Using the Extract Command 247

    Setting Up an Extract Range 247

    Creating an Extract Table 249

    Writing a Computed Criterion 252

Using the Computed Criterion   255

Performing the Delete Command   256

    Planning Ahead for a Delete Operation   257

    Completing the Delete Operation   259

12 Using the Built-in Database Functions   *261*

Understanding Database Functions   262

    The Arguments of the Database Functions   263

Setting Up a Statistical Table for the Database   264

    Entering the Functions   265

    Changing the Selection Criterion   269

    Specifying an Exact-Match Criterion   270

Part V: Streamlining Your Work with Macros   *275*

13 Recording Macros in Excel   *277*

Preparing a Worksheet for Developing Macros   280

Using the Recorder   282

    The Record Command   283

    Recording Your First Macro   287

    Examining the Macro Sheet   290

    Testing the Macro   292

Developing Other Macro Tools   294

    Creating a Number Formatter   294

    Creating a Title Macro   296

    Saving the Macro Sheet   303

Using the Run Command   303
Ideas for Additional Macros   303

Index   306

Introduction

Microsoft Excel, version 1.5, is a popular spreadsheet program designed for the Apple Macintosh computer. The program combines a complete set of spreadsheet operations, a powerful graphics package, a database manager, and a simple "macro" programming language—all in one integrated software environment. You can use version 1.5 of Excel on any Macintosh that has 512K or more of random-access memory, and at least one 800K disk drive. In addition, this latest version of the program extends Excel's support of computer hardware to include such features as color display and hard-disk data storage.

Whether you are working with version 1.5 or with an earlier version of the program, *The ABC's of Excel on the Macintosh* will introduce you to the most important features of this software package. In a series of hands-on exercises, you will efficiently master all of these general tasks:

- Designing and building worksheets for your own numeric applications.

- Creating presentation-quality charts and graphs from your own worksheet data.

- Working with databases, and performing basic operations such as searching, sorting, extracting, and deleting data records.

- Generating your own automatic macro programs to streamline your work in the Excel environment.

Each chapter in this book presents a short, self-contained lesson that you will probably be able to complete in a single sitting. The hands-on exercises appear as sequences of numbered steps that you should perform on your own computer. Screen illustrations accompany each exercise; as you go through a given exercise, you can check your progress by comparing your own computer screen with the illustrations presented in the book. (Depending on the type of display you are using, you may occasionally find small differences between the screens presented in this book and the organization of your own computer screen.)

This book is divided into five parts. Part I introduces you to the general types of applications you can perform in Excel. You'll learn about the features that Excel offers for working with your documents, including worksheets, charts, and databases.

Part II concentrates on the essential worksheet operations in Excel. For example, you'll learn how to

- Manage worksheet windows.
- Enter data values into the worksheet and format the data to suit your application.
- Create and copy formulas.
- Investigate "what-if" scenarios.
- Use Excel's large library of built-in functions.
- Perform disk and printer operations.

Part III shows you how to build presentation-quality charts from your worksheet data. You'll learn to take advantage of Excel's sophisticated charting package to modify and customize the charts you create.

Part IV teaches you about databases in Excel. You'll learn how to create and define a database, and how to express *criteria* for selecting records in a database. Then you'll master each of the essential database operations available in Excel: searching, extracting, and deleting records, and using Excel's special built-in database functions.

Part V introduces you to Excel's automatic macro-recording facility. In this book's final chapter you'll learn to create your own library of *macros*—useful tools that will simplify all of your work in Excel. This chapter stops short of pushing you into any advanced programming topics; rather, you'll concentrate on mastering the automatic Macro Recorder that is built into Excel.

If you have just purchased Excel, you should make a copy of the Excel program before you begin this book. Whether you are using a hard disk or an 800K removable disk, you should copy the following two files onto your working disk from the original disk you receive in the Excel package:

- The main Excel program file, called *Microsoft Excel.*
- The help file, called *Excel.Help.*

On the Macintosh desktop, you will use the mouse to drag the icons for these two files to the icon for your hard disk or 800K disk. Here are the steps:

1. Insert the original Excel program disk into an available disk drive. (If you have a system with two 800K drives, insert a blank disk into the other drive.)

2. Double click the icon representing the original program disk. This opens the window for this disk and shows you the disk's contents.

3. Position the mouse pointer over the Excel program icon. (Glance forward to Figure 1.14 if you want to see what the program icon looks like.) Hold down the mouse button, and drag the program icon to the icon representing the disk onto which you want to copy the program.

4. Release the mouse button, and wait for the computer to complete the copy operation.

5. Perform the same steps (3 and 4) to copy the help file onto your working program disk.

At the end of Chapter 1 you'll learn how to start up the program, and you'll begin your first hands-on exercise with Microsoft Excel.

PART I

Welcome to Excel

1

Your First Look at Excel

Featuring:

Worksheets
Charts
Database operations
On-line help in Excel
Excel's menu system

Within a single menu-driven environment, Microsoft Excel for the Apple Macintosh computer combines the functions and operations of three tools:

- A spreadsheet

- A chart generator

- A database manager

In this first chapter you'll learn what these three components do, and you'll begin to find out what you have in store as an Excel user. After this chapter, the remainder of the book concentrates on the details of *how* to make Excel work for you; but before you start working on those details, it's important to sit back and let your imagination wander through the endless possible uses for Excel in your personal and business life.

As is true of all good computer tools, Excel becomes more and more valuable to you as your skill in using it increases. This chapter suggests some elementary uses for Excel, as well as several more sophisticated applications. For the moment, imagine yourself as a seasoned Excel user, ready to start thinking about your own individual applications for the program. Don't worry just yet about the *how* of Excel use; concentrate for a while on the *what*.

What Excel Can Do for You

Think of any group of numbers that you have gathered and used during the course of your work at home or office. The numbers might represent any subject at all—from household financial information to business accounting records to scientific or statistical data. We frequently see such numbers arranged in rows and columns. For example, the following table of numbers contains nine rows and four columns:

26.93	14.23	4.31	13.21
20.32	9.14	0.00	6.35
28.96	11.43	0.25	8.89

4.32	14.74	12.70	7.61
15.24	27.44	27.95	20.83
36.06	35.31	42.42	29.97
18.29	25.65	20.14	20.82
14.73	30.12	57.63	49.79
23.12	26.67	27.18	25.40

You can assume that the rows and columns represent categories of some kind, and that the numbers have some central theme or reason for being arranged together in table form. However, without descriptive labels or a title, the numbers have no particular meaning or context.

Given a tabular set of numbers like this, there are several general kinds of tasks that you can perform to make the numbers meaningful, readable, and useful. Specifically, you can

- Supply labels for the rows and columns, along with a title or other text describing the table.

- Modify the format of the numbers to show what the values actually represent—for example, supply a dollar-and-cent format, a percent format, or a rounded integer format.

- Calculate additional values based on the table of numbers: totals, averages, percentages, or other statistical calculations.

- Produce a variety of pictorial charts and graphs to clarify the significance of the numbers—for example, bar charts, pie charts, or line charts.

- Treat the table as a *database*, in which each row represents a *record* of information; you might then want to select records according to stated selection criteria, for use in particular operations.

- Print the table on paper, along with associated charts or other documents.

- Store the table on disk for future use.

Microsoft Excel is a tool designed to help you perform all of these tasks simply and reliably. Jobs that would take days to accomplish by hand, or many hours with a pocket calculator, can be completed in minutes using Excel. You can begin solving problems with Excel as soon as you have the program running on your computer—even before you understand all the categories of operations that Excel can perform. On the other hand, the more you learn about Excel, the more effectively you can use its integrated tools in coordination with each other.

Like other Macintosh application programs, Excel presents documents as individual windows on the "desktop" represented by the display screen. There are three kinds of Excel documents:

- *Worksheets* designed for storing and performing operations on tables of numbers. (Under certain special conditions that we'll begin discussing in this chapter, a worksheet can also contain a database.)

- *Chart* documents displaying pictorial representations of the numbers stored in a worksheet.

- *Macro sheets* that store one or more *macros*—programs you write to automate operations in the Excel environment. (Chapter 13 introduces the subject of macros.)

You can open and work with any number of these documents on the desktop at a time, up to the memory capacity of your computer.

The primary type of document for most of your work in Excel is the worksheet. A new worksheet is organized as a vast array of empty rows and columns. The intersection of a row and a column is called a *cell*; into a cell you can enter a number, a label, or even a formula that performs a particular calculation. When you first start Excel, a worksheet named simply *Worksheet1* appears on the desktop, as shown in Figure 1.1. Notice that Excel identifies the columns of a worksheet with letters and the rows with numbers. What you see on the screen is actually only a small window to a much larger worksheet; you can use the worksheet window to view any part of the worksheet that you want to work with.

We'll begin exploring the characteristics of worksheets in detail in Part II of this book. By the way, you may often hear the terms *spreadsheet* and *worksheet* used almost synonymously. The Excel documentation distinguishes between the two terms in the following way: A *worksheet* is the document into which you enter tables of numbers,

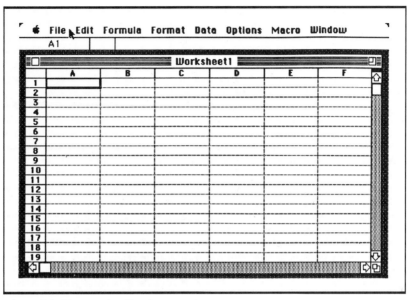

Figure 1.1: *The opening Excel screen*

labels, and formulas; a *spreadsheet* is a generic name for the Excel program itself, which allows you to work with worksheets, charts, and databases.

Figure 1.2 shows a portion of a worksheet that contains the table of numbers we looked at earlier in this chapter. In the upcoming sections of this chapter—and throughout this book—we'll imagine several diverse applications for these numbers; we'll invent a variety of different contexts in turn for the one data set.

The examples in this chapter introduce many of the Excel features that we'll be examining in detail later in this book. Here we'll concentrate on the contents of completed applications rather than on the process of producing them. Significantly, the worksheets we'll examine are displayed without the column letters, the row numbers, and the lined grid system that appear in Figures 1.1 and 1.2. Excel provides this grid for your convenience, to help you develop information on a worksheet; but the program does not insist that you retain the grid once your work is complete. You can always remove the grid display, both on the screen and on finished worksheets that you print onto paper.

Let's begin with an application involving personal finances; then we'll examine some business and scientific applications.

	A	B	C	D
1	26.93	14.23	4.31	13.21
2	20.32	9.14	0.00	6.35
3	28.96	11.43	0.25	8.89
4	4.32	14.74	12.70	7.61
5	15.24	27.44	27.95	20.83
6	36.06	35.31	42.42	29.97
7	18.29	25.65	20.14	20.82
8	14.73	30.12	57.63	49.79
9	23.12	26.67	27.18	25.40

Figure 1.2: A table of numbers stored in a worksheet

Managing Your Personal Finances with Excel

For the first exercise, imagine that you operate a small consulting business out of your home. You normally keep track of your business expenses simply by filing all your paper receipts, in no particular order, in a manila folder named *Expenses*. But you have decided to go back and examine your expenses for the last four weeks more systematically. Let's say the numbers in Figure 1.2 represent your dollar expenses for the four weeks, in nine specific categories. You would like to compute the total of each expense category, and the average weekly expense. In addition, you would like to see how each expense category relates to the total expenses for the period.

To prepare for these tasks, enter the table of numbers into an Excel worksheet document. You create a column of expense category names just to the left of the first column of numbers, and a row of column headings above the numbers. You also make room for a title. Finally, you instruct Excel to calculate a new column of numbers— specifically, the total of each expense category for the entire four-week period, as shown in Figure 1.3.

Calculating Totals

Creating the final column of totals is a simple but interesting task; you enter a formula into the worksheet to find the sum of the four numbers in each row of the table. A *formula* in Excel is simply an arithmetic expression, using familiar operations such as addition, subtraction, multiplication, and division. In response to a formula entry, Excel performs a calculation using specified numbers on the worksheet.

```
                          Four-Week  Expense  Records

                     Week  #1    Week  #2    Week  #3    Week  #4  Total  Expenses
  Books/Magazines      $26.93      $14.23       $4.31      $13.21        $58.68
  Business Lunches     $20.32       $9.14       $0.00       $6.35        $35.81
  Car Expenses         $28.96      $11.43       $0.25       $8.89        $49.53
  Computer supplies     $4.32      $14.74      $12.70       $7.61        $39.37
  Messengers           $15.24      $27.44      $27.95      $20.83        $91.46
  Office Supplies      $36.06      $35.31      $42.42      $29.97       $143.76
  Postage              $18.29      $25.65      $20.14      $20.82        $84.90
  Repairs              $14.73      $30.12      $57.63      $49.79       $152.27
  Telephone            $23.12      $26.67      $27.18      $25.40       $102.37
```

Figure 1.3: Expenses calculated in an Excel worksheet

You begin by writing a formula that calculates the sum of the four weekly expense amounts for the first category, *Books/Magazines.* You enter this formula into the cell located just to the right of the fourth expense amount in the first row of your table. As soon as you enter the formula, Excel instantly performs the expressed calculation and displays the result in the cell. In other words, entering a formula into a worksheet cell produces a specific displayed result.

After finding the total for the first expense category, you can simply copy the same formula down the worksheet, into every cell of the Total Expenses column. The result is a column of expense totals that takes only a few seconds to produce. The ability to copy formulas from one cell to another in a worksheet is one of the most important operations in any spreadsheet program; as we will see in Chapters 3 and 4, Excel makes this operation very easy to perform.

Excel also allows you to perform specific formatting operations on your data. For example, you can express the numbers on your expenses worksheet in dollar-and-cent format (such as $27.95). Furthermore, you can display the text in the worksheet (the title, column headings, and row labels) in combinations of boldface type and italics.

Creating a Pie Chart

The next task you want to perform is to produce a pie chart representing the total expenses for the four-week period. As you'll learn in Chapter 6, creating a chart in Excel is extremely simple; simply select the numbers and labels from which you want to build the chart, and then instruct

Excel to open a new chart document. Excel automatically draws the chart in the new document. You can select from among an impressive variety of chart types available in Excel, and you can perform many versatile formatting operations to customize your chart.

For example, Figure 1.4 shows a pie chart for your expense totals. Each wedge of the pie represents one of the nine expense categories. A *legend* located at the right of the chart identifies each category and shows a sample of the corresponding wedge pattern in the chart. Around the circumference of the pie, Excel has automatically supplied the percentages corresponding to the wedges of the pie.

Imagine that you want to emphasize one particular category in the chart—your telephone expenses for the period. To do so, you can pull the wedge representing this category slightly away from the center of the pie and write a short note with an arrow pointing to the wedge, as shown in Figure 1.4. Again, all of these operations require only a few seconds to perform. We'll explore these and other charting activities in Chapter 7.

Sorting and Expanding the Worksheet

Returning to the worksheet, you decide that it would be useful to rearrange the table by the numbers in the Total Expenses column. Specifically, you would like the largest total expense category to appear at

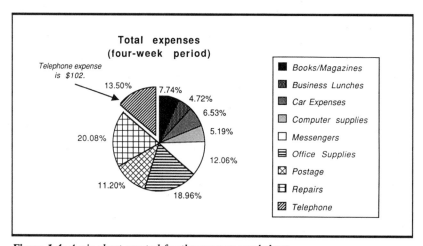

Figure 1.4: A pie chart created for the expense worksheet

the top of the table and the smallest at the bottom. To accomplish this, you perform a *descending sort* operation, using the Total Expenses column as the *key* to the sort. Given your sorting instructions, Excel rearranges the data almost instantly; the result appears in Figure 1.5. We'll discuss sorting operations in Chapter 10.

Finally, you decide to include some additional calculations in your table. A row of totals at the bottom of the table will supply the total expenses for each individual week as well as the grand total for the entire four-week period. A Percent column will show how each individual expense category relates to this four-week total. Finally, an Average column will give the average weekly expense for each category as well as for the total row.

These new calculations all appear in Figure 1.6. (As you can see, your total expenses for the period were $758.15, and your average weekly expenses were $189.54.) Again, these calculated values are very simple to produce: enter a formula into one cell, then copy the formula down a column or across a row.

As we begin examining specific worksheet formulas in Chapters 3 and 4, we'll see that individual data values in a formula are typically represented by *references* to the cells in which the values reside. In general, a reference is a way of expressing the location of a particular cell in a worksheet. For example, the cell at the intersection of column D and row 9 is named D9. A reference to D9 in a formula is one way of identifying the value currently stored in cell D9.

This leads us to a very important characteristic of worksheets. Whenever you change the value stored in a given cell, Excel

Four-Week Expense Records					
	Week #1	Week #2	Week #3	Week #4	Total Expenses
Repairs	$14.73	$30.12	$57.63	$49.79	$152.27
Office Supplies	$36.06	$35.31	$42.42	$29.97	$143.76
Telephone	$23.12	$26.67	$27.18	$25.40	$102.37
Messengers	$15.24	$27.44	$27.95	$20.83	$91.46
Postage	$18.29	$25.65	$20.14	$20.82	$84.90
Books/Magazines	$26.93	$14.23	$4.31	$13.21	$58.68
Car Expenses	$28.96	$11.43	$0.25	$8.89	$49.53
Computer Supplies	$4.32	$14.74	$12.70	$7.61	$39.37
Business Lunches	$20.32	$9.14	$0.00	$6.35	$35.81

Figure 1.5: The expense worksheet sorted by the Total Expenses column

	Four-Week Expense Records						
	Week #1	Week #2	Week #3	Week #4	Total Expenses	Percent	Average
Repairs	$14.73	$30.12	$57.63	$49.79	$152.27	20.08%	$38.07
Office Supplies	$36.06	$35.31	$42.42	$29.97	$143.76	18.96%	$35.94
Telephone	$23.12	$26.67	$27.18	$25.40	$102.37	13.50%	$25.59
Messengers	$15.24	$27.44	$27.95	$20.83	$91.46	12.06%	$22.87
Postage	$18.29	$25.65	$20.14	$20.82	$84.90	11.20%	$21.23
Books/Magazines	$26.93	$14.23	$4.31	$13.21	$58.68	7.74%	$14.67
Car Expenses	$28.96	$11.43	$0.25	$8.89	$49.53	6.53%	$12.38
Computer Supplies	$4.32	$14.74	$12.70	$7.61	$39.37	5.19%	$9.84
Business Lunches	$20.32	$9.14	$0.00	$6.35	$35.81	4.72%	$8.95
TOTALS	$187.97	$194.73	$192.58	$182.87	$758.15	100.00%	$189.54

Figure 1.6: Additional calculations for the expense worksheet

automatically recalculates formulas that depend, directly or indirectly, on that value. For instance, if you change the value stored in cell D9, Excel recalculates any worksheet formulas that contain a reference to D9. The cells that contain the recalculated formulas will instantly show the new result. We commonly refer to this feature as the *what-if* facility of a spreadsheet program. You can use what-if operations to find out what happens to a worksheet if you change one or more data values upon which calculations depend.

Performing What-If Operations

Let's look at a very simple example of this feature in the weekly expense worksheet. Imagine that you have completed all the calculations that you wanted to produce for the table—the columns representing totals, percentages, and averages for the expense categories, and the row of weekly totals. After doing all this work, you discover an overlooked expense receipt that had fallen to the floor while you were compiling your original data. It turns out that the expense amount in week #3 for the *Books/Magazines* category should be $24.31, not $4.31 as it currently appears.

You look in dismay at your worksheet, noting all the calculations that will have to be redone as a result of this single omission: the total expense at the bottom of the column for week #3 will change, as will the totals and averages for both the Books/Magazines category and the entire four-week period. Furthermore, *all* of the numbers in the

Percent column will change, since these values depend on the total expenses for the period.

Does this mean that you have to start your work over again, practically from the beginning? No, the solution to this problem is much simpler. Thanks to Excel's what-if facility, you can revise your entire worksheet by simply making one change in the original data. Excel automatically recalculates all the relevant formulas as a result of the change.

Figure 1.7 shows what happens when you change the expense figure in the Books/Magazines category in the column for week #3. (To help you see the changes that have occurred, the new values appear in boldface in this particular figure.) Comparing this new version of the worksheet with Figure 1.6, you can see that all the related calculations have been redone, including totals, averages, and percentages. Furthermore, Excel also modifies any charts that you have built from this worksheet. Clearly the ability to recalculate formulas—finding quick solutions to "what-if" scenarios—is one of Excel's most important and useful features. We'll look much more carefully at this operation in Part II.

Let's quickly review the tasks that we have seen illustrated in this expense worksheet. Many things have happened to the original data shown back in Figure 1.2. To accomplish these changes, we have used the appropriate worksheet operations to

- Insert rows and columns for labels and headings

- Format numbers in the dollar-and-cent format

Four-Week Expense Records

	Week #1	Week #2	Week #3	Week #4	Total Expenses	Percent	Average
Repairs	$14.73	$30.12	$57.63	$49.79	$152.27	19.57%	$38.07
Office Supplies	$36.06	$35.31	$42.42	$29.97	$143.76	18.47%	$35.94
Telephone	$23.12	$26.67	$27.18	$25.40	$102.37	13.16%	$25.59
Messengers	$15.24	$27.44	$27.95	$20.83	$91.46	11.75%	$22.87
Postage	$18.29	$25.65	$20.14	$20.82	$84.90	10.91%	$21.23
Books/Magazines	$26.93	$14.23	**$24.31**	$13.21	**$78.68**	10.11%	**$19.67**
Car Expenses	$28.96	$11.43	$0.25	$8.89	$49.53	6.37%	$12.38
Computer Supplies	$4.32	$14.74	$12.70	$7.61	$39.37	5.06%	$9.84
Business Lunches	$20.32	$9.14	$0.00	$6.35	$35.81	4.60%	$8.95
TOTALS	$187.97	$194.73	**$212.58**	$182.87	**$778.15**	100.00%	**$194.54**

Figure 1.7: The expense worksheet showing a what-if calculation

- Format text in boldface and italics
- Calculate rows and columns of values: totals, averages, and percentages
- Sort the worksheet by a selected column
- Produce a pie chart
- Perform "what-if" calculations

Later in this book we'll go through all of these operations step by step. But for now, let's continue exploring possible applications for the Excel program.

Producing Scientific Worksheets

The next example shows how Excel proves useful in the process of compiling data and calculating statistics for a scientific application. Imagine that you are working on a research project that requires seasonal precipitation statistics for several large U.S. cities. You have begun gathering the data, and you have organized the information in an Excel worksheet, as shown in Figure 1.8. (You may recognize the numbers in this worksheet. The table contains the same numeric data as in the previous example, but the numbers are displayed in integer format. When you select this format, Excel automatically rounds numbers to the nearest integer, for display purposes only. The numbers actually stored in memory—and used in calculations—are the same as before.)

	Average Precipitation in Major U.S. Cities *(centimeters)*			
	Dec/Jan/Feb	Mar/Apr/May	Jun/Jul/Aug	Sep/Oct/Nov
Honolulu	27	14	4	13
Los Angeles	20	9	0	6
San Francisco	29	11	0	9
Denver	4	15	13	8
St. Louis	15	27	28	21
New Orleans	36	35	42	30
Cleveland	18	26	20	21
Miami	15	30	58	50
New York	23	27	27	25

Figure 1.8: An annual-precipitation worksheet

You have two assignments in this project. First, you are to create a bar chart that clearly shows both the relative seasonal precipitation levels for each individual city and the relative total precipitation levels for the group of cities. Second, you are to compute three statistical values describing each city's seasonal precipitation—the average, the variance, and the standard deviation. (These latter two statistics show how a group of values are grouped around their own average.)

Producing a Bar Chart

The chart in Figure 1.9 shows the solution to your first assignment. Again, creating a chart from an Excel worksheet is a simple matter: you select the numbers and labels you want to include in the chart and open a new chart document. After Excel draws the initial chart, you can select the appropriate chart type and perform any number of formatting operations to make the chart conform precisely to your requirements.

In this case a *stacked bar chart* fits the application best. Each vertical bar in the chart represents the total annual precipitation for a given city in the study. Patterns inside a given bar represent the seasonal precipitation that makes up the annual total for a city. (The legend identifies the seasonal periods represented by each pattern in a bar.) In Chapter 6 you will see exactly how easy it is to produce a graph like this one. Excel's charting ability is one of the most engaging features of this integrated package.

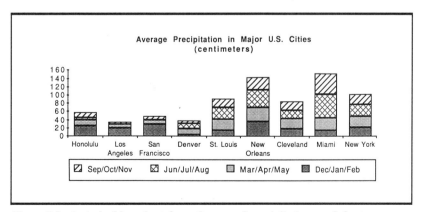

Figure 1.9: A stacked bar chart from the annual-precipitation worksheet

Calculating Statistics

Returning to the worksheet itself, you next have the task of calculating statistics from the raw data. Fortunately, Excel provides a special group of convenient tools called *functions*, designed to help you perform particular calculations. Each of these tools has a name and performs a predefined operation on worksheet data; we'll examine many of these functions in subsequent chapters of this book. For example, one of the simplest and most frequently used functions is named SUM. As its name suggests, this function adds together a sequence of numbers and displays the result of the addition in a worksheet cell.

Excel also includes built-in functions for all three statistical values you need to produce in the precipitation worksheet: AVERAGE, VAR (for the variance), and STDEV (for the standard deviation). You can use these three functions in formulas to produce the three columns of calculated values shown in Figure 1.10. If you have ever tried to perform manual calculations for the variance and standard deviation of a set of values, you will appreciate the presence of these functions in Excel's extensive library of built-in functions.

In the next exercise our table of numbers will become the annual sales records of a group of salespeople.

Using Excel in Business

Imagine that you are a sales manager for a small company, and you have been tracking the performance of a group of salespeople over the past four quarters. Figure 1.11 shows the database that you have developed for the names, regions, and quarterly sales levels of your salespeople. (Sales amounts in this table are expressed in units of a thousand dollars; for example, the figure 29.97 represents $29,970.)

In essence, the term *database* is simply another name for a table of data, in which each column in the table is identified by a unique heading. We generally use a special set of vocabulary to describe the elements of a database table:

- A *field* is one column of information in the database. For example, the salesperson database contains seven fields—for

Average Precipitation in Major U.S. Cities (centimeters)					-------Seasonal	Statistics------	
	Dec/Jan/Feb	Mar/Apr/May	Jun/Jul/Aug	Sep/Oct/Nov	Average	Variance	Stand. Dev.
Honolulu	27	14	4	13	14.670	86.654	9.309
Los Angeles	20	9	0	6	8.953	72.058	8.489
San Francisco	29	11	0	9	12.383	145.039	12.043
Denver	4	15	13	8	9.843	22.544	4.748
St. Louis	15	27	28	21	22.865	36.357	6.030
New Orleans	36	35	42	30	35.940	26.014	5.100
Cleveland	18	26	20	21	21.225	9.845	3.138
Miami	15	30	58	50	38.068	375.970	19.390
New York	23	27	27	25	25.593	3.277	1.810

Figure 1.10: Statistical calculations for the annual-precipitation data

Name	Region	First	Second	Third	Fourth	Totals
Baker, J.	North	26.93	14.23	4.31	13.21	$58.68
Smith, D.	Midwest	20.32	9.14	0.00	6.35	$35.81
Flint, M.	West	28.96	11.43	0.25	8.89	$49.53
Brown, S.	Southeast	4.32	14.74	12.70	7.61	$39.37
Vern, Q.	South	15.24	27.44	27.95	20.83	$91.46
Marlow, I.	North	36.06	35.31	42.42	29.97	$143.76
Harper., L.	West	18.29	25.65	20.14	20.82	$84.90
Fleming, N.	Midwest	14.73	30.12	57.63	49.79	$152.27
White, W.	South	23.12	26.67	27.18	25.40	$102.37

Figure 1.11: The salesperson database

the name, region, first-quarter sales, second-quarter sales, third-quarter sales, fourth-quarter sales, and total sales levels of each person in the table.

- A *field name* is the heading at the top of a given column. The field names identify and describe the data stored in the fields of the database. For example, the field names in the salesperson database are *Name, Region, First, Second, Third, Fourth,* and *Totals.*

- A *record* is one row of data in the database, usually containing one data entry in each of the field columns. For example, each record in the salesperson database contains seven items of information about a given salesperson.

Defining a Database in Excel

In Excel you can define a database explicitly by following these general steps:

1. Create a rectangular data table on a worksheet, and organize the table in the form of a database. Make sure you identify each field of the database with a unique column heading.

2. Select the entire database area on the worksheet, and tell Excel that you want to treat this area as a database.

We'll examine the steps of this procedure in more detail in Chapter 10. For now, let's see why it is an advantage to define a worksheet table as a database.

Excel offers a variety of important operations that are available only for a database. These operations all involve selecting a group of records in the database as the target of a specific action. To perform any of these operations you must define not only the database itself, but also a set of *criteria* that Excel can use for selecting particular records from the database. When you have defined both a database and a group of selection criteria, you can instruct Excel to perform the following tasks:

- Find each record that matches the criteria.

- Extract a copy of each record that matches the criteria, and store the extracted records at another location in the worksheet.

- Delete records that match the criteria.

- Perform statistical calculations on numerical values contained in records that match the criteria.

For the statistical calculations, Excel provides a special set of built-in functions that work only on a defined database. For example, DSUM finds the sum of the values in a selected numeric database field, but only adds the values of records that match the current selection criteria.

We'll discuss all these operations in Chapters 11 and 12. For now, let's return to the salespeople database for a quick example of one of the available operations—*Extract*.

Extracting Data from a Database

Imagine that you want to find the names of all salespeople who have annual sales levels over $90,000. To do this, you designate three different areas on your worksheet:

- The database itself
- The area that contains an expressed selection criterion
- The area that will be the destination of the extracted data

You can examine these three areas in Figure 1.12. The database appears the same as before, at the left side of the worksheet. In the upper-right corner of the worksheet you can see two entries:

Totals

>90

This is the selection criterion that instructs Excel to select all those records in which the Totals field contains a value greater than 90.

Just below the selection criterion you can see the result of the Extract operation. Excel has made copies of data from four records in the database; these four records represent the sales people who have made more than $90,000 in sales for the year. Of course, this example is a very small database; you can imagine how useful the Extract operation could prove to be in a larger collection of information.

Defining a worksheet table as a database does not preclude performing other kinds of operations on the table. For example, in Figure 1.13 the salesperson worksheet has been revised and expanded to present a variety of other calculations for the salespeople's records.

Name	Region	First	Second	Third	Fourth	Totals		Totals
Baker, J.	North	26.93	14.23	4.31	13.21	$58.68		>90
Smith, D.	Midwest	20.32	9.14	0.00	6.35	$35.81		
Flint, M.	West	28.96	11.43	0.25	8.89	$49.53		**Top Salespeople**
Brown, S.	Southeast	4.32	14.74	12.70		7.61	$39.37	
Vern, Q.	South	15.24	27.44	27.95	20.83	$91.46		*Name* *Totals*
Marlow, I.	North	36.06	35.31	42.42	29.97	$143.76		Vern, Q. $91.46
Harper., L.	West	18.29	25.65	20.14	20.82	$84.90		Marlow, I. $143.76
Fleming, N.	Midwest	14.73	30.12	57.63	49.79	$152.27		Fleming, N $152.27
White, W.	South	23.12	26.67	27.18	25.40	$102.37		White, W. $102.37

Figure 1.12: The Extract operation used with the salespeople database

	Bonus Table							
Sales	*Bonus*							
0.00	0.25							
50.00	1.00							
75.00	1.50							
100.00	2.25							
125.00	3.00							
150.00	3.50							

Quarterly Sales by Salesperson
(thousands of dollars)

Name	First	Second	Third	Fourth	Totals	Salary	Bonus	Salary+Bonus
Baker, J.	26.93	14.23	4.31	13.21	$58.68	$14.93	$1.00	$15.93
Smith, D.	20.32	9.14	0.00	6.35	$35.81	$13.79	$0.25	$14.04
Flint, M.	28.96	11.43	0.25	8.89	$49.53	$14.48	$0.25	$14.73
Brown, S.	4.32	14.74	12.70	7.61	$39.37	$13.97	$0.25	$14.22
Vern, Q.	15.24	27.44	27.95	20.83	$91.46	$16.57	$1.50	$18.07
Marlow, I.	36.06	35.31	42.42	29.97	$143.76	$19.19	$3.00	$22.19
Harper., L.	18.29	25.65	20.14	20.82	$84.90	$16.25	$1.50	$17.75
Fleming, N.	14.73	30.12	57.63	49.79	$152.27	$19.61	$3.50	$23.11
White, W.	23.12	26.67	27.18	25.40	$102.37	$17.12	$2.25	$19.37
Totals	$187.97	$194.73	$192.58	$182.87	$758.15			

Figure 1.13: A lookup table added to the salespeople database

Specifically, this new worksheet shows quarterly and annual sales totals, along with salary and bonus calculations. Notice in particular that a bonus table has been inserted into the worksheet above the database; this becomes a *lookup table* for finding the correct bonus for each salesperson, based on total sales for the year. We'll return to this worksheet—and discuss the idea of a lookup table—in Chapter 5.

This ends our brief tour of the three major components of Microsoft Excel. We have seen examples of worksheets, charts, and a database application. The upcoming chapters will guide you through many individual, hands-on exercises, and you'll learn exactly how to perform the various tasks we have reviewed here.

Much of your work in Excel depends on options that are available in Excel's menu system. Let's take a first look at the Excel desktop and menus.

Beginning Your Work with Excel

Now is the time to start up the Excel program on your computer if you have not done so already. (If you have not yet installed Excel for your computer, you may want to turn to the introduction for instructions.) Open the Excel program disk onto the Macintosh desktop and find the Excel icon. Figure 1.14 shows the icon for version 1.5 of Excel on the left, and the icon for previous versions on the right. *Double-click* the icon with the mouse—that is, move the mouse pointer over the icon and click the mouse button twice in quick succession. After a short time the Excel program will take control of your computer, and your screen will look like Figure 1.1.

You control activities in Excel via a set of menus represented at the top of the desktop. If you have already had experience with another application program on the Apple Macintosh computer, you will find that you already know how to perform many basic operations in Excel. You generally follow two basic steps to accomplish individual tasks:

1. Select an object on the desktop (for example, a document, a worksheet cell, a range of worksheet cells, a portion of a chart, and so on).

2. Pull down a menu and select an option to perform a specific operation on your selection.

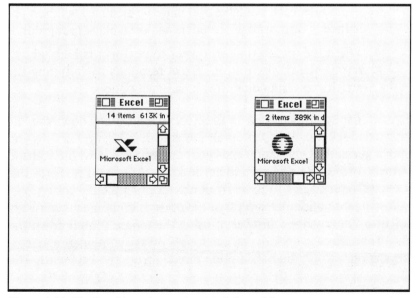

Figure 1.14: *The Excel icon for version 1.5 (left) and for previous versions (right)*

We'll see many variations of these two simple steps as we examine the various components of Excel.

To make selections on the desktop and to perform menu options, use the keyboard or the mouse, or a combination of both. Often, you will have a choice between a mouse technique and a keyboard technique for performing the same operation. As you can see in Figure 1.1, the following menu line appears at the top of the screen when you first start Excel:

File   Edit   Formula   Format   Data   Options   Macro   Window

All of these titles represent *pull-down menus*. To view a particular menu and select an option, you perform the following steps:

1. Move the mouse pointer to the title of the menu you want to work with. (As you use the mouse to move around the desktop, you will find that the mouse pointer takes on a variety of different shapes and forms. When positioned over a menu title, the pointer appears as an upward-pointing arrow.)

2. Hold down the mouse button to pull the menu down onto the desktop.

3. Move the mouse down to select a menu option. As you move the mouse, each available option in the menu list will be highlighted in turn, with white letters against a black background.

4. When the option that you want to perform is highlighted, release the mouse button. Excel responds by initiating the activity corresponding to your selected option.

As a first experiment with an Excel menu, try pulling down the File menu and selecting the Quit option, as shown in Figure 1.15. As you might guess, the Quit option ends your current session with Excel and returns you to the original Finder desktop. After you perform this exercise, return again to Excel by double-clicking the Excel icon.

You might notice that several of the options in the File menu have keyboard alternatives. Instead of using the mouse to pull down the menu and select an option, you can simply press a combination of two keys at once to perform the option directly from the keyboard. The

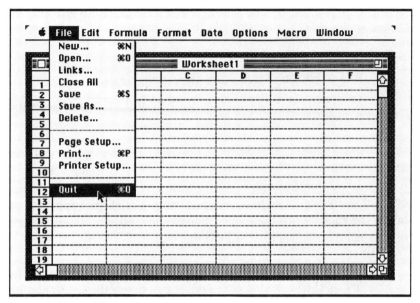

Figure 1.15: *The File menu*

first key in the combination is always the *Command key* (represented by the ⌘ icon). For example, to perform the Quit command directly from the keyboard, you hold down the Command key and then press the Q key at the same time. In this book a keyboard sequence such as this one is represented in the following form:

⌘-Q

As you start working with menus, you should know that Microsoft Excel has a sophisticated on-line Help facility. This feature can often provide you with quick but satisfactory answers to questions that might come up while you are working inside the Excel environment. In the next section you'll see how to access this Help facility.

Getting On-Line Help in Excel

There are two ways to ask Excel for help on a particular topic. The first is to invoke the About Excel command, located in the Apple menu (represented by the small apple icon at the beginning of the menu line):

1. Move the mouse pointer to the apple icon, and press the mouse button to pull down the Apple menu.

2. Select the About Excel... option and release the mouse button.

In response, the *dialog box* for the Help facility appears on the screen, as shown in Figure 1.16. This box tells you which version of Excel you are working with and the portion of your computer's memory that is still available. In addition, a list of Help topics appears in a box at the right side of the screen. You can use either of the following mouse techniques to *scroll* through this list:

• Click the down scroll arrow (at the lower-right corner of the list box) to examine options further down the list or the up scroll arrow to move up the list.

• Drag the scroll box up or down the scroll bar to move to a particular position in the list.

(You'll learn more about scrolling in Chapter 2.)

To get information on a given topic, select the topic in the list and then click the Help button at the bottom of the dialog box. (Alternatively, you can simply double-click an option in the list.) Excel presents a new box containing the Help information that you requested.

Excel also offers *context-sensitive help*. This means that you can automatically elicit help on a given topic without having to go through the About Excel... option. To do so, follow these steps:

1. Press the ⌘-? keyboard combination (that is, the command key and the question-mark key); the mouse pointer becomes a question mark.

2. Pull down a menu and select a menu option (or click an object on the desktop). In response, Excel displays a Help box describing the option or object you have selected.

To experiment with this technique, let's view the context-sensitive help for the Quit command. Press ⌘-? and then pull down the File

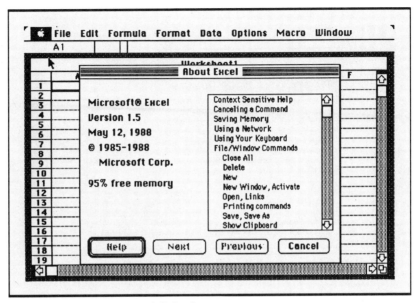

Figure 1.16: *The About Excel dialog box*

menu and select Quit. The Help box shown in Figure 1.17 appears on the screen. After you read the Help information, you can click the Cancel button to return to the Excel desktop. Note that Excel does not actually perform a menu option that you select for context-sensitive help.

Take advantage of context-sensitive help frequently during your work. You will find that it provides good, concise information about the operations of Excel.

The final section of this chapter presents a very brief summary of the Excel menu system.

A First Look at the Excel Menus

You'll be working with options located in each one of the Excel menus as you continue in this book. For now, take a moment to browse through the menus; pull down each menu in turn and examine the options displayed in the menu list.

You might notice that some menus display one or more options in light gray text. This indicates that the option is not available for use at

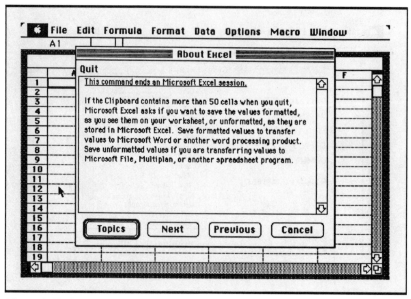

Figure 1.17: Context-sensitive help for the Quit command

the moment. Some options require specific conditions for performance; we'll see some options like this in Part II.

Each menu option represents a command that you give Excel to perform a particular operation. You'll notice that some commands are followed by ellipses (...) and some are not. When you select a command that is followed by ellipses, Excel subsequently displays a *dialog box* on the screen, offering you additional options by which you define the final result of an operation. A command that is not followed by ellipses results in an immediate action whenever you select it.

The following list summarizes the Excel worksheet menus:

- The File menu allows you to open new documents, to open documents that you have previously created and saved on disk, and to save your current work to disk. In addition, the File menu gives you three commands for sending documents to the printer. Finally, as we have seen, the File menu's Quit command ends a session with Excel.

- The Edit menu gives you commands for moving and copying information in a worksheet and for clearing information from one or more cells. Other commands allow you to insert or delete entire columns or rows in a worksheet. Edit also has an Undo command, which you can often—but not always—use to back out from a step that you have just performed.

- The Formula menu allows you to create names to represent cells or groups of cells on a worksheet. As we'll see in Chapter 5, this technique can simplify your work with formulas in a worksheet. This menu also gives you easy access to Excel's library of built-in functions and offers several other tools that help you build formulas.

- The Format menu has several important commands that allow you to specify how data should appear in a worksheet. You can control the format, the alignment, and the style of numbers and text on a worksheet.

- The Data menu has a collection of commands that you use to work with a database. This menu also has a Sort command that allows you to rearrange data in a worksheet.

- The Options menu has a variety of commands that control and modify some important aspects of Excel's behavior.

- The Macro menu allows you to create and work with macro programs, as we'll see in Chapter 13.

- The Window menu displays a list of all the documents currently open on the desktop and allows you to select any one of them for viewing or action.

Before you move on to the next chapter, you might want to take some time to read Excel's context-sensitive Help screens for a selection of menu commands. Here are some commands you could read about to prepare for Part II:

- The New, Open, Save, and Print commands in the File menu

- The Delete, Insert, Fill Right, and Fill Left commands in the Edit menu

- The Number, Style, and Column Width commands in the Format menu

PART II

Your First Look at Excel

2

Managing Worksheet Windows

Featuring:

Scrolling a worksheet

Selecting cells and ranges

Moving and sizing windows

Opening and closing documents

As we saw in Chapter 1, Excel displays worksheets inside *windows* on the desktop. An Excel window is an extremely versatile tool for viewing information; using the mouse and the keyboard, you can change the shape, size, position, and contents of a window. You can perform the following tasks:

- *Scroll* the window to view different portions of the worksheet

- *Size* the window to change its proportions and make it larger or smaller

- *Move* the window to a new position on the desktop, so that you can examine more than one window at a time

In this chapter, you'll see how to perform these operations in Excel. You'll also learn how to select cells inside the worksheet, and how to close and open a worksheet window.

The Elements of a Window

Figure 2.1 shows the opening screen that you are now already familiar with. Around the perimeter of a window, Excel displays an assortment of icons and shapes, representing the tools you use for scrolling, sizing, and moving the window. You don't need to know what these tools are called in order to use them successfully; all the same, you will want to become familiar with their names in order to understand the upcoming discussion. Refer to Figure 2.1 as you read the following summary:

- The *title bar* is the horizontal stripe at the top of the worksheet window. In the middle of the title bar, Excel always displays the name of the document; Figure 2.1 shows the default name of the first worksheet, *Worksheet1*.

- The small white square located at the left end of the title bar is called the *close box*. You use this box to close the worksheet window.

- The square icon located at the opposite end of the title bar is called the *zoom box*. You can use this box to expand the worksheet window over the entire available desktop space or to restore the original size of the window.

- The vertical gray stripe located at the right side of the window and the horizontal gray strip bordering the bottom of the window are the *scroll bars*. The arrow icons located at the top and bottom of the vertical scroll bar and at the left and right ends of the horizontal scroll bar are the *scroll arrows*. The *scroll boxes* are the white squares at the top and left of the vertical and horizontal scroll bars, respectively. You can make the scroll box slide down or across the scroll bars. All of these tools are designed for scrolling the worksheet.

- The small icon located at the far lower-right corner of the window is the *size box*; this is a tool for sizing the window.

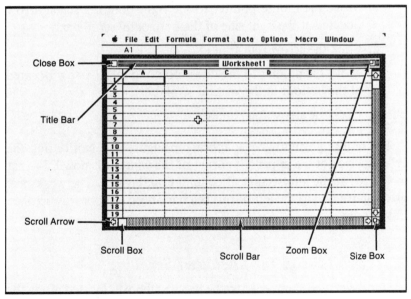

Figure 2.1: *Tools available in Excel's opening screen*

When positioned inside the worksheet, the mouse pointer takes the shape of a small square cross. However, the pointer changes to an arrow when you use the mouse to select and activate one of the scrolling, sizing, or moving tools located around the perimeter of the window. Let's see how these tools work.

Scrolling a Worksheet Window

To scroll the worksheet by one row or column at a time, you simply click one of the scroll arrows with the mouse. Each time you click the down scroll arrow, the top row of the worksheet disappears from sight and a new row appears at the bottom of the worksheet. Likewise, each time you click the right-pointing scroll arrow, the left column of the worksheet disappears and a new column appears at the right side of the worksheet. For example, watch the worksheet carefully as you perform these steps:

1. Move the mouse pointer to the right-pointing scroll arrow (located at the right side of the horizontal scroll bar).

2. Click the arrow four times.

3. Move the pointer to the down-pointing scroll arrow (located at the bottom of the vertical scroll bar).

4. Click the arrow four times.

The resulting window view appears in Figure 2.2. Notice that the cell displayed at the upper-left corner of the window is now E5—that is, the cell at the intersection of column E and row 5. The worksheet areas above and to the left of this cell have been temporarily scrolled out of sight.

Using Scroll Boxes for Localized Scrolling

Notice what has happened to the two scroll boxes located inside the scroll bars. The horizontal scroll box has moved a little more than halfway across the horizontal scroll bar, and the vertical scroll box has dropped about a quarter of the way down the vertical scroll bar. The positions of these two boxes inside their respective scroll bars indicate the current scroll position of the worksheet. To learn more about the scroll boxes, try this exercise:

1. Position the mouse pointer over the horizontal scroll box, press the mouse button, and move the box all the way over to the right side of the scroll bar. This is called *dragging* the scroll box.

2. Drag the vertical scroll box all the way to the bottom of the vertical scroll bar, using the same procedure as above.

Figure 2.3 shows the result. Cell H20 is now displayed at the upper-left corner of the window, and the worksheet display goes down to cell M38 at the lower-right corner.

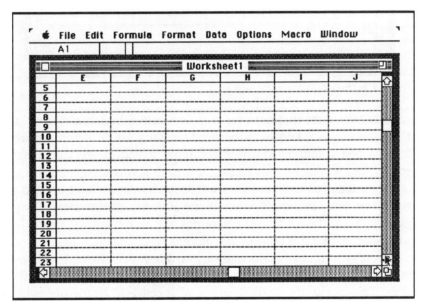

Figure 2.2: *Clicking the scroll arrows*

Of course, cell M38 is not the last cell available in the worksheet— far from it. To prove this to yourself, all you have to do is click the down scroll arrow and the right scroll arrow several more times; you'll see that the worksheet window continues scrolling down and to the right. So why have the scroll boxes stopped the scrolling at cell H20, and what exactly is the purpose of the scroll boxes?

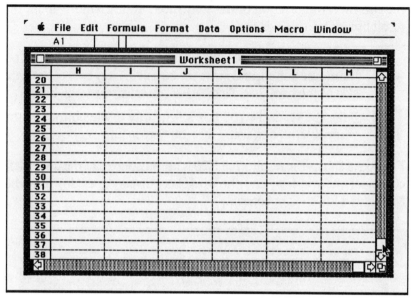

Figure 2.3: *Dragging the scroll boxes for localized scrolling*

To answer these questions we turn to a convenient new feature of Excel, version 1.5, known as *localized scrolling*. By default, dragging a scroll box results in localized scrolling, which means that Excel scrolls your worksheet only inside the area that you are actually using in the current application. For example, let's say you have created a worksheet that contains 10 columns and 30 rows of data values. Dragging the scroll boxes to their extremes will move your view of the worksheet within this table of 10 columns and 30 rows.

Before you enter any information into a new worksheet, Excel designates the first 8 columns and the first 20 rows as the default active area. This is why the scrolling stops with cell H20 in the upper-left corner when you move the two scroll boxes all the way down and to the right.

You'll have opportunities to experiment further with the effects of localized scrolling as you begin building your first worksheet in Chapter 3. For now, perform the following steps to scroll the worksheet back to cell A1:

1. Move the mouse pointer into the vertical scroll bar (any location above the current position of the scroll box) and click. The scroll box automatically jumps to the top of the bar.

2. Move the mouse pointer to the beginning of the horizontal scroll bar, and click twice. The scroll box jumps to the beginning of the bar.

As you can see, clicking inside the scroll bars has the effect of scrolling the worksheet an entire window of rows or columns at a time. At this point, cell A1 should once again appear at the upper-left corner of the worksheet window.

Scrolling Over the Entire Worksheet

Excel also gives you another way to use the scroll boxes, allowing you to scroll over the entire range of the worksheet rather than just the current active area. Scrolling over the whole worksheet requires two simultaneous actions: you hold down either of the two Shift keys on your keyboard, at the same time using the mouse to drag the scroll box.

While you are in the process of scrolling the worksheet, Excel displays the current scroll position—that is, the current column letter or row number—in the upper-left corner of the screen, so that you'll know exactly how far you have scrolled. To see this feature, keep your eye on the rectangular display area located at the upper-left corner of the desktop (just below the menu line) as you perform these steps:

1. Hold down either of the Shift keys.

2. Using the mouse, drag the scroll box all the way across the horizontal scroll bar.

3. Drag the other scroll box all the way down the vertical scroll bar.

Figure 2.4 shows the resulting view of the worksheet. Notice that the far corner of the entire worksheet is cell IV16384: the intersection of column IV and row 16384. As you have already seen, Excel identifies the first 26 columns of the worksheet with the letters A to Z. After these columns, each column is identified by a pair of letters: AA to AZ, BA to BZ, CA to CZ, and so on up to IV. This system gives a total of 256 columns.

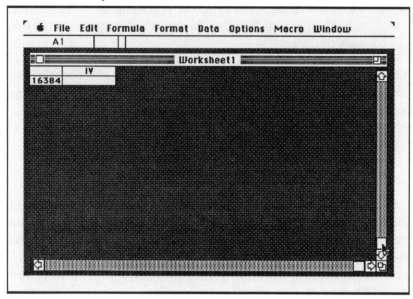

Figure 2.4: *Scrolling over the entire worksheet*

Multiplying 256 by 16384—that is, the number columns by the number of rows—you will see that an Excel worksheet has a range of over four million cells. Of course, the amount and type of information you can store in a given worksheet depends on the amount of memory in your computer.

As mentioned earlier, releases of Excel prior to version 1.5 do not have localized scrolling. If you are working in one of these older versions, you will find that dragging the scroll box always scrolls you through the entire worksheet rather than through the current active cells.

Scrolling Back to the Beginning of the Worksheet

There are several ways for you to scroll back to the beginning of the worksheet. Here are the techniques we have discussed so far:

- Click the up scroll arrow and the left scroll arrow multiple times, to scroll one row or column at a time.

- Click inside the vertical or horizontal scroll bars to scroll one window of rows or columns at a time.

- Drag the scroll boxes back to their original positions at the top and left side of their respective scroll bars.

An additional technique that you can use to scroll the worksheet is to use the Show Active Cell command in the Formula menu.

Using the Show Active Cell Command

The *active cell* is the one cell that is currently selected for accepting a data value. When you first open a new worksheet, Excel automatically selects A1 as the active cell. (Later in this chapter, you'll learn techniques for selecting a new active cell.) As you can see in Figure 2.1, the active cell has a dark black border. In addition, Excel displays the address of the current active cell in the upper-left corner of the desktop, just below the menu line.

The active cell does not change when you use the scroll bar tools to scroll the worksheet. In fact, Figure 2.4 shows that you can scroll all the way to the far corner of the worksheet without changing the status of the active cell. Since A1 is still the active cell, you can scroll quickly back to the beginning of the worksheet, so that the cell A1 is once again at the upper-left corner of the worksheet window, by performing these steps:

1. Pull down the Formula menu. (Move the mouse pointer to the menu's title and press the mouse button.)

2. Select the last command in the menu, Show Active Cell.

3. Release the mouse button.

Figure 2.5 shows how the Formula menu appears as you perform this command. As a result of the operation, the worksheet window appears once again as shown in Figure 2.1.

Now let's discuss techniques for selecting cells inside a worksheet window.

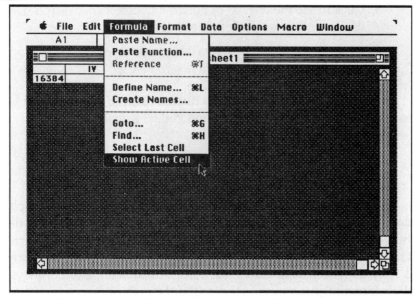

Figure 2.5: *Performing the Show Active Cell command*

Selecting a Single Cell

As you'll learn in Chapter 3, the process of entering data into a worksheet cell consists of two general steps:

1. Select and activate the cell into which you want to store a data value.

2. Enter a data value into the cell from the keyboard.

Keep in mind that the active cell on a worksheet is the one into which Excel is prepared to accept data. For your convenience, Excel gives you a variety of ways to activate individual cells while you are entering data. You can use either the mouse or the keyboard to select cells, as we'll discuss in the upcoming sections of this chapter.

Using the Mouse to Activate a Cell

The mouse provides a direct technique for activating a particular cell on the worksheet. To make a selection, you simply move the pointer to the target cell and click the mouse button. Of course, if the target cell is not currently visible inside the worksheet window, you'll have to scroll the worksheet first. For example, to select cell H25 on the worksheet, you would follow these steps:

1. Scroll the worksheet until H25 is visible in the window. (Use any of the scrolling techniques you have learned.)

2. Position the mouse pointer over the target cell.

3. Click the mouse button.

Figure 2.6 shows the result of this elementary but essential activity. Notice the two changes that have taken place on the desktop:

- Cell H25 is now enclosed in a dark border, the visual marker for an active cell.

- The address of the new active cell is displayed at the upper-left corner of the desktop.

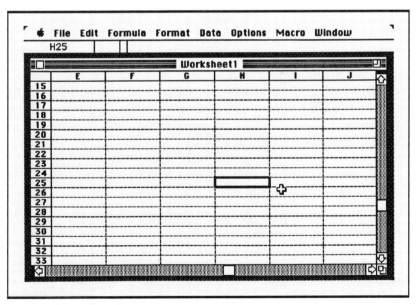

Figure 2.6: *Changing the active cell on a worksheet*

Using the mouse is convenient and fast when you want to select a cell that is far away from the current cell selection. However, when you are entering data you will sometimes want a faster way to select consecutive or adjacent cells—for example, when you are entering an entire column or row of data in one input sequence. In this case, you'll prefer to use the keyboard to activate cells.

Using the Keyboard to Activate Cells

Excel provides four distinct keyboard techniques for activating a cell that is adjacent to the currently selected cell:

- Press the Enter key to activate the cell located immediately below the current cell.

- Press Shift-Enter to activate the cell above the current cell.

- Press the Tab key to activate the cell to the right of the current cell.

- Press Shift-Tab to activate the cell to the left of the current cell.

Take a few moments now to experiment with each of these operations. You'll find that Excel automatically scrolls the worksheet, if necessary, to display a consecutive or adjacent cell that is not currently displayed in the window. For example, let's say your worksheet appears as in Figure 2.6. You can perform the following steps as an experiment with the Return key:

1. Press Return eight times, to activate each consecutive cell from H26 to H33 in turn.

2. Press Return another time to scroll the worksheet by one row and to activate cell H34.

The Return key and Tab key actually perform dual roles in the data-entry process; in addition to activating a nearby cell, each of these keys also completes the current data entry. We'll explore this point further in Chapter 3.

Using the Goto Command

The Goto command in the Formula menu provides a quick way to activate and display a cell that does not currently appear inside the worksheet window. You can now perform the following steps to activate cell A1 and to scroll the window back to its original view of the worksheet:

1. Pull down the Formula menu, and select the Goto command. A *dialog box* appears on the screen.

2. From the keyboard, enter the address of the cell that you want to activate—in this case A1, as shown in Figure 2.7.

3. Press Return (or click OK with the mouse) to complete the operation.

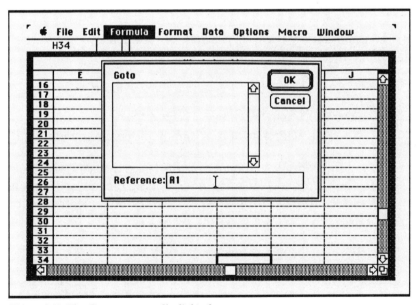

Figure 2.7: *The Goto command's dialog box*

When you pull down the Formula menu, you'll notice that Excel provides a keyboard alternative for the Goto command. You can bring up the Goto dialog box directly by pressing the ⌘-G keyboard combination.

Take a moment to study the elements of the Goto command's dialog box. In the upper-right corner of the box are two *buttons* that you can click with the mouse: OK, to complete the operation, or Cancel, to back out of the operation. At the bottom of the dialog box there is an *edit box* into which you enter the target cell reference. The rest of the space is occupied by a *list box*, which is currently empty. You'll learn more about the Goto command in later chapters.

In a number of Excel operations, you need to be able to select an entire *range* of cells rather than just a single cell. A range is a rectangular area on the worksheet, consisting of a number of consecutive and/or adjacent cells. We'll discuss techniques for selecting ranges in the following section.

Selecting a Range of Cells

You can select a vertical, horizontal, or rectangular range of cells, including the following groupings:

- A range of consecutive cells in a given column

- A range of adjacent cells in a given row

- A rectangular range of cells in multiple columns and rows

To do so, simply drag the mouse over the range that you wish to select. To select a rectangular range of cells, drag the mouse from one corner of the range to the opposite corner. For example, try the following steps to select the range from B4 to E10:

1. Position the mouse pointer over cell B4.

2. Hold down the mouse button, and drag the mouse pointer to cell E10. Before you release the mouse button, notice that Excel displays the following message at the upper-left corner of the desktop (in the space where the address of the active cell normally appears):

   7R × 4C

   This tells you that the range you are currently selecting contains seven rows and four columns.

3. Release the mouse button.

When you complete these steps, your worksheet will appear as shown in Figure 2.8. The range selection appears as a rectangle of black cells inside the worksheet window.

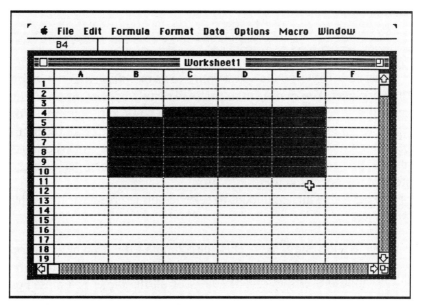

Figure 2.8: *Selecting a range of cells*

Changing the Active Cell in a Range

Inside the selected range, cell B4 is the active cell, shown as the one white cell in the range. When you select a range, the first cell that you click with the mouse initially becomes the active cell. However, you can use the Return key or the Tab key to activate another cell inside the range. For example, try this experiment:

1. Press the Return key six times to activate cells from B4 to B10.

2. Press the Return key again to activate the next cell in the range, C4.

3. Keep pressing Return until you have gone through all four columns of cells in the range, and cell E10 is active.

4. Press Return a final time to jump back to cell B4.

As you can see, pressing Return moves you cell by cell through each column of the selected range, and then finally back to the beginning. Alternatively, the Tab key moves you row by row through the range. Shift-Return and Shift-Tab move backward through the range.

Selecting Entire Rows or Columns

Excel also allows you to select entire rows or columns as ranges on the worksheet. You may want to perform certain operations on all the cells of a given row, column, or range of rows and columns. For example, you might want to specify a display format for all the numbers that you enter into a particular column on the worksheet. As always, you must first select the target range and then perform the steps of the operation itself.

Use the following techniques to select columns, rows, or the entire worksheet:

*   To select one column, click the column's letter heading at the top of the worksheet. To select a range of adjacent columns, drag the mouse over the letter headings of all the target columns. For example, Figure 2.9 shows a worksheet in which columns B, C, and D have been selected.

*   To select one row, click the row's numeric heading, at the left side of the worksheet. To select a range of consecutive rows, drag the mouse down the headings of all the target rows. Figure 2.10 shows a selection of rows 7 through 11.

*   To select the entire worksheet, click the small rectangle located at the intersection of the row and column headings. Figure 2.11 shows a selection of the entire worksheet. (The mouse pointer is still positioned over the rectangle that you use to select the entire worksheet.)

You'll see specific applications for these range selections in later chapters. We'll end this chapter with a quick look at a few more window techniques—specifically, techniques for sizing, moving, opening, and closing windows.

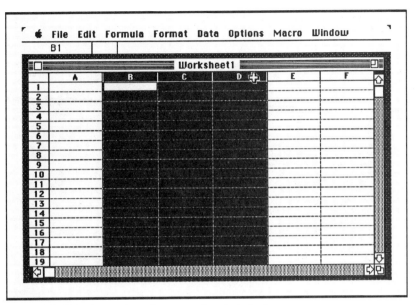

Figure 2.9: Selecting entire columns on the worksheet

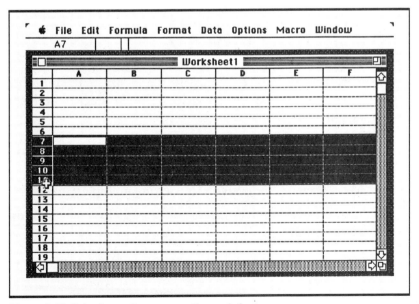

Figure 2.10: Selecting entire rows on the worksheet

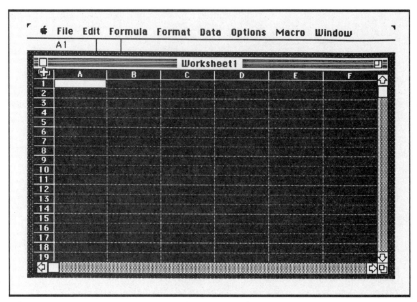

Figure 2.11: *Selecting the entire worksheet*

Sizing and Moving a Window

Sometimes you may need to change the shape, size, and position of a particular worksheet window on the desktop, in order to perform any of the following format changes:

- Display and examine a small essential portion of the worksheet, and temporarily hide other portions from view

- Make room on the desktop for viewing multiple windows

- Improve the convenience and clarity of the desktop arrangement

You can use the mouse to size and move the worksheet window on the desktop. You'll recall that the size box is the small square icon located at the far lower-right corner of the worksheet window (see Figure 2.1). To make the window smaller, drag this box up and to the left.

For example, let's say you want a window that displays a three-column by ten-row portion of the worksheet. To size the window appropriately, perform these steps:

1. Position the mouse pointer over the size box.

2. Hold down the mouse button as you drag the size box up and to the left. A ghost image of the new worksheet boundaries appears superimposed over the current worksheet, as shown in Figure 2.12.

3. When you have arrived at the new worksheet size that you want to work with, release the mouse button. You can see the result of the operation in Figure 2.13.

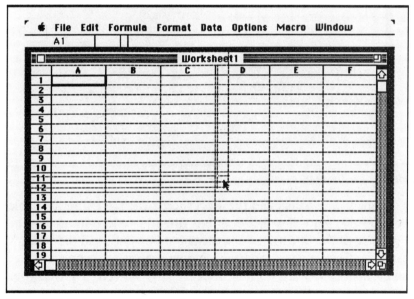

Figure 2.12: *Sizing the worksheet window*

Now let's say you want to move the worksheet window to the approximate center of the desktop. To perform this task, drag the worksheet's title bar using the following steps:

1. Position the mouse pointer over the title bar.

2. Drag the window to the center of the desktop. A thin black border represents the new position of the window, as shown in Figure 2.14.

3. Release the mouse button to complete the move. Figure 2.15 shows the changes to the desktop.

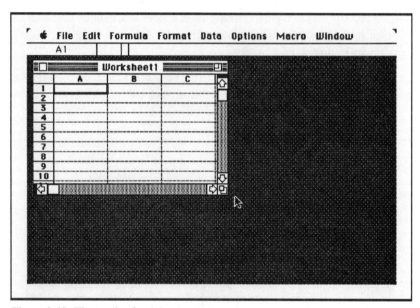

Figure 2.13: *The result of a sizing operation*

A quick way to expand the worksheet over the entire available desktop area is to click the zoom box (the square icon located at the right side of the title bar). Click the zoom box once and the window expands. Click it again, and the window returns to its previous size and shape. If you are working with an early version of Excel, your windows may not have zoom boxes. In this case, you must use an alternative technique to zoom the window: double-click the title bar— that is, position the mouse pointer over the title bar and quickly click the mouse button twice in succession.

Opening a New Window and Closing a Window

Excel allows you to work with multiple worksheets on the desktop at once. Use the New command (in the File menu) to open additional

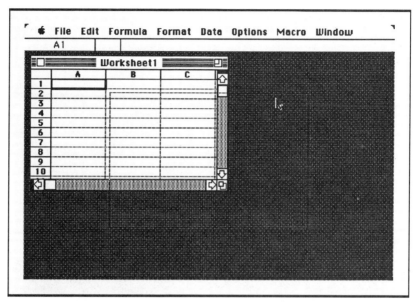

Figure 2.14: *Moving the window*

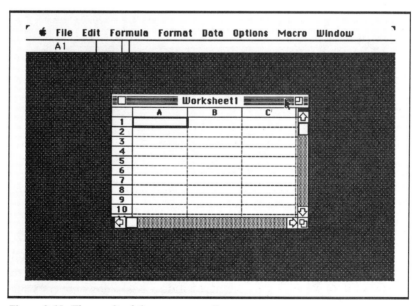

Figure 2.15: *The result of the move operation*

new worksheets onto the desktop. You can use either of the following techniques to invoke the New command:

- Use the mouse to pull down the File menu and select New.

- Press ⌘-N from the keyboard.

In either case, the New dialog box appears on the screen, as shown in Figure 2.16. This box gives you a choice among the three different types of document windows you can open: a worksheet, a chart, or a macro sheet. By default, Excel expects that you want to open a new worksheet, so all you have to do is press Return (or click the OK button) to complete the operation.

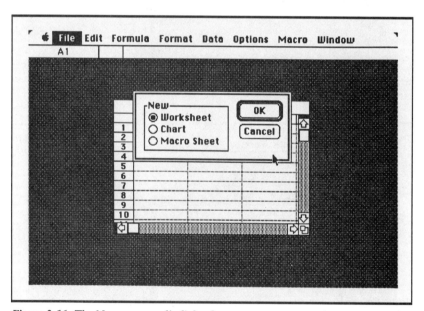

Figure 2.16: *The New command's dialog box*

A new worksheet appears on the desktop, named Worksheet2. (Subsquent new worksheets that you open onto the desktop are called Worksheet3, Worksheet4, and so on.) Since you have changed the size and position of Worksheet1, the new window completely covers your original worksheet. However, you can use the Window menu to select and activate the hidden window.

The Window menu presents a list of all the windows that are currently open on the desktop (Figure 2.17). To view a hidden window, you simply select the window from the list. For example, follow these steps to view the hidden Worksheet1:

1. Pull down the Window menu and select Worksheet1 from the list of document names.

2. Release the mouse button.

Worksheet1 will appear superimposed over the larger Worksheet2 window.

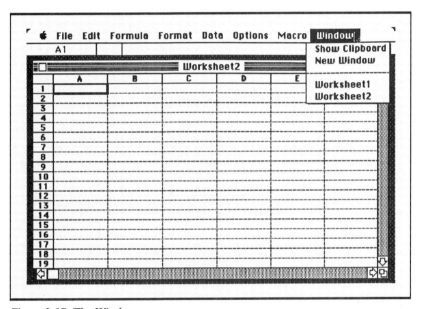

Figure 2.17: The Window menu

You can close a document by simply clicking the window's close box, located at the left side of the title bar. If you have not done any work on the window yet, Excel closes the window immediately. For example, to close Worksheet2, perform the following steps:

1. Position the mouse pointer over the close box (see Figure 2.1).

2. Click the mouse button.

Since you have not done any work yet on Worksheet2, the window disappears immediately. In contrast, if you had already entered data into the worksheet, Excel would ask you if you wanted to save the document onto disk.

You have learned a large variety of window operations: scrolling the worksheet; activating cells and selecting ranges; sizing, moving, and zooming the window; opening a new window; and closing a window. You'll continue to practice these operations in Chapter 3, as you begin building your first worksheet.

3

Building
a Worksheet

*F*eaturing:

*Entering and
formatting data*

*Creating and copying
formulas*

*Saving and printing a
worksheet*

This chapter guides you through the first steps of developing a practical worksheet application. Specifically, you'll create a worksheet that records weekly business expenses, organized by categories. You'll learn how to enter data into worksheet cells, and how to perform several menu operations to change the appearance of the data. You'll also create a simple formula on the worksheet and then copy the formula down the cells of a column. Finally, you'll learn how to print and save your worksheet. In short, this chapter introduces you to the basic skills you'll need to build successful worksheets.

Entering Data Into a Worksheet

For this chapter's exercise, we'll start again with Excel's first worksheet window, named Worksheet1. If you have quit Excel since the previous chapter, start the program up again now. (If your work from Chapter 2 is still displayed on the screen and the desktop looks like Figure 2.15, click the zoom box of Worksheet1 to expand the window over the entire desktop space.)

We'll be working with the small table of numbers that we first examined in Chapter 1:

26.93	14.23	4.31	13.21
20.32	9.14	0.00	6.35
28.96	11.43	0.25	8.89
4.32	14.74	12.70	7.61
15.24	27.44	27.95	20.83
36.06	35.31	42.42	29.97
18.29	25.65	20.14	20.82
14.73	30.12	57.63	49.79
23.12	26.67	27.18	25.40

Your first activity in this chapter will be to enter these numbers into the worksheet. (You'll also save them as a file on disk so that you can reuse this table in other exercises later in this book.) As you enter the numbers, you'll learn editing techniques for correcting any data-entry errors that you might make. Then you'll begin developing a version of the weekly expense worksheet, first described in Chapter 1. For a review of this worksheet—and a preview of this chapter's hands-on exercise—take a quick look back at Figure 1.3.

Entering a Column of Numbers

There are two steps in the process of entering a data value into a selected worksheet cell:

1. Activate the cell into which you want to enter a value.

2. Enter the value itself from the keyboard.

The data table you'll be working with in this chapter contains nine rows and four columns of numeric values. You'll enter these values into cells ranging from A1 down to D9, activating each cell in turn inside this range.

To start out, select cell A1 (if this cell is not already active on your worksheet) and begin entering the digits of the first data value:

26.93

As you type this value from the keyboard, notice the changes that take place on the desktop. The value itself appears in two places while you type (see Figure 3.1): inside the worksheet cell itself, and inside the horizontal work space located immediately below the desktop menu. This latter space, called the *formula bar*, is a very important part of the desktop. Let's see how it works.

Any time you enter a numeric value, a text value, or a formula into a worksheet cell, the entry appears on the formula bar. You can use the formula bar to examine your entry and to edit it as you type from the keyboard. A blinking vertical line inside the formula bar is the *cursor* that marks your current position in the entry. Each time you type a character or digit from the keyboard, the cursor moves forward. Alternatively, you can press the Backspace key to move the cursor backward and to erase the last character you typed. (You can also double-click the formula bar with the mouse to select a single entry or a word of text. Subsequently pressing the Backspace key erases the highlighted portion of the formula bar.)

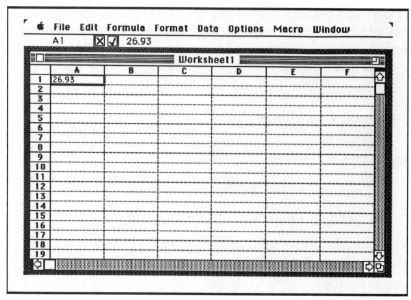

Figure 3.1: *Entering a value into a worksheet cell*

When the formula bar is active, Excel offers you tools for confirming or cancelling the current data-entry process. These tools are represented by two small boxes located just to the left of the data-entry point in the formula bar, as you can see in Figure 3.1. These boxes serve important purposes in the process of entering a data value:

- The first box, filled with an X, is called the *cancel box*. You can click this box with the mouse to cancel the current entry if you change your mind at some point in the process. (Alternatively, you can cancel an entry directly from the keyboard by pressing the ⌘-. key combination—the Command key along with the period key.) No matter how many digits or characters you have entered from the keyboard, Excel deactivates the formula bar when you click the cancel box. The active cell reverts to its previous contents; if the cell was empty, it remains empty.

- The second box, enclosing a check-mark, is the *enter box*. You can click this box to complete a data entry. In response, Excel stores the entry in the active cell and deactivates the formula bar.

The equivalent action from the keyboard is pressing the Enter key, which completes an entry without moving to a new cell.

Returning now to your work on Worksheet1, make sure you have typed the first number of the data table correctly, and then click the enter box next to the formula bar. Watch what happens on the desktop. The cancel box and enter box disappear, signifying that the formula bar is no longer active; however, the formula bar still displays the value you have just entered.

Cell A1 remains the active cell and Excel displays the number 26.93 at the right side of the cell. This automatic alignment illustrates an important point: by default, Excel *right-justifies*—aligns the right edge of the rightmost digit at the rightmost point—a numeric value that you enter into a cell. You'll learn later in this chapter how to change the alignment of a data value in a cell.

As you may recall from Chapter 2, there are several different ways to complete your data entry and select an adjacent cell, using the Tab key or the Return key. To review, the Tab key completes the entry and activates the next cell to the right in the current row; Shift-Tab activates the cell to the immediate left; the Return key activates the next cell down the current column; and Shift-Return activates the cell immediately above in the column.

To continue the expenses worksheet, use the Return key to enter the remaining eight numbers into the first column of the table, from cells A2 to A9. Type the column as follows:

	A
1	26.93
2	20.32
3	28.96
4	4.32
5	25.24
6	36.06
7	18.29
8	14.73
9	23.12

After you enter a group of numeric values like this one, you will normally want to look back to check your work. The final results of a worksheet application are only as accurate as the original data that you supply. For this reason, it is important to check your data before you begin calculating values.

If you proofread this column against the original data table in Figure 1.3, you'll notice that the fifth entry—in cell A5—is not correct. We have supplied the number 25.24, whereas the value in the original table is 15.24. (In this case the error is intentional; however, input errors are probably the single most important cause of inaccuracies in worksheet applications.) We'll look at ways to correct this entry in the next section.

Editing an Entry

One simple way to correct a typographical error is to reenter the value into the cell. For example, you could activate cell A5 and simply enter the correct value, 15.24. As a result, the previous value is replaced by the new entry.

A more sophisticated technique is to use the formula bar to change individual digits or characters in an entry. This technique is most appropriate when the entry in a cell is long or complex. Nonetheless, to get some practice, we'll use this technique to change the value currently stored in cell A5 using the following steps:

1. Activate cell A5. As usual, the contents of the active cell appear inside the formula bar.

2. Point to the formula bar and click. This activates the formula bar and displays the cancel box and the enter box, as shown in Figure 3.2. Inside the formula bar, the mouse pointer is a short vertical line with inverted arrowheads on each end.

3. Use the mouse to select the first digit of the entry in the formula bar: Position the pointer between the 2 and the 5, hold down the mouse button, and drag the pointer to the left. The first digit, 2, is highlighted against a black background, as shown in Figure 3.3.

4. From the keyboard, enter the correct digit, 1. This entry takes the place of the highlighted digit in the formula bar.

5. Complete the entry either by clicking the enter box or pressing the Enter key. The worksheet now appears as shown in Figure 3.4.

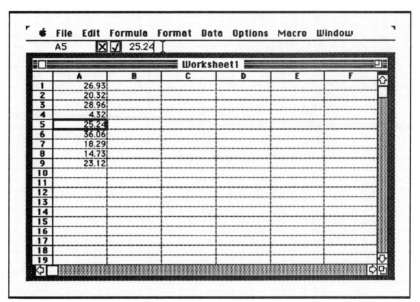

Figure 3.2: *Activating the formula bar*

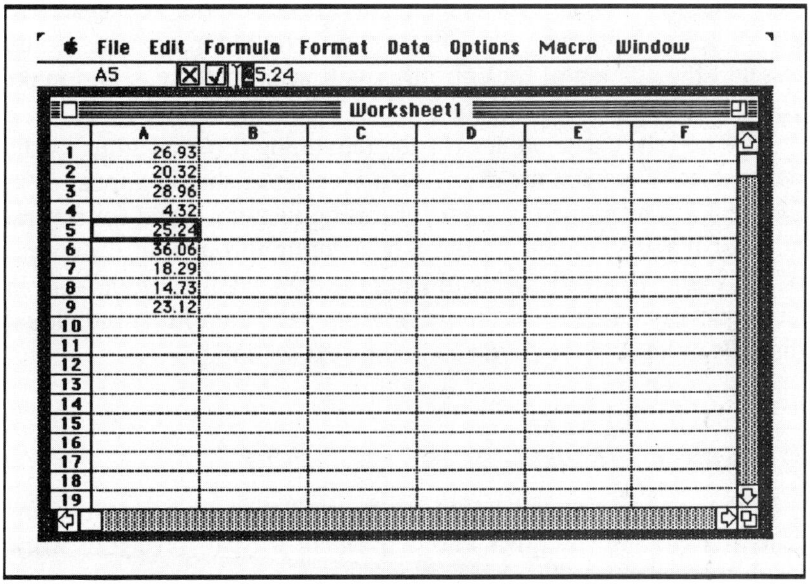

Figure 3.3: *Editing a data value in the formula bar*

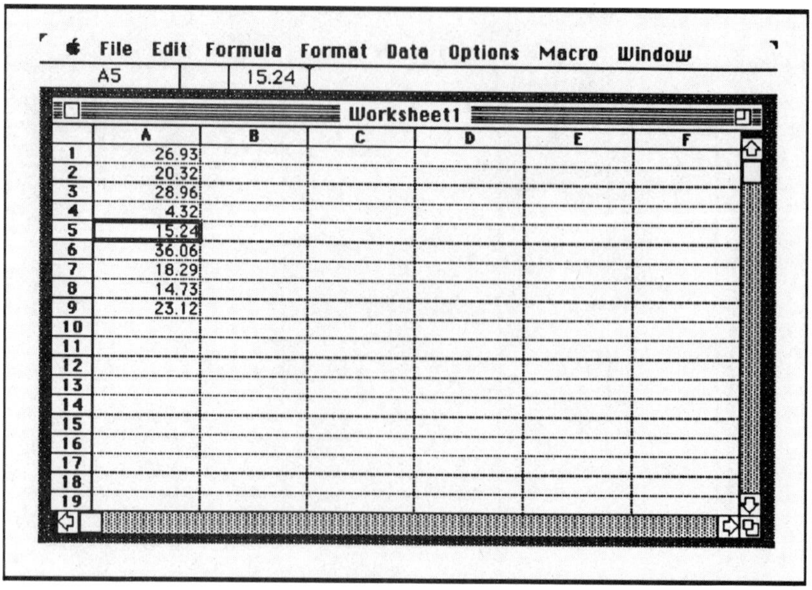

Figure 3.4: *Completing the edit operation*

As this exercise demonstrates, the formula bar is a versatile tool that you can use to edit the contents of any cell on the worksheet. To do so, select the target cell, activate the formula bar, use the mouse to select the portion of the entry that you want to change, and make your changes from the keyboard.

Now enter the data values for the remaining three columns of the data table. When you are done, your worksheet should appear as in Figure 3.5. This is the raw data for this application—and for several additional applications that you'll be creating throughout the course of this book. To avoid having to enter the data again for your work in subsequent chapters, you should now save the data in an individual disk file of its own. You'll do so in the next section.

Saving the Worksheet for the First Time

Like most major application programs for the Macintosh computer, Excel gives you quick and convenient ways to save your work on disk. You'll usually want to perform save operations at several points during the development of a worksheet, so that you can be rela-

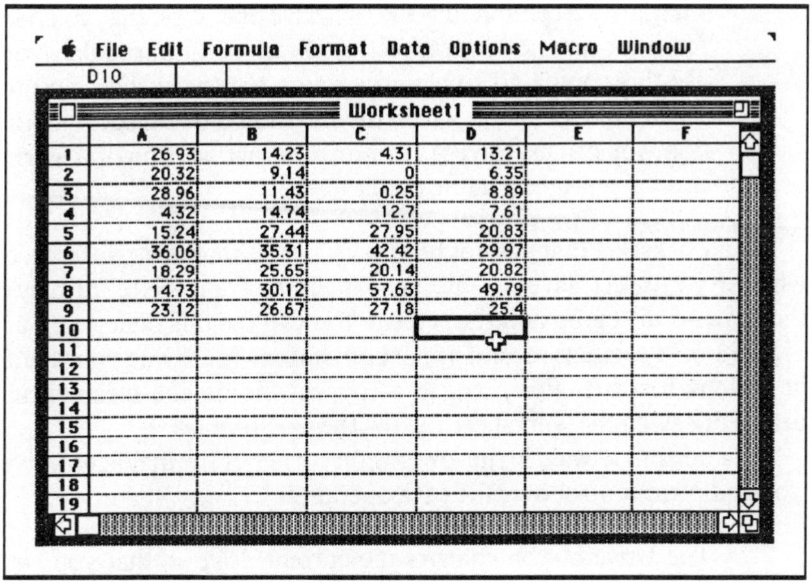

Figure 3.5: *The completed worksheet data*

tively sure that you will not lose any work that you have already completed.

If you pull down the File menu—that is, position the mouse pointer over the word *File* in the menu line and click the mouse button—you'll find that Excel offers two different commands for saving files to disk:

Save   ⌘S
Save As...

These commands are designed for use in two distinct situations, which we can summarize as follows:

- The Save command saves the current version of your worksheet in a file on disk. You will use Save only after you have already saved the worksheet at least once before. As a result of this command, the existing worksheet file stored on disk is replaced by the new version of your worksheet, as currently displayed on the desktop. Notice that the Save command has a keyboard alternative (⌘-S), so that you can perform this important operation conveniently and frequently.

- The Save As command is the first save operation that you perform for any new worksheet application. In particular, you use this command to assign a name to a worksheet and to specify the format in which the file should be saved. In addition, you can use Save As to store a second version of a worksheet under a new name on disk.

For a worksheet that has not been saved yet, it makes no difference whether you select Save or Save As—in either event, Excel displays the Save As dialog box on the screen. You can see this dialog box in Figure 3.6. It contains several important options for saving your data in various formats. For now, let's concentrate on the mechanical details of saving the worksheet file for the first time.

Four buttons located in the lower-right corner of the dialog box give you complete control over the save operation:

- The Drive button changes the current drive so that you can choose any available disk device for saving your file.

- The Eject button allows you to eject the disk from the current drive, so that you can insert another disk for saving your file.

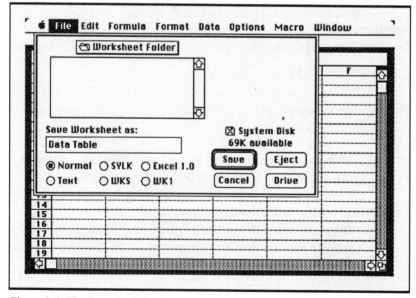

Figure 3.6: *The Save As dialog box*

- The Save button performs the save operation.

- The Cancel button cancels the operation.

We'll save the worksheet in its current form in a file named *Data Table*. Follow these steps to save the file:

1. Use the Drive and Eject buttons, if necessary, to select the drive and disk on which you want to save your file.

2. Enter the name **Data Table** as the name of the worksheet.

3. Click the Save button to complete the operation.

Back on the desktop, you'll see that the new name of the worksheet is *Data Table*.

Next we'll begin transforming this table of raw data into a real worksheet application.

Inserting a Column and Entering Labels

To identify the expense categories in this worksheet, the first thing we need to do is make room for a column of labels at the left side of the data table. We'll use the Insert command from the Edit menu to accomplish this. This command inserts one or more rows or columns at a specified location in the worksheet. In this case, we want to insert a new blank column at the location of column A, and move the data table to the right by one column.

Here are the steps for performing this operation:

1. Use the mouse to click the heading of column A, selecting the entire column.

2. Pull down the Edit menu, and select the Insert command. (Alternatively, you can use the keyboard combination ⌘-I to perform the Insert command.)

The result of these steps appears in Figure 3.7. The data table is now stored in the range of cells from B1 to E9, and column A is blank. We'll enter a series of labels into this column, identifying the nine expense categories.

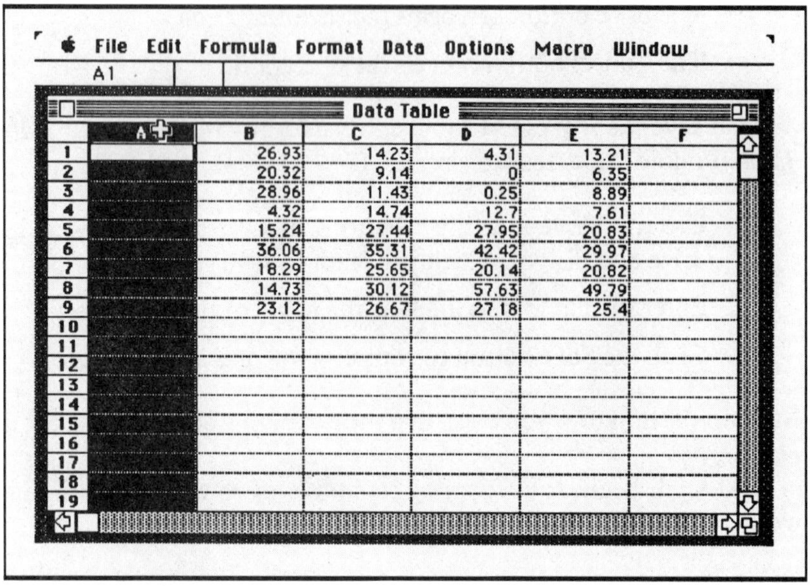

Figure 3.7: *Inserting a column*

Begin by activating cell A1, and then enter the following labels into cells A1 to A9:

Books/Magazines
Business Lunches
Car Expenses
Computer Supplies
Messengers
Office Supplies
Postage
Repairs
Telephone

You'll notice that Excel left-justifies each text value in its respective cell.

Unfortunately, column A is not wide enough to display the longest of these labels in full. Since column B already contains other data, Excel is limited to the current width of column A for displaying the labels. For this reason, you'll want to increase the width of column A. In addition, you may want to decrease the width of columns B through E, since the numeric data values do not seem to require the full default column width. In the next section you'll learn two ways to change column widths.

*A*djusting Column Widths

Most new Excel users—especially those who have already worked with some other spreadsheet program—are delighted to find out how easy it is to change the width of a column. You can use the mouse in Excel to drag the vertical border line (located at the right side of a given column) in either direction. Dragging to the right increases the width, and dragging to the left decreases the width.

To perform this operation, begin by positioning the mouse pointer directly over the short vertical line located between one column heading and the next. For example, if you want to change the width of column A, you select the border line between the A heading and the B heading. As you do so, the mouse pointer changes its shape again, becoming a small cross with arrow heads pointing to the right and to the left, as shown in Figure 3.8. When this special icon appears on the desktop, you know that you have positioned the mouse pointer correctly for a column width adjustment.

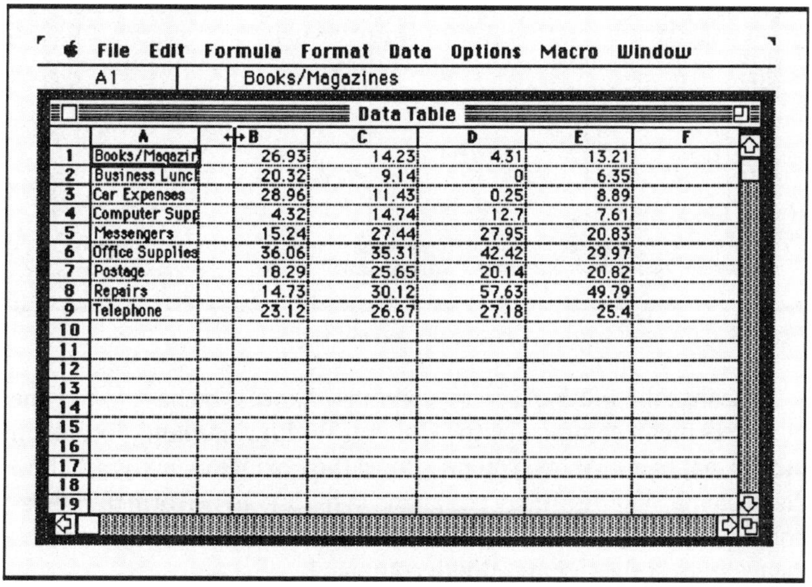

	A	**B**	**C**	**D**	**E**	**F**
1	Books/Magazir	26.93	14.23	4.31	13.21	
2	Business Lunc	20.32	9.14	0	6.35	
3	Car Expenses	28.96	11.43	0.25	8.89	
4	Computer Supp	4.32	14.74	12.7	7.61	
5	Messengers	15.24	27.44	27.95	20.83	
6	Office Supplies	36.06	35.31	42.42	29.97	
7	Postage	18.29	25.65	20.14	20.82	
8	Repairs	14.73	30.12	57.63	49.79	
9	Telephone	23.12	26.67	27.18	25.4	

Figure 3.8: Using the mouse to increase the width of a column

Here are the steps for increasing the width of column A so that the entire width of each label will come into view:

1. Position the mouse pointer over the line between the A heading and the B heading.
2. Hold down the mouse button, and drag the pointer to the right by about half an inch.
3. Release the mouse button.

When you complete these steps, your worksheet should appear as shown in Figure 3.9. If you are not happy with the resulting width, you can simply repeat the process.

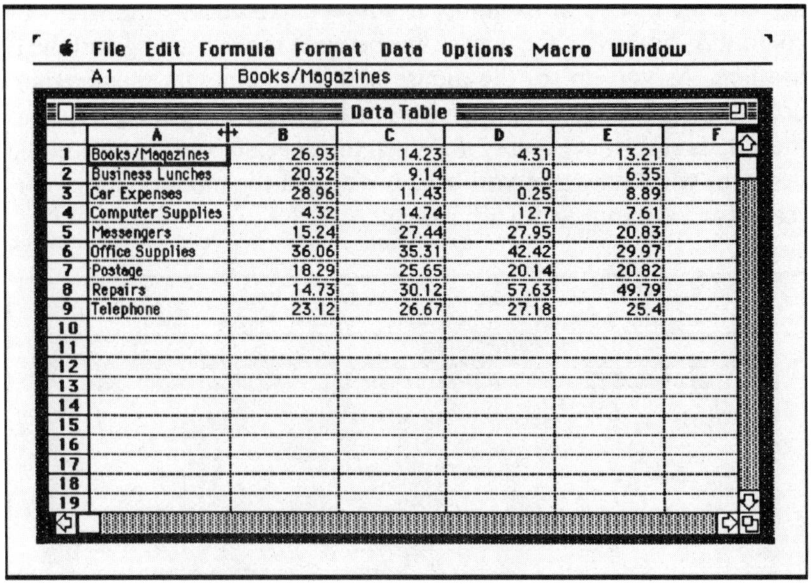
File Edit Formula Format Data Options Macro Window
A1
Books/Magazines
Data Table
A B C D E F
1 Books/Magazines 26.93 14.23 4.31 13.21
2 Business Lunches 20.32 9.14 0 6.35
3 Car Expenses 28.96 11.43 0.25 8.89
4 Computer Supplies 4.32 14.74 12.7 7.61
5 Messengers 15.24 27.44 27.95 20.83
6 Office Supplies 36.06 35.31 42.42 29.97
7 Postage 18.29 25.65 20.14 20.82
8 Repairs 14.73 30.12 57.63 49.79
9 Telephone 23.12 26.67 27.18 25.4
10
11
12
13
14
15
16
17
18
19

Figure 3.9: Column A after changing the column width

To change the width of several columns at once, you have to use one of Excel's menu commands: the Column Width command, located in the Format menu. When you pull down the Format menu, you'll find that Column Width is the last command in the list. To perform the operation, you first select the columns that will be affected by the operation, then you select the Column Width command.

For example, here are the steps for decreasing the widths of columns B through E by half:

1. Drag the mouse pointer over the B, C, D, and E headings to highlight the four target columns.

2. Pull down the Format menu, and select the Column Width command. As you can see in Figure 3.10, the default width of worksheet columns in Excel is 10.

3. From the keyboard, enter a new value of 5 for the width.

4. Click the OK button (or press the Return key) to complete the operation. You can see the resulting column widths in Figure 3.11.

As a result of these column adjustments, the worksheet is easier to read; the labels on the left are displayed in their full lengths, and the numeric data takes up no more room than is necessary. Next we'll turn to the problem of selecting a consistent display format for the numbers.

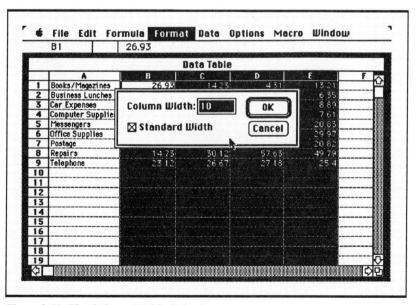

Figure 3.10: The Column Width dialog box

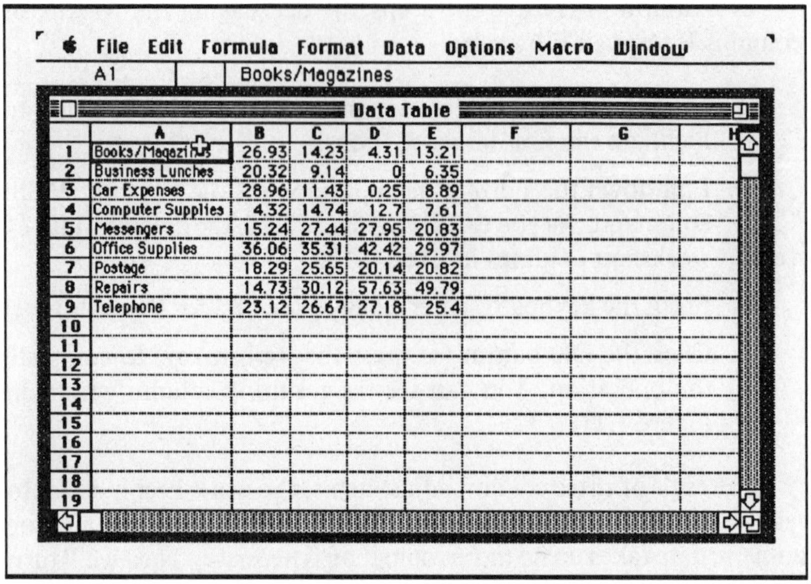

Figure 3.11: *Changing the widths of four columns at once*

Formatting Numbers

If you look carefully at the data table, you'll see that there are some inconsistencies in the way the numbers are displayed. For example, here are the first four numbers in the third column of numbers:

4.31
0
0.25
12.7

The decimal points are not aligned in this column; in fact, one of the numbers shows no decimal point at all. By default Excel supplies only as many decimal places as are necessary to match the accuracy of the original numeric data entry.

To make these numbers easier to read and compare we would like to have exactly two digits after the decimal point in every case. In addition, since the numbers represent your expenses, expressed in dollars and cents, it would be helpful to supply a dollar sign in the display format.

Excel offers a considerable list of predefined numeric formats for you to work with. You gain access to these formats via the Number command in the Format menu. In this exercise we'll look at only one of the formats, but we'll be returning to the Number command many times in the course of this book.

To format a group of numbers, you first select the target range on the worksheet, and then you perform the Number command. Here are the steps you should perform to format the expense data:

1. Use the mouse to select the worksheet range from B1 to E9. This is the range that contains the numeric data.

2. Pull down the Format menu and select the Number command. The resulting dialog box, with its list of available formats, appears in Figure 3.12. (If you want to look through the predefined formats that Excel offers, you can scroll the list by clicking the scroll arrows or dragging the scroll box.)

3. Select the format that produces dollar-and-cent numeric displays:

   $#,##0.00;($#,##0.00)

   The various symbols of this predefined format indicate that Excel will supply a dollar sign (and a comma if necessary), along with a fixed two-digit decimal portion. (The second format, enclosed in parentheses, indicates that any negative numbers will appear in parentheses.) When you click this format with the mouse, Excel highlights the format (white text against a black background), and also displays the format inside the input box.

4. Click the OK button or press the Return key to complete the operation.

You may be a bit surprised by the result of this operation. As you can see in Figure 3.13, some of the numbers appear as expected in the dollar-and-cent format. But the majority of the cells in the selected range now contain strings of # characters.

Don't be alarmed by this result. These special characters are simply Excel's way of telling you that the columns are not wide enough to display the numbers in their new format. We have now seen how Excel

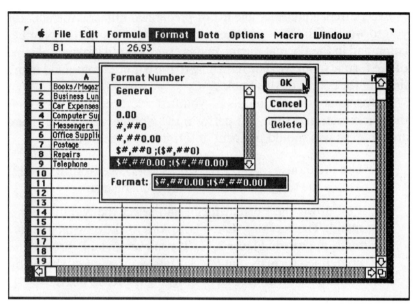

Figure 3.12: The Number command's dialog box

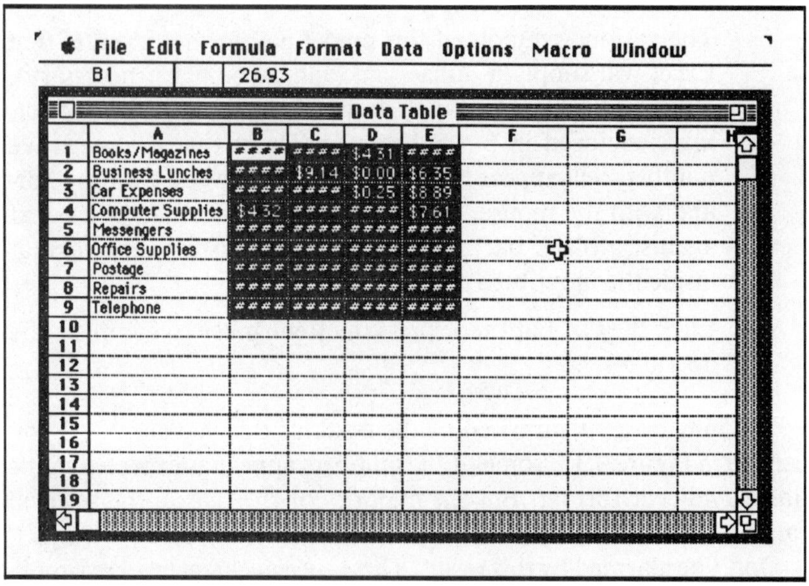

Figure 3.13: Columns that are too narrow indicated on the worksheet

handles both text values and numeric values when the columns are too narrow:

- If a column is too narrow to display a text value (and the adjacent cells to the right already contain data values), Excel simply displays as much of the text as will fit in a given cell.

- If a column is too narrow to display a numeric entry, Excel indicates the problem by displaying a string of # symbols in the cells that are too small. This is what has happened in the expense worksheet.

To solve this problem, all you have to do is increase the width of columns B through E. You previously set the width at 5. Now pull down the Format menu again, select the Column Width command, and reset the width at 6. This increased width is enough to display all of the numbers successfully in the dollar-and-cent format, as you can see in Figure 3.14. Notice also in the figure that the formula bar always displays the actual unformatted number that is stored in the active cell.

File	**Edit**	**Formula**	**Format**	**Data**	**Options**	**Macro**	**Window**

| | D4 | | 12.7 | | | | |

Data Table

	A	B	C	D	E	F	G
1	Books/Magazines	$26.93	$14.23	$4.31	$13.21		
2	Business Lunches	$20.32	$9.14	$0.00	$6.35		
3	Car Expenses	$28.96	$11.43	$0.25	$8.89		
4	Computer Supplies	$4.32	$14.74	$12.70	$7.61		
5	Messengers	$15.24	$27.44	$27.95	$20.83		
6	Office Supplies	$36.06	$35.31	$42.42	$29.97		
7	Postage	$18.29	$25.65	$20.14	$20.82		
8	Repairs	$14.73	$30.12	$57.63	$49.79		
9	Telephone	$23.12	$26.67	$27.18	$25.40		
10							
11							
12							
13							
14							
15							
16							
17							
18							
19							

Figure 3.14: The worksheet adjusted to an appropriate column width

Now that you've gone this far with the expense worksheet, you should perform another Save As operation. Be careful *not* to select the Save command in this case, since you do not want to replace the existing Data Table file with the new version of the worksheet. Instead, you'll want to create a different file on disk for storing the expenses worksheet. At the end of this exercise, you will have created two separate files:

- The Data Table file, for storing the unformatted numeric data table

- The Expenses file, for storing the complete expense worksheet

Pull down the File menu again and select the Save As command. Enter **Expenses** as the new name for the worksheet, and click the Save button. This operation leaves the original Data Table file intact, and produces a new file for the current version of the worksheet.

So far you've entered a table of numbers into the worksheet, inserted a column of labels, and formatted the numbers in an appropriate manner. The next step in developing the expenses worksheet is to produce a column of calculated totals, so that you can see the total amount for each expense category. During this step, you will produce your first worksheet formula. In Chapter 4 you'll learn much more about formulas; but this short exercise gives you an introduction to the power of formulas in Excel.

Creating Formulas in a Worksheet

As we discussed in Chapter 1, a formula can perform operations based on data stored in a worksheet. The result is displayed in the cell where the formula itself is entered. All the common arithmetic operations are available for you to use in building formulas, using their standard operators (shown here in parentheses): addition (+), subtraction (−), multiplication (*), division (/), and exponentiation (^).

The *operands*—the parts of an arithmetic formula that are operated *on*—can include both literal numeric values that you enter into the formula directly from the keyboard and references to worksheet cells that contain numeric data. For example, a reference to B5 in a formula refers to the data value that is currently stored in cell B5. An expression such as B5 + 2 therefore means, "Add 2 to the value currently stored in cell B5."

To inform Excel that you are going to enter a formula into the current active cell, you always begin the entry with an equal sign (=). Once you have typed the equal sign, Excel provides several techniques that you can use to build the elements of your formula. Probably the two most common activities are

- Entering the elements of the formula, including numeric operands, references, and the symbols for operations, directly from the keyboard

- Using the *pointing* technique to incorporate references into a formula

We'll explore the pointing technique in the next section.

Creating a Formula by Pointing

While you are building a formula, you can use the mouse to point to a cell that you want to include as an operand. In response, Excel inserts the reference to the cell directly into your formula. This efficient technique saves you the trouble of typing the reference address of the cell from the keyboard. Keep in mind that a cell reference represents the value that is actually stored inside the cell.

In the expenses worksheet, the formula that we develop to calculate the total expense for a given category should simply add the four weekly expense amounts in the category. For example, the following formula would compute the total for the *Books/Magazines* expense in row 1:

$$= B1 + C1 + D1 + E1$$

Since the four weekly expense amounts for this category are stored in cells B1, C1, D1, and E1, the sum of these four values gives the total for the category.

To compute and display the total for the first expense category, let's enter this formula into cell F1. Here are the steps for building the formula:

1. Activate cell F1.

2. Type an equal sign (=) as the first character of the entry.

3. Position the mouse pointer over cell B1, and click the mouse button. Excel encloses the cell in a moving dotted border to show that you have selected the cell as an operand of your formula. (This special moving border is called a *marquee*.) In the formula bar Excel enters a reference to cell B1:

   = B1

4. Position the mouse pointer over cell C1, and click the mouse button again. In the formula bar Excel enters a plus sign and a reference to cell C1:

   = B1 + C1

   This step illustrates a very convenient feature: if you do not specify an operation while you are pointing to cells, Excel assumes that you want to add the operands, and therefore automatically supplies a plus sign.

5. Position the mouse pointer over cell D1, and click the mouse, then over E1 and click the mouse again. Figure 3.15 shows how the desktop appears at this point in the process. Notice that the formula is complete, but cell E1 is still enclosed in its marquee.

6. Press the Enter key to enter the formula into the active cell, F1.

In response to this formula entry, Excel performs the specified additions and displays the result in cell F1: 58.68. Now we want to enter similar formulas into all of the cells in column F—from F2 to F9—to calculate the total of each expense category. Fortunately, we do not have to build each formula individually. Instead, Excel supplies a very straightforward technique for copying the existing formula down the column; this technique uses the Fill Down command from the Edit menu. In general, Fill Down copies an entry from the top of a columnar range selection into every cell down the column. Let's see how this command works for copying our formula.

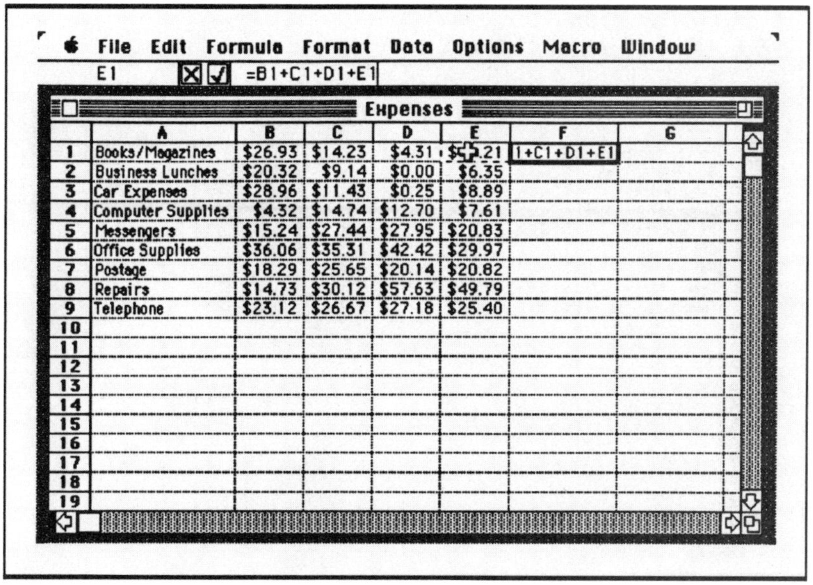

Figure 3.15: *Building a formula by pointing*

Copying the Formula Down a Column

To copy the formula in cell F1 into the range of cells from F2 to F9, perform these two simple steps:

1. Use the mouse to select the range from F1 to F9.

2. Pull down the Edit menu and select the Fill Down command (or simply press the keyboard alternative, ⌘-D).

In response to these steps, Excel copies the formula from the top of the range down the column. Furthermore, Excel automatically adjusts the cell references appropriately for each copy of the formula. You can see the result in Figure 3.16. On your own screen, you should explore the formulas that Excel has created during the Fill Down operation. For example, if you activate cell F2 and examine the formula it contains, you will see

$$= B2 + C2 + D2 + E2$$

In other words, this formula adds the four expense amounts stored in row 2. Likewise, you will find that each of the formulas in the column adds the numeric values in the corresponding row.

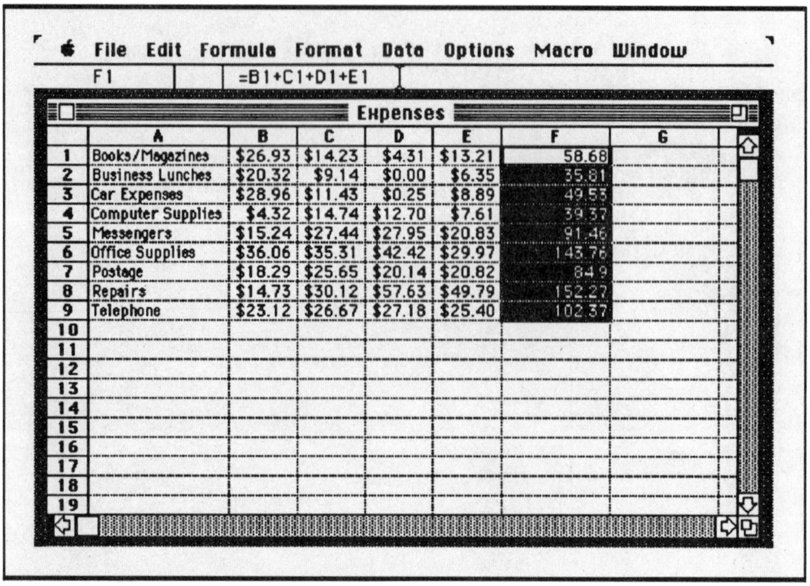

Figure 3.16: *Copying the formula down the column*

We call the operands of the original formula *relative references*, because Excel automatically adjusts them relative to their new positions during a copy operation. You'll learn more about the relative reference—and its counterpart, the *absolute reference*—in Chapter 4.

For now let's quickly perform a few more tasks to complete the expenses worksheet. In the process, you'll have the chance to review some of the skills you've already developed in this chapter, and you'll also learn about a few new Excel features.

*C*ompleting the Worksheet

First, you'll want to format the numbers in the totals column in the same dollar-and-cent format as the rest of the worksheet. Here are the steps:

1. Select the range of cells from F1 to F9.

2. Pull down the Format menu and select the Number command.

3. Select the predefined dollar-and-cent format.

4. Click the OK button to complete the operation.

Next, you should incorporate column headings and a title into the worksheet. To do this, you'll have to insert three rows above the current data table.

Inserting Rows at the Top of the Worksheet

Here are the steps for inserting new rows and entering labels at the top of the worksheet:

1. Select rows 1 through 3 by dragging the mouse pointer down the first three row headings.

2. Pull down the Edit menu and select the Insert command (or simply press ⌘-I). Three empty rows appear above the data table.

3. Select cell B1 and enter the following text:

   Four-Week Expense Records

   Since the cells to the right of B1 are empty, Excel displays the entire text of this title, even though the title is much too big to fit into one cell.

4. Enter the following column headings into cells B3 through F3:

   Wk1   Wk2   Wk3   Wk4   Totals

   Remember to use the Tab key to enter each text value and activate the next cell to the right.

As a finishing touch, you can now take advantage of two commands located in the Format menu to change the type style and the alignment of the text located in the first three rows of the worksheet. You have seen how the Numbers command changes the format of numeric values. Now you'll use the Style and Alignment commands to change the appearance of text values.

*C*hanging Text Styles

The Style command in the Format menu command allows you to display values in boldface and/or italic type styles. The Alignment command in the same menu gives you options for reorienting the position of a data value inside its cell. Both of these commands are very easy to use, but can produce rather dramatic results. They present dialog boxes on the screen with a variety of options.

Both commands are available for use on either numeric values or text values, as shown in the following exercise:

1. Select the range of cells from B1 to F3.

2. Pull down the Format menu and select the Style command.

3. In the resulting dialog box (shown in Figure 3.17), click both the Bold and the Italic options. An X appears in the box next to each option.

4. Click OK to complete the operation. As a result, the text in the first three rows of the worksheet appears in boldface italics.

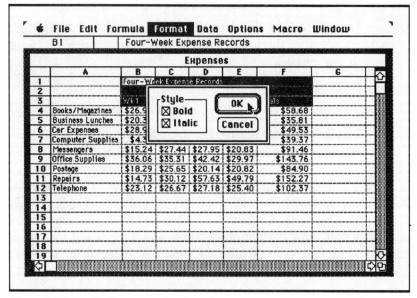

Figure 3.17: *The Style command's dialog box*

5. Select the text of the column headings—the range of cells from B3 to F3.

6. Pull down the Format menu and select the Alignment command.

7. Click the Right option, as shown in Figure 3.18. This option right-justifies the text values in their cells, thus aligning them with the numbers below.

8. Click OK to complete the operation.

9. Press ⌘-S to save this latest version of your worksheet to disk.

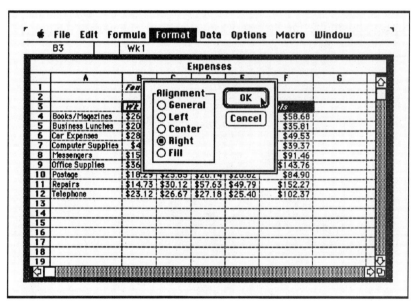

Figure 3.18: The Alignment command's dialog box

Finally, you're ready to print the worksheet for the first time.

*P*rinting the Worksheet

Excel offers many different printing options that allow you to plan and control the way worksheets are sent to your printer. We'll explore some of these options in later chapters. For now, you can quickly perform the following steps to print the expenses worksheet:

1. Make sure your printer is turned on and ready to print.

2. Pull down the File menu and select the Print command.

3. On the subsequent dialog box, simply click the OK button to initiate the printing operation.

Figure 3.19 shows the printed worksheet. Examining this document, you can review the many tasks you've mastered in this chapter: entering and formatting numbers and text; changing column widths; building and copying formulas; inserting columns and rows; and changing the alignment and type style of text values. You'll continue to expand and refine these worksheet skills in the next two chapters.

Expenses

	A	B	C	D	E	F
1		Four-Week Expense Records				
2						
3		Wk1	Wk2	Wk3	Wk4	Totals
4	Books/Magazines	$26.93	$14.23	$4.31	$13.21	$58.68
5	Business Lunches	$20.32	$9.14	$0.00	$6.35	$35.81
6	Car Expenses	$28.96	$11.43	$0.25	$8.89	$49.53
7	Computer Supplies	$4.32	$14.74	$12.70	$7.61	$39.37
8	Messengers	$15.24	$27.44	$27.95	$20.83	$91.46
9	Office Supplies	$36.06	$35.31	$42.42	$29.97	$143.76
10	Postage	$18.29	$25.65	$20.14	$20.82	$84.90
11	Repairs	$14.73	$30.12	$57.63	$49.79	$152.27
12	Telephone	$23.12	$26.67	$27.18	$25.40	$102.37

Figure 3.19: Printing the worksheet

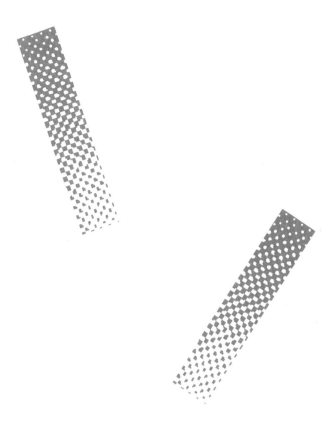

4

Working with Formulas and Functions

Featuring:

Working with absolute
and relative
references

Using built-in
functions

Testing what-if
scenarios

Controlling output to
the printer

You have already mastered the essential skills necessary for building a worksheet application, but there is still much more to learn about the power of formulas in Excel. In this chapter you'll find out the difference between relative and absolute references, and you'll learn how to incorporate any of Excel's built-in worksheet functions into a formula. You'll also acquire some first-hand experience with the important *what-if* feature of the spreadsheet program. Finally, at the end of this chapter you'll see how to use the Page Setup and Print commands to control the way Excel sends a worksheet to the printer.

In Chapter 3 you saved two different worksheet files to disk—the Data Table worksheet, which contains a simple table of numeric data; and the Expenses worksheet, which is the application that you developed during the course of the chapter. To begin your work now, you'll open up the Data Table worksheet and begin developing a new application with the data it contains.

Specifically, this chapter will guide you though the steps for creating a quarterly sales worksheet. As suggested in Chapter 1, you'll imagine yourself the sales manager for a small company, responsible for watching over the performance of a group of nine salespeople. (To review the general appearance of the application, look back at Figures 1.12 and 1.13.)

Creating the Sales Data Worksheet

The first task at hand is to reopen the Data Table worksheet, so that you can once again use it as the raw data of an application. To open a worksheet that you have previously saved as a disk file, use the Open command in the File menu.

Opening a Worksheet File from Disk

Here are the steps for opening the Data Table worksheet:

1. Pull down the File menu and select the Open command. The resulting dialog box should be similar to the one shown in Figure 4.1.

2. Use the Drive and Eject buttons, if necessary, to locate the correct drive or to eject a disk so that you can insert the disk that contains the data file.

3. When you see the name Data Table in the list of files, position the mouse pointer over the name and click the mouse button to select the name.

4. Click the Open button to open the file onto the desktop.

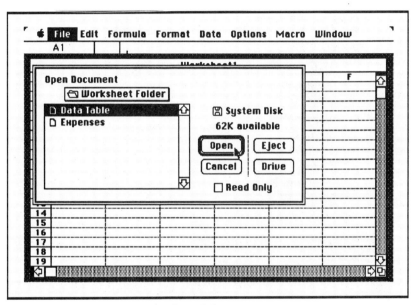

Figure 4.1: *Opening a worksheet from disk*

The worksheet appears on the desktop in the same form as when you originally saved it (Figure 3.5). You can now begin transforming this data into a worksheet named Sales Data; in the process, you'll have the opportunity to review just about everything you learned in Chapter 3.

Reviewing the Basic Worksheet Skills

Your goal in this beginning exercise is to create the worksheet that appears in Figure 4.3. Notice that the rows of the worksheet now represent sales data for the nine salespeople, and the columns represent quarterly sales in units of $1,000. Column F gives the total annual sales for each person.

Here are the steps for creating this worksheet; refer back to Chapter 3 if you need to review some steps in more detail:

1. Use the mouse to select column A, and press ⌘-I to insert a new column at the left side of the worksheet.

2. Select rows 1 through 4, and press ⌘-I again to insert four new rows at the top of the worksheet.

3. In cells A5 through A13 enter the names of the nine salespeople:

    Baker, J.
    Smith, D.
    Flint, M.
    Brown, S.
    Vern, C.
    Marlow, I.
    Harper, L.
    Fleming, N.
    White, W.

4. Select the range of cells from A5 to A13, and use the Style command in the Format menu to display the nine names in boldface type.

5. Use the mouse to select columns B through E, and perform the Column Width command in the Format menu to reduce the width of these columns to 6.

6. In cell E1, enter the title of the worksheet:

    Quarterly Sales by Salesperson

    Since the title is too long to fit in cell E1, Excel displays it across the boundaries of the cells to the right.

7. In cell E2, enter the following note, describing the units represented by the numeric data:

    (thousands of dollars)

    Your worksheet should now look like Figure 4.2.

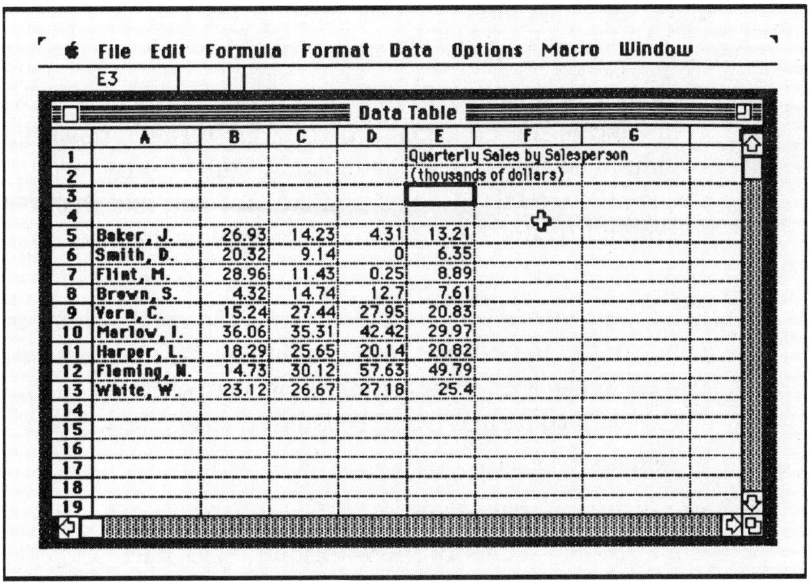

	A	B	C	D	E	F	G
1					Quarterly Sales by Salesperson		
2					(thousands of dollars)		
3							
4							
5	Baker, J.	26.93	14.23	4.31	13.21		
6	Smith, D.	20.32	9.14	0	6.35		
7	Flint, M.	28.96	11.43	0.25	8.89		
8	Brown, S.	4.32	14.74	12.7	7.61		
9	Vera, C.	15.24	27.44	27.95	20.83		
10	Marlow, I.	36.06	35.31	42.42	29.97		
11	Harper, L.	18.29	25.65	20.14	20.82		
12	Fleming, N.	14.73	30.12	57.63	49.79		
13	White, W.	23.12	26.67	27.18	25.4		
14							
15							
16							
17							
18							
19							

***Figure 4.2:** The worksheet title before reformatting*

8. Select the range of cells from E1 to E2; then pull down the Format menu and select the Alignment command. Click the Center option in the Alignment dialog box, and then click the OK button. In response, Excel centers the two title lines horizontally around column E.

9. Use the Style command in the Format menu to display the top title line in boldface italics, and then use the command again to display the second line (the explanation of units) in italics.

10. Enter the following column labels into cells B4 through F4:

    First Second Third Fourth Totals

    Use the Alignment command in the Format menu to right-justify each of these labels in its cell. Then use the Style command in the Format menu to display all the labels in boldface type.

11. Select cell F5, and use the mouse to point to the cells B5, C5, D5, and E5 in succession, thus entering the following formula into cell F5:

    = B5 + C5 + D5 + E5

Excel then computes the total sales for the first salesperson, 58.68 (representing $58,680 in the context of this worksheet).

12. Select the range of cells from F5 to F13, and use the Fill Down command in the Edit menu to copy the formula down the column. Use the Number command in the Format menu to display these totals in dollar-and-cent format, and the Style command in the Format menu to display them in bold-face type.

13. Select the range of cells from B5 to E13, and use the Numbers command in the Format menu to display the numbers with two decimal places. To accomplish this step, select the following predefined format from the Number dialog box:

   0.00

14. Pull down the File menu and select the Save As command. Enter the new name for the worksheet, **Sales Data**, and click the Save button to save the current version of the worksheet.

Figure 4.3 shows the starting point for your work in this chapter.

	A	B	C	D	E	F	G
1				*Quarterly Sales by Salesperson*			
2				*(thousands of dollars)*			
3							
4		First	Second	Third	Fourth	Totals	
5	Baker, J.	26.93	14.23	4.31	13.21	$58.68	
6	Smith, D.	20.32	9.14	0.00	6.35	$35.81	
7	Flint, M.	28.96	11.43	0.25	8.89	$49.53	
8	Brown, S.	4.32	14.74	12.70	7.61	$39.37	
9	Vera, C.	15.24	27.44	27.95	20.83	$91.46	
10	Marlow, I.	36.06	35.31	42.42	29.97	$143.76	
11	Harper, L.	18.29	25.65	20.14	20.82	$84.90	
12	Fleming, N.	14.73	30.12	57.63	49.79	$152.27	
13	White, W.	23.12	26.67	27.18	25.40	$102.37	
14							
15							
16							
17							
18							
19							

Figure 4.3: The Sales Data worksheet

More about Entering Formulas

In Chapter 3 you learned how to incorporate references into a formula. A reference inside a formula represents a value that is stored at the corresponding cell address. Whenever you intend to copy such a formula to other cells, you have to anticipate exactly how you want Excel to copy references from one cell to the next; you have to distinguish between *relative references* and *absolute references*. Let's see exactly what these terms mean.

Relative and Absolute References

You can see how Excel has copied the references in the totals column of the Sales Data worksheet. The formula you originally entered into cell F5 is

= B5 + C5 + D5 + E5

But when you perform the Fill Down command to copy the formula down the totals column, Excel adjusts each reference for the corresponding row of sales figures. For example, here is how the formulas appear in cells F6, F7, and F8:

= B6 + C6 + D6 + E6
= B7 + C7 + D7 + E7
= B8 + C8 + D8 + E8

As you can see, Excel has automatically incremented the row numbers in the four references of these formulas. The reference to B6 has become B7 for the formula in row 7, B8 for the formula in row 8, and B9 for the formula in row 9. Likewise, each of the other references has been adjusted appropriately. These operands are called *relative references*, because Excel automatically adjusts them relative to the cell location that receives the formula.

When you point to a cell while you are building a formula, Excel's default behavior is to insert a relative reference into the formula bar. However, in some worksheet applications you'll want to prevent the automatic adjustments that normally occur when relative references are copied from one cell to another. Rather, you'll want to treat a particular cell reference as the unchanging location of a specific value in a formula. To do this, you must transform the operand into an *absolute reference* while you are building your formula.

In Excel's notation for an absolute reference, a dollar sign appears before both the column letter and the row number. For example, here is an absolute reference to cell B1:

$B$1

Excel provides a convenient menu command that you can use to convert a relative reference into an absolute reference while you are building a formula: the Reference command in the Formula menu. (You'll practice using this command shortly.) When you subsequently copy the formula from one cell to another, Excel treats the absolute reference as a fixed address, representing the value stored in unchanging location on the worksheet.

The best way to learn the difference between relative and absolute references is by looking at an example.

Calculating Salaries

Let's say you want to create a column on the Sales Data worksheet that shows the salary each salesperson has earned during the four quarters displayed on the worksheet. In your current salary structure, each person on your sales staff earns $1,000 per month (or $12,000 per year) as a base salary, plus 5% commission on sales. You want to incorporate these figures into a formula that will calculate each person's annual earnings.

One approach is to incorporate the salary structure figures literally into the formula that you write. For example, you could write the formula for the first salesperson as follows:

12 + .05*F5

Since cell F5 contains the first salesperson's total annual sales, this formula represents the following steps:

1. Multiply the person's annual sales by .05 (that is, by 5%).

2. Add 12 (representing $12,000) to the result of the multiplication.

Controlling the Order of Operations

At this point, we should take a brief look at how Excel performs calculations. When you create a formula that contains more than one arithmetic operation, Excel follows the standard algebraic rules for determining which operation to perform first: multiplication and division operations are performed before addition and subtraction. If you want to be explicit about the order of operations in a formula, you can always supply parentheses in the formula:

= 12 + (.05*F5)

You can also supply parentheses to specify a nonstandard order of operations. Excel always performs operations that are enclosed in parentheses before other operations in the formula. You'll see an example of this in Chapter 5.

Building a More Useful Salary Formula

The initial salary formula that we have developed has two major disadvantages:

- Since the base salary and commission figures are not displayed on the worksheet itself, these values are, in effect, hidden inside the formula. A person looking at the table would have no way of knowing how the salary column is calculated.

- The design of the formula does not allow you to perform what-if experiments. If you should want to explore possible changes in the base salary and/or the commission rate, you would have to rewrite and recopy the formula itself.

We can solve both of these problems by designating cells on the worksheet for storing the base salary and the commission. Then we'll write a formula that refers directly to these cell locations. Let's use the range of four cells from A1 to B2 for this purpose. In column A we'll enter explanatory labels, and in column B we'll store the salary structure figures, as follows:

	A	B
1	**Base salary**	**12**
2	**Commission**	**5%**

Enter these values into the worksheet. Use the Style command in the Format menu to display the labels in boldface type. When you enter the numeric value **5%** into cell B2, notice that Excel immediately recognizes the meaning of the percent sign. Although the value is displayed as a percentage in the cell itself, the formula bar displays the number as a decimal: 0.05. When you incorporate this value into a formula, you can therefore be confident that the percent operation will be performed correctly.

Now you are ready to build the salary formula, using references to cell B1 for the base salary and B2 for the commission rate. Clearly you want Excel to treat these two references as the fixed addresses of their respective numeric values. When you copy the salary formula down a column, you do not want these two references to be adjusted in any way. For this reason, you must incorporate these operands into the formula as absolute references.

Use column G for the salary calculation. Enter the label **Salary** into cell G4, and use the Style command to display the text in boldface type. Then perform the Alignment command to right-justify the label in its cell. Next, select cell G5, and proceed as follows:

1. To begin the formula, enter an equal sign from the keyboard.

2. Position the mouse pointer over cell B1, and click the mouse button. As usual, Excel enters a relative reference to this cell into the formula bar:

   = B1

3. While the cursor in the formula bar is still located immediately after the reference to B1, pull down the Formula menu and select the Reference command. This command transforms the relative reference B1 into an absolute reference:

   = $B$1

   As you have seen, the dollar signs are Excel's way of indicating that this is a fixed reference to a particular column-and-row location on the worksheet.

4. Click cell B2. Excel incorporates a plus sign and a reference to the selected cell into the formula:

   = $B$1 + B2

5. Once again, pull down the Formula menu and select the Reference command (or use the keyboard alternative, ⌘-T). The second operand also becomes an absolute reference:

   = $B$1 + $B$2

6. Enter an asterisk (∗) from the keyboard, the symbol for multiplication in Excel.

7. Click cell F5, the cell that contains the total annual sales for the first salesperson. Excel incorporates this final reference into the formula, as you can see in Figure 4.4. This last operand should remain a relative reference; when you copy the formula down the column, you will want Excel to adjust this reference appropriately for each salesperson.

8. Click the enter box, or press the Enter key to complete the formula entry. The result of the formula for the first salesperson is 14.934, indicating that this person earned $14,934 in salary and commission for the year.

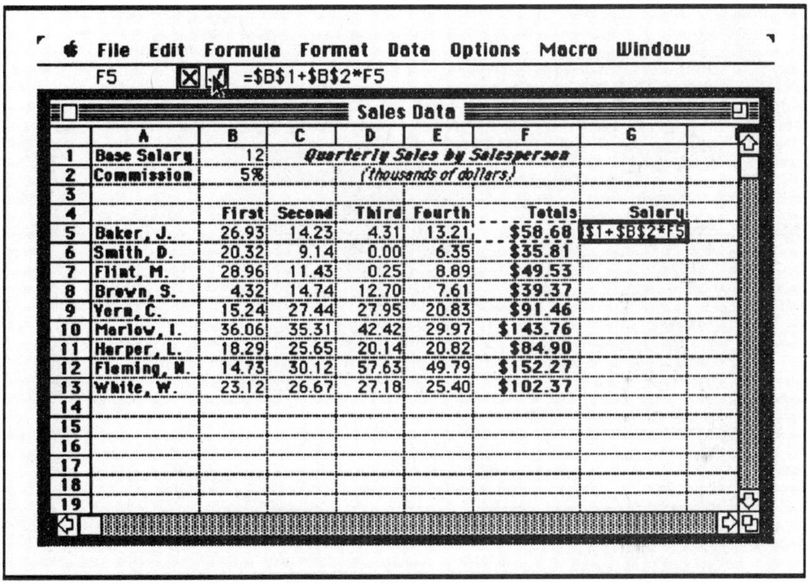

Figure 4.4: A worksheet formula combining relative and absolute references

Copying the Formula down the Column

Now that you have carefully distinguished between absolute and relative references in the salary formula, you can confidently copy the formula down column G to calculate salaries for the rest of the sales staff:

1. Select the range of cells from G5 to G13.

2. Pull down the Edit menu and select the Fill Down command (or simply press ⌘-D from the keyboard).

3. Use the Number command in the Format menu to display the numbers in this column in a consistent dollar-and-cent format.

Figure 4.5 shows the result of this copied formula. An interesting exercise at this point is to examine the formulas that Excel has copied into each cell down the column. The absolute references in the formula remain unchanged for each copy, whereas the relative reference

⌘ File Edit Formula Format Data Options Macro Window
G5   =$B$1+$B$2*F5

Sales Data

	A	B	C	D	E	F	G
1	Base Salary	12	*Quarterly Sales by Salesperson*				
2	Commission	5%	*(thousands of dollars)*				
3							
4		First	Second	Third	Fourth	Totals	Salary
5	Baker, J.	26.93	14.23	4.31	13.21	$58.68	$14.93
6	Smith, D.	20.32	9.14	0.00	6.35	$35.81	$13.79
7	Flint, H.	28.96	11.43	0.25	8.89	$49.53	$14.48
8	Brown, S.	4.32	14.74	12.70	7.61	$39.37	$13.97
9	Vern, C.	15.24	27.44	27.95	20.83	$91.46	$16.57
10	Marlow, I.	36.06	35.31	42.42	29.97	$143.76	$19.19
11	Harper, L.	18.29	25.65	20.14	20.82	$84.90	$16.25
12	Fleming, N.	14.73	30.12	57.63	49.79	$152.27	$19.61
13	White, W.	23.12	26.67	27.18	25.40	$102.37	$17.12
14							
15							
16							
17							
18							
19							

Figure 4.5: Copying the salary formula down the column

is adjusted according to the row location. For example, here are the formulas copied into cells G6, G7, and G8:

= $B$1 + $B$2 * F6
= $B$1 + $B$2 * F7
= $B$1 + $B$2 * F8

These formulas precisely match the requirements of the application at hand, and clearly illustrate the difference between absolute and relative references.

By the way, Excel also allows *mixed references* for use in more complex worksheet applications. When copied to a new cell, a mixed reference remains fixed in one dimension, and is adjusted for the other dimension. The notation for a mixed reference uses a single dollar sign to indicate the fixed dimension. For example, the reference $M20 is fixed for the column dimension ($M) and relative for the row dimension (20). Conversely, M$20 is relative for the column and fixed for the row. Mixed references can prove essential when you plan to copy a formula in two directions at once—that is, both across rows and down columns.

The next step in developing the Sales Data worksheet is to create a row of totals across the bottom of the data table. To accomplish this, you'll use one of Excel's many *built-in functions*.

Calculating with Built-in Functions

We want to design the bottom row of the worksheet to include totals for all of the numeric columns, including

- The total sales for each of the four quarters
- The total sales for the entire year
- The total salaries and commissions paid to the salespeople

To compute these total values you'll first enter a formula in cell B14 and then copy the formula across row 14.

You'll recall that the formula for the total annual sales column simply adds together the individual quarterly sales amounts. This kind of formula is reasonably convenient for finding the sum of three or four numbers, but would become very unwieldy for a larger group of operands. Fortunately, Excel supplies a special tool that computes the sum of an entire range of numbers. This tool is the built-in function SUM.

As we discussed briefly in Chapter 1, Excel has a large library of built-in worksheet functions that perform a variety of different operations conveniently and reliably. Each function has a distinct name. In addition, a function typically requires you to supply specific types of data values as operands for the function to work with. These values are called the *arguments* of the function.

The SUM function requires one or more numeric arguments, or a range of numeric arguments. As with all functions, you supply the arguments in parentheses immediately after the function's name. If there are multiple arguments, you use a comma to separate each argument from the next. For example, here is a formula that finds the sum of the values stored in cells B7 and E12, and then adds 5 to the result:

= SUM(B7,E12,5)

Like any other formula in Excel, the expression begins with an equal sign.

SUM is one of the simplest, but most commonly used, of all the built-in functions. Other, more complex, functions require specific types of arguments in a defined order; if you confuse the order of the arguments, these functions produce unpredictable results. We'll examine other built-in functions in Chapter 5. In the meantime, a quick exercise with the SUM function will give you the opportunity to learn the general technique for using functions.

To build a formula that contains a built-in function, you can either type the function's name directly from the keyboard or select the name from a list presented in Excel's Paste Function command. This command, located in the Formula menu, is simply a shortcut for entering the name of a function into a worksheet. Let's see how it works.

Using the Paste Function Command

Before you begin building the row of totals, select cell A14 and enter the word **Totals** into the cell. Then use the Style command in the Format menu to display this label in boldface italic type.

Next select cell B14, and perform the following steps:

1. Pull down the Formula menu and select the Paste Function command. The resulting dialog box presents a scrollable list

of all the built-in functions available for the worksheet. The function names are in alphabetical order.

2. Use the scroll box and/or the scroll arrows to scroll down to the SUM function. (Alternatively, you can press the **S** key at the keyboard; in response, Excel scrolls down to the first function name that begins with the letter S. You then have to scroll a bit further to find SUM.)

3. Position the mouse pointer over the SUM function name, and click the mouse button. Excel highlights the function in white text against a black background, as shown in Figure 4.6.

4. Click the OK button to incorporate the selected function into your formula. Since you haven't yet typed the equal sign to start the formula, Excel supplies it for you, along with the name of the function:

   = SUM( )

   Excel positions the formula bar's cursor right between the two parentheses, making it easy for you to begin entering arguments for the formula.

5. Select the range of cells from B5 to B13. Excel places a marquee around this range (as shown in Figure 4.7), and automatically enters the range reference as the argument of the SUM function:

   = SUM(B5:B13)

   In the notation for a range reference, a colon separates the first cell of the range from the last cell.

6. Click the enter box (or press the Enter key) to complete the formula entry.

The result of this formula is 187.97 (representing $187,970)—the total sales by all salespeople for the first quarter. Finally, you can use the Fill Right command (in the Edit menu) to copy this formula across row 14:

1. Select cells B14 to G14.

2. Pull down the Edit menu and select Fill Right (or press ⌘-**R** from the keyboard).

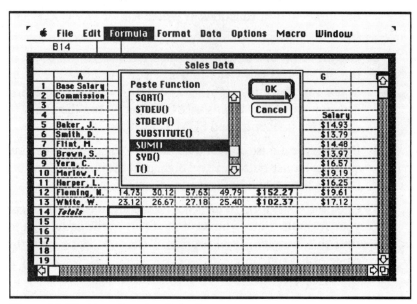

Figure 4.6: *The Paste Function dialog box*

♣ File Edit Formula Format Data Options Macro Window

B5   ☒ ☑ =SUM(B5:B13)

Sales Data

	A	B	C	D	E	F	G
1	Base Salary	12	*Quarterly Sales by Salesperson*				
2	Commission	5%	*('thousands of dollars)*				
3							
4		First	Second	Third	Fourth	Totals	Salary
5	Baker, J.	26.93	14.23	4.31	13.21	$58.68	$14.93
6	Smith, D.	20.32	9.14	0.00	6.35	$35.81	$13.79
7	Flint, M.	28.96	11.43	0.25	8.89	$49.53	$14.48
8	Brown, S.	4.32	14.74	12.70	7.61	$39.37	$13.97
9	Vern, C.	15.24	27.44	27.95	20.83	$91.46	$16.57
10	Marlow, I.	36.06	35.31	42.42	29.97	$143.76	$19.19
11	Harper, L.	18.29	25.65	20.14	20.82	$84.90	$16.25
12	Fleming, N.	14.73	30.12	57.63	49.79	$152.27	$19.61
13	White, W.	23.	26.67	27.18	25.40	$102.37	$17.12
14	*Totals*	B5:B13)					
15							
16							
17							
18							
19							

Figure 4.7: *Building a formula with the SUM function*

3. Use the Number command (in the Format menu) to display cells F14 and G14 in dollar-and-cent format.

4. Use the Style command (in the Format menu) to display the total in cell F14 in boldface type.

5. Press ⌘-S to save the latest version of the worksheet to disk.

The complete worksheet appears in Figure 4.8. You can see the calculated totals below all of the numeric columns, including the last two columns, which themselves contain calculated data. This worksheet now presents an ideal environment in which to test Excel's *what-if* facility. The next exercise in this chapter shows you how to perform such experiments.

	A	B	C	D	E	F	G
1	Base Salary	12	*Quarterly Sales by Salesperson*				
2	Commission	5%	*(thousands of dollars)*				
3							
4		First	Second	Third	Fourth	Totals	Salary
5	Baker, J.	26.93	14.23	4.31	13.21	$58.68	$14.93
6	Smith, D.	20.32	9.14	0.00	6.35	$35.81	$13.79
7	Flint, M.	28.96	11.43	0.25	8.89	$49.53	$14.48
8	Brown, S.	4.32	14.74	12.70	7.61	$39.37	$13.97
9	Vern, C.	15.24	27.44	27.95	20.83	$91.46	$16.57
10	Marlow, I.	36.06	35.31	42.42	29.97	$143.76	$19.19
11	Harper, L.	18.29	25.65	20.14	20.82	$84.90	$16.25
12	Fleming, N.	14.73	30.12	57.63	49.79	$152.27	$19.61
13	White, W.	23.12	26.67	27.18	25.40	$102.37	$17.12
14	*Totals*	187.97	194.73	192.58	182.87	$758.15	$145.91

Figure 4.8: Copying the row of totals

Testing What-if Scenarios

Imagine the following situation. As sales manager, you are considering ways to restructure the salary and commission rates for your employees; specifically, you would like to lower the base salary, and increase the commission. Your goal is not necessarily to change the total amount of salary and commission paid to the nine salespeople, but rather to distribute the amount in a way that provides greater incentive for high performance. In short, you would like to see your best salespeople earn more, and your weakest people earn less.

To decide exactly how to restructure this system, you've decided to see what would have happened to last year's salaries under different terms. The scenario you would like to try first is this: What would the salaries look like if you doubled the commission rate to 10% and cut the annual base salary in half, to $6,000?

Thanks to the way you have designed the Sales Data worksheet, you can examine this scenario almost instantly. Recall the following two features of your worksheet:

- You have placed the base salary and the commission rate figures at the upper-left corner of the worksheet, in cells B1 and B2, where you can easily revise them.

- You have written formulas that depend directly or indirectly on the values stored in these two cells. The individual annual salary amounts in cells G5 to G13 depend directly on the base salary and commission rate. Furthermore, the total annual salary for all nine salespeople—calculated as the sum of the cells in the range G5:G13—depends indirectly on the salary terms.

What allows you to test your salary scenario is the fact that each time you make a change in either the base salary in cell B1 or the commission rate in cell B2, Excel will *automatically* recalculate all the formulas that depend on these two amounts, displaying the newly calculated salaries instantly on the worksheet.

Try it now. Follow these steps to double the commission rate and cut the base salary in half:

1. Select cell B1, and enter a new value of **6** (representing $6,000) for the base salary.

2. Select cell B2, and enter a new value of **10%** (including the % sign) for the commission rate. (Notice that Excel displays the correct decimal equivalent, 0.1, in the formula bar.)

Figure 4.9 shows the result of these two changes. All the numbers in column G have been recalculated using the new salary terms. As you can see, this scenario begins to meet your goals for the change: the strongest salespeople earn more, and the weakest earn less. However, you have also decreased the total annual salary paid to all your staff by over $15,000. To correct this situation you might try examining either of the following scenarios:

- An annual base salary of $8,000, and a commission rate of 10%.
- An annual base salary of $6,000, and a commission rate of 12%.

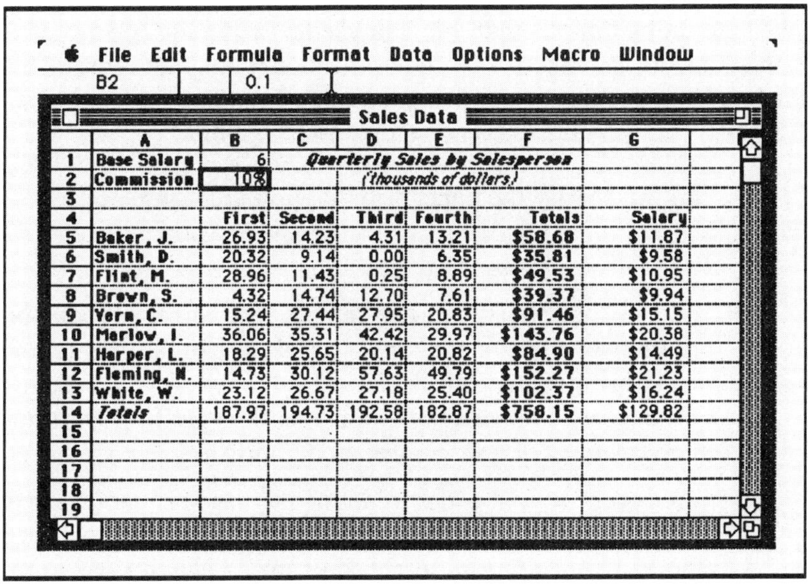

	A	B	C	D	E	F	G
1	Base Salary	6	*Quarterly Sales by Salesperson*				
2	Commission	10%	*(thousands of dollars)*				
3							
4		First	Second	Third	Fourth	Totals	Salary
5	Baker, J.	26.93	14.23	4.31	13.21	$58.68	$11.87
6	Smith, D.	20.32	9.14	0.00	6.35	$35.81	$9.58
7	Flint, M.	28.96	11.43	0.25	8.89	$49.53	$10.95
8	Brown, S.	4.32	14.74	12.70	7.61	$39.37	$9.94
9	Vera, C.	15.24	27.44	27.95	20.83	$91.46	$15.15
10	Marlow, I.	36.06	35.31	42.42	29.97	$143.76	$20.38
11	Harper, L.	18.29	25.65	20.14	20.82	$84.90	$14.49
12	Fleming, N.	14.73	30.12	57.63	49.79	$152.27	$21.23
13	White, W.	23.12	26.67	27.18	25.40	$102.37	$16.24
14	*Totals*	187.97	194.73	192.58	182.87	$758.15	$129.82
15							
16							
17							
18							
19							

Figure 4.9: *Testing your what-if scenario*

Both of these scenarios end up with approximately the same total salary as on the original worksheet. Of course, in the end it is up to you to decide exactly how to restructure the salary terms. But Excel can quickly give you a wealth of relevant information to use in making the decision.

In the last section of this chapter you'll learn more about the options Excel gives you for printing a worksheet.

Controlling the Printing Process

You printed your worksheet in Chapter 3 by simply pulling down the File menu, selecting the Print command, and clicking the OK button. The result was a printed document that looked almost the same as the worksheet on the desktop—complete with gridlines, letter column headings (A, B, C, and so on), and numbered rows. Now you'll learn how to increase your own control over the output to the printer.

Using the Page Setup Command

The Page Setup command in the File menu supplies a number of very interesting options that you can use to define the format of a printed document. Figure 4.10 shows the dialog box that appears on the screen when you invoke this command. Examine this box carefully, and you will notice several categories of options:

- You can specify the paper size that you are using, and Excel will determine page breaks accordingly. The default size is *US Letter*—8½-by-11-inch paper.

- You can choose between the default vertical orientation for printing your document, or a special horizontal orientation that actually prints your document sideways down the length of the paper. The latter option is especially useful for fitting many columns of a worksheet all on one sheet of paper.

- You can use special codes to define the page header (the text that Excel prints at the top of every page) and the page footer (the text that appears at the bottom of every page). For example, the default *&f* code prints the title of the document as the header. The *Page &p* code prints the page number as the footer. You can edit these codes, or delete them altogether.

- You can change the default settings for the left, right, top, and bottom margins.

- You can omit the row and column headings and the gridlines from the printed document.

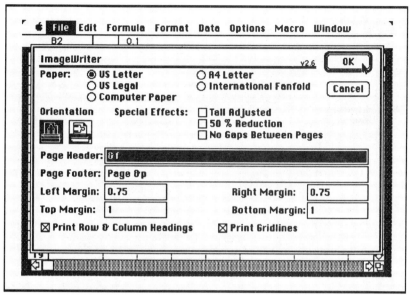

Figure 4.10: The Page Setup dialog box

As an exercise with this command, try performing the following steps:

1. Pull down the File menu and select Page Setup.

2. Use the mouse to click the Print Row & Column Headings option. This option is on by default; clicking it turns it off, making the X in the small box located at the left of the option disappear.

3. Click the Print Gridlines option, also turning it off.

4. Press the Backspace key to delete the highlighted text located inside the Page Header box.

5. Drag the mouse over the Page Footer box to highlight the text located inside the box, and press the Backspace key to delete the contents altogether.

When you complete these steps, the dialog box will appear as shown in Figure 4.11. In summary, you have specified that you want to omit the header, the footer, the row and column headings, and the gridlines

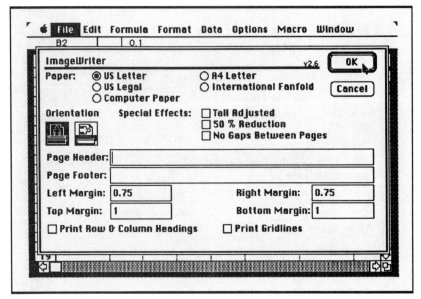

Figure 4.11: Changing the Page Setup options

from your printed document. Your selected options will take effect the next time you print the worksheet.

Next, we'll take another look at the Print command.

Using the Print Command

Figure 4.12 shows the dialog box that appears on the screen when you invoke the Print command from the File menu. This box also includes some interesting and important options:

- When you are working with an Apple ImageWriter printer, you can choose among three different print qualities: the Best option gives you near-letter-quality output, but prints rather slowly; the Faster option gives somewhat less quality in less printing time; and the Draft option produces a rough document very quickly using standard dot-matrix printer quality.

- You can specify the portion of the document that you wish to print. (The default is All—that is, the entire document.)

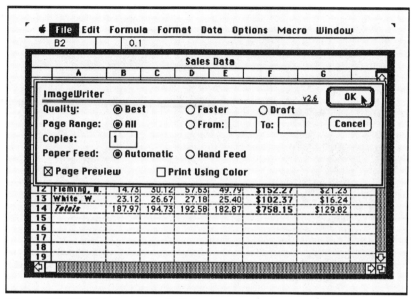

Figure 4.12: The Print command's dialog box

- You can check the Page Preview option; as a result, Excel displays a preview of your printed document on the screen. You use this preview to check whether everything is formatted just as you want it before you actually print the document.

Now that you have specified your formatting options in the Page Setup command, you are ready to print the Sales Data worksheet using the following steps:

1. Pull down the File menu and select the Print command (or simply press ⌘-**P**).

2. Use the mouse to click the Page Preview command. An X appears in the small box located to the left of the option, as shown in Figure 4.12.

3. Click the OK button to begin the preview. Excel displays the preview page as shown in Figure 4.13. When you move the mouse over the area covered by this page, the pointer takes the shape of a small magnifying glass icon. Accordingly, you can position this pointer over a particular part of the worksheet that you would like to see, and click the mouse to magnify the area. Click again to return to the small preview page.

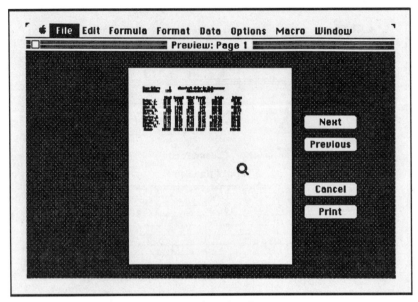

Figure 4.13: *Previewing a document to be printed*

4. If you are satisfied with the format of the worksheet, click the Print button to send the document to your printer. Otherwise, click Cancel to return to the desktop. (The Next and Previous buttons on the preview screen are for paging through a multi-page document.)

Earlier versions of Excel do not offer a Print button on the preview screen. If you are working in one of these versions, you have to exit from the preview and then invoke the Print command a second time to print your document.

Figure 4.14 shows the printed Sales Data worksheet. As a result of the options selected with the Page Setup command, Excel has printed the document without column letters, row numbers, or gridlines.

*C*losing the Worksheet

If you now click the close box on the Sales Data worksheet, Excel prompts you to specify whether or not you want to save the changes in

Base Salary		6	*Quarterly Sales by Salesperson*				
Commission		10%	*(thousands of dollars)*				
	First	Second	Third	Fourth		Totals	Salary
Baker, J.	26.93	14.23	4.31	13.21		$58.68	$11.87
Smith, D.	20.32	9.14	0.00	6.35		$35.81	$9.58
Flint, M.	28.96	11.43	0.25	8.89		$49.53	$10.95
Brown, S.	4.32	14.74	12.70	7.61		$39.37	$9.94
Vern, C.	15.24	27.44	27.95	20.83		$91.46	$15.15
Marlow, I.	36.06	35.31	42.42	29.97		$143.76	$20.38
Harper, L.	18.29	25.65	20.14	20.82		$84.90	$14.49
Fleming, N.	14.73	30.12	57.63	49.79		$152.27	$21.23
White, W.	23.12	26.67	27.18	25.40		$102.37	$16.24
Totals	187.97	194.73	192.58	182.87		$758.15	$129.82

Figure 4.14: The printed Sales Data worksheet

the worksheet:

Save changes in "Sales Data"?

This prompt appears even if you have made no actual changes inside the worksheet since the last save operation. The reason is that Excel normally saves your Page Setup options along with the worksheet. When you change these options, Excel needs to know whether you want to save the changes before closing the document window.

As you can see in Figure 4.15, the message window that appears on the screen has three buttons:

- Click Yes to save the current version of the worksheet before closing it.

- Click No to abandon the current version of the worksheet.

- Click Cancel to return to the desktop without closing the worksheet.

If you click the Yes button, the Page Setup options will be saved, and will take effect once again when you next load the worksheet onto the desktop from disk.

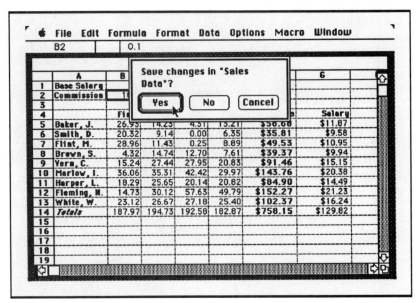

Figure 4.15: Closing the worksheet

In Chapter 5 you'll continue working with formulas and built-in functions, and you'll learn some very useful ways to work with dates in a worksheet.

5

Learning More about Formulas and Functions

Featuring:

Performing a
cut-and-paste
operation

Defining names for
worksheet ranges

Using lookup
functions

Working with date
values

You've already learned to create and copy formulas using combinations of absolute references, relative references, and built-in functions. In this chapter you'll expand your understanding of formulas and functions even further. In particular, you'll find out how to use a rather elaborate variety of built-in function called a *lookup function*; and you'll explore the results of formulas that perform *date arithmetic.*

Along the way, you'll pick up some simple but important new worksheet skills. These include

- Performing *cut-and-paste* operations
- Defining *meaningful names* for worksheet ranges
- Dividing the worksheet window into *panes*

You'll continue developing the Sales Data worksheet from Chapter 4 as you work through the exercises presented in this chapter. Your first task is to prepare the worksheet for some additional columns of calculations.

Continuing the Sales Data Worksheet

Near the end of Chapter 4 you experimented on the Sales Data worksheet with various what-if scenarios, to determine the possible effects of a revised salary structure. Now you'll restore the worksheet to the original salary terms that were in effect during the past year, and you'll add a column to the worksheet for calculating year-end bonuses.

Open the Sales Data worksheet on the desktop (if it is not already displayed there) and begin your work by quickly performing the following mechanical tasks:

1. Enter the original base salary amount and commission rate back into the worksheet; the value for cell B1 is **12** (for $12,000), and the value for cell B2 is **5%**.

2. Use the mouse to select rows 1 through 6, and press ⌘-I to insert six rows at the top of the worksheet. (This new space is for a bonus *lookup table* that you'll be entering into the worksheet.)

3. Click the zoom box (at the upper-right corner of the worksheet window) to expand the worksheet over the entire available desktop space.

4. Use the mouse to reduce columns F and G to the smallest width possible for displaying the numbers those columns contain.

5. Select column H and use the Column Width command (in the Format menu) to reduce the width to 5.

6. Select column I and use Column Width to reduce the width to 6.

When you have completed these operations, the worksheet should appear as shown in Figure 5.1. Thanks to the zoomed window and the reduced column widths, you can view columns A through I on the worksheet. This is room enough for you to accomplish all of your work in the upcoming exercise without having to scroll the window back and forth.

	A	B	C	D	E	Fourth	Totals	Salary	H	I
File Edit Formula Format Data Options Macro Window										
E7			Quarterly Sales by Salesperson							
				Sales Data						
	A	B	C	D	E	F	G	H	I	
1										
2										
3										
4										
5										
6										
7	Base salary	12	*Quarterly Sales by Salesperson*							
8	Commission	5%	*(thousands of dollars)*							
9										
10		First	Second	Third	Fourth	Totals	Salary			
11	Baker, J.	26.93	14.23	4.31	13.21	$58.68	$14.93			
12	Smith, D.	20.32	9.14	0.00	6.35	$35.81	$13.79			
13	Flint, M.	28.96	11.43	0.25	8.89	$49.53	$14.48			
14	Brown, S.	4.32	14.74	12.70	7.61	$39.37	$13.97			
15	Vera, C.	15.24	27.44	27.95	20.83	$91.46	$16.57			
16	Marlow, I.	36.06	35.31	42.42	29.97	$143.76	$19.19			
17	Harper, L.	18.29	25.65	20.14	20.82	$84.90	$16.25			
18	Fleming, N.	14.73	30.12	57.63	49.79	$152.27	$19.61			
19	White, W.	23.12	26.67	27.18	25.40	$102.37	$17.12			
20	*Totals*	187.97	194.73	192.58	182.87	$758.15	$145.91			

Figure 5.1: *Revising the Sales Data worksheet*

You'll be entering the bonus lookup table into the range C1:D8. However, part of the title of the worksheet is currently displayed inside this range. To make room for the bonus table, you'll have to move the title over to the right by a couple of columns. In Excel you use the Cut and Paste commands in the Edit menu to move information from one range to another inside the worksheet. Let's see how these commands work.

Performing a Cut-and-Paste Operation

Pull down the Edit menu and examine the second, third, and fourth commands displayed in the menu list:

Cut	**⌘-X**
Copy	**⌘-C**
Paste	⌘-V

The Cut command works in conjunction with the Paste command to *move* information from a source range to a destination range. Likewise, the Copy command combines with the Paste command to *copy* information from a source to a destination. Notice that the Paste command is currently inactive (that is, the command is displayed in light gray type inside the menu list); it remains so until you perform either the Cut or the Copy command.

Briefly, here is how you perform the move and copy operations:

- To move data from one range to another, select the source range (the range that contains the information that you want to move) and perform the Cut command. Then you select the destination range and perform the Paste command. A move operation leaves the source range empty.

- To copy data from one range to another, you select the source range and perform the Copy command. Then you select the destination and perform the Paste command. A copy operation leaves the source range intact.

As you have already seen on several occasions, the Fill Right and Fill Down commands (in the Edit menu) are also useful for copying data or formulas from one place to another. When you want to copy across a row or down a column, these commands are very efficient alternatives to the two-step copy-and-paste operation. Thanks to the convenience of Fill Right and Fill Down, you may seldom find a need to use the Copy and Paste commands.

However, cut-and-paste is a quick and useful way to move information from one place to another, as you'll see in the following exercise. Perform these steps to move the worksheet title lines from their current position in column E to a new position in column G:

1. Select the range E7:E8, which contains the two title lines (even though the titles are displayed over several cells).

2. Pull down the Edit menu and select the Cut command (or simply press ⌘-X). Excel places a marquee around the selected range.

3. Activate cell G7, the top cell of the destination range. At this point your worksheet should appear as shown in Figure 5.2.

4. Pull down the Edit menu and select the Paste command (or press ⌘-V). Excel moves the two title lines to their new position in column G. After the move the two lines retain their original type styles (boldface and italics), and their alignment (centered).

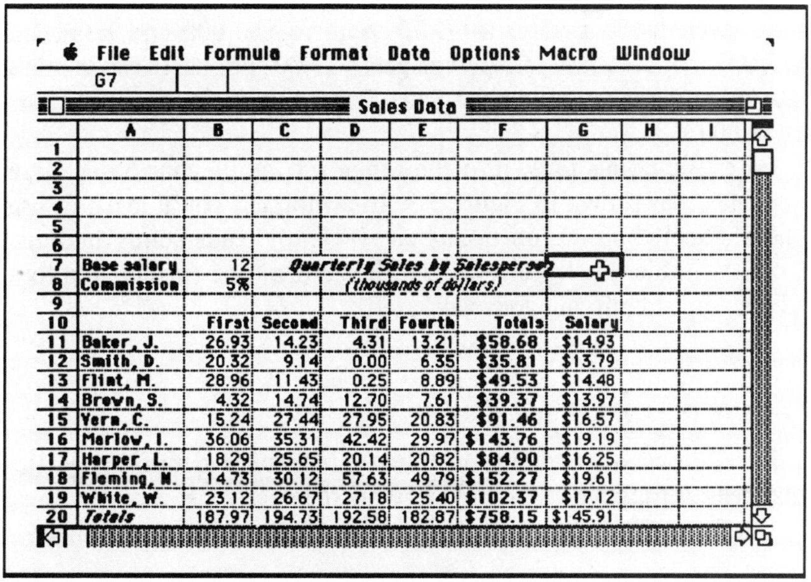

Figure 5.2: Moving text values from one range to another

Now there is room on the worksheet to place the bonus table in the range C1:D8. The bonus table is a two-column structure that shows the bonuses that you plan to award to your salespeople according to their sales levels:

Bonus Table

Sales	Bonus
0.00	0.25
50.00	1.00
75.00	1.50
100.00	2.25
125.00	3.00
150.00	3.50

This is called a *lookup table*. The quintessential example of a lookup table—an example that most people are all too familiar with—is the income tax table. On a tax table you search for your income level in the first column, and then you look across to the right to find the tax that you owe. Likewise, you can read values from the bonus table as follows: Search for the level of a salesperson's individual sales in the first column, and then look across to the second column for the corresponding bonus amount.

For instance, consider the first salesperson, who has a sales level of $58,680 for the year. The lookup table gives a bonus of $1,000 to any sales level that is greater than or equal to $50,000 and less than $75,000. Thus the first salesperson gets a $1,000 bonus. (Keep in mind that all numeric values on the Sales Data worksheet represent units of $1,000.)

Enter the bonus table into the range C1:D8 of your Sales Data worksheet, as shown in Figure 5.3. In a moment you'll learn to use one of Excel's built-in functions that efficiently reads bonus amounts from this table. First, however, you'll perform one further step that will end up simplifying your work.

Naming a Worksheet Range

Excel allows you to define meaningful names for identifying particular cells or ranges of cells on your worksheet. In most cases your use of this feature is optional; however, defining names on a worksheet—

	A	B	C	D	E	F	G	H	I
1			Bonus Table						
2			Sales	Bonus					
3			0.00	0.25					
4			50.00	1.00					
5			75.00	1.50					
6			100.00	2.25					
7	Base salary	12	125.00	3.00	*Quarterly Sales by Salesperson*				
8	Commission	5%	150.00	3.50	*(thousands of dollars)*				
9									
10		First	Second	Third	Fourth	Totals	Salary		
11	Baker, J.	26.93	14.23	4.31	13.21	$58.68	$14.93		
12	Smith, D.	20.32	9.14	0.00	6.35	$35.81	$13.79		
13	Flint, M.	28.96	11.43	0.25	8.89	$49.53	$14.48		
14	Brown, S.	4.32	14.74	12.70	7.61	$39.37	$13.97		
15	Vera, C.	15.24	27.44	27.95	20.83	$91.46	$16.57		
16	Marlow, I.	36.06	35.31	42.42	29.97	$143.76	$19.19		
17	Harper, L.	18.29	25.65	20.14	20.82	$84.90	$16.25		
18	Fleming, N.	14.73	30.12	57.63	49.79	$152.27	$19.61		
19	White, W.	23.12	26.67	27.18	25.40	$102.37	$17.12		
20	*Totals*	187.97	194.73	192.58	182.87	$758.15	$145.91		

Figure 5.3: *The bonus lookup table added to the worksheet*

especially on a complex worksheet—can result in clearer and more reliable applications.

Names are particularly useful in building formulas. For example, you'll recall the formula that you originally created to calculate the base salary plus commission for each of your salespeople. This formula currently appears in cell G11 as

= $B$7 + $B$8 * F11

(Notice that Excel has automatically adjusted the references in this formula as a result of the new rows that you have inserted at the top of the worksheet.) Imagine how much clearer this formula would be if the various cell locations were represented by meaningful names:

= Base + Commission * Sales

You can use the Define Name command in the Formula menu to define a name for any cell or range of cells on the worksheet. The most convenient way to use this command is to begin by selecting the cell or range for which you want to define a name, and then to invoke the Define Name command.

As an experiment with this command, let's assign a name to the bonus table, in the range C3:D8. The process is quick and simple:

1. Use the mouse to select the range C3:D8.

2. Pull down the Formula menu and select the Define Name command.

3. Enter the name **Bonus** into the Name box, as shown in Figure 5.4. Notice that Excel has already inserted the current range selection into the *Refers to:* box; furthermore, the range is expressed as an absolute reference, $C$3:$D$8.

4. Click the OK button (or press Return from the keyboard) to complete the operation.

The existence of this new name has no immediate effect on the appearance or structure of the worksheet. However, the name is now available for use in formulas that you write. In addition, Excel supplies another command in the Formula menu—the Paste Name command—that gives you quick access to all of the names you have defined for a given worksheet. As you'll see in the next section, the name makes the lookup table itself easier to use.

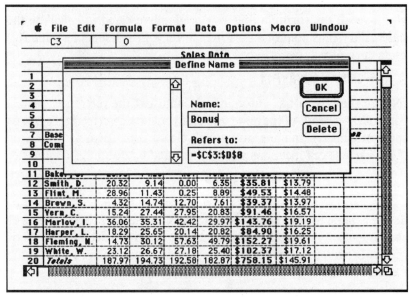

Figure 5.4: The Define Name command's dialog box

Using a Lookup Function

Excel's built-in LOOKUP function is designed to perform a lookup operation on a table that you have entered into your worksheet. (Actually, Excel has two other functions that are similar to LOOKUP. They are named HLOOKUP and VLOOKUP, and are designed to work with various shapes and forms of lookup tables. LOOKUP happens to be the simplest of these three functions to use for the Sales Data worksheet.)

Unlike the SUM function, which takes multiple numeric arguments in any order, the LOOKUP function requires two arguments in a specific order. We can represent the function's format as follows:

LOOKUP(*LookupValue, LookupTable*)

In other words, the first argument is the value that LOOKUP searches for in the lookup table, and the second argument is the range location of the lookup table itself.

For example, we can use the following formula to find the bonus for the first salesperson in the worksheet:

=LOOKUP(F11,$C$3:$D$8)

In response to this formula, Excel searches down the first column of the lookup table ($C$3:$C$8) for the level of the first salesperson's annual sales amount (F11). The LOOKUP function returns the corresponding bonus amount from the second column of the table ($D$3:$D$8).

Of course, since you have assigned a name to the lookup table, you can simplify the LOOKUP formula as follows:

=LOOKUP(F11,Bonus)

Recall that the name *Bonus* is the same as an *absolute* reference to the range of the bonus table, $C$3:$D$8. When you ultimately copy this formula down a column of the worksheet, Excel will therefore treat the lookup table as a fixed range. Let's enter the formula into the worksheet now.

Entering the Bonus Formula on the Worksheet

We'll use column H for displaying the bonuses, and column I for the total income (salary plus bonus) of each salesperson. Begin by entering appropriate labels at the top of these two columns: **Bonus** in cell H10, and **Total** in cell I10. Use the Style command and the Alignment command in the Format menu to display these labels in boldface type and to right-justify them in their respective cells. Then select the range H11:I20, and use the Number command to assign the dollar-and-cent format to these cells. Excel allows you to format a range before you actually enter data into it. The numbers that you then enter into these cells will appear in the format you have chosen.

Next select cell H11 and perform these steps:

1. Pull down the Formula menu and select the Paste Function command. Scroll down to LOOKUP in the function list, and use the mouse to highlight this name. Click the OK button to enter the function name into your formula. The formula bar appears as follows:

    = LOOKUP( )

2. Click cell F11 with the mouse to enter this cell reference as the first argument of the function. Then type the comma key to separate the first argument from the second:

    = LOOKUP(F11,)

3. Pull down the Formula menu and select the Paste Name command. This command provides a list of all the cell or range names that are currently defined for the worksheet. At the moment there is only one name, Bonus. Select the name, and click the OK button to paste the name into your function. The formula bar appears as follows:

    = LOOKUP(F11,Bonus)

4. Press Enter to complete the formula entry.

As you can see in Figure 5.5, the LOOKUP function finds the correct bonus for the first salesperson: $1,000. By the way, the Formula menu's Paste Function command and Paste Name command are designed to simplify the process of building a formula; their use is completely optional. A perfectly acceptable alternative technique for building the bonus formula is simply to enter the entire expression directly from the keyboard, starting with an equal sign. Try it if you want; as long as you type the formula correctly, the result will be the same as before.

```
  ┌─────────────────────────────────────────────────────────────────┐
  │  ▪  File  Edit  Formula  Format  Data  Options  Macro  Window    │
  │  ┌──────────┐         ┌──────────────────────┐                   │
  │  │   H11    │         │ =LOOKUP(F11,Bonus)    │                  │
  └─────────────────────────────────────────────────────────────────┘
```

	A	B	C	D	E	F	G	H	I
1			*Bonus Table*						
2			*Sales*	*Bonus*					
3			0.00	0.25					
4			50.00	1.00					
5			75.00	1.50					
6			100.00	2.25					
7	Base salary	12	125.00	3.00		*Quarterly Sales by Salesperson*			
8	Commission	5%	150.00	3.50		*(thousands of dollars)*			
9									
10		First	Second	Third	Fourth	Totals	Salary	Bonus	Total
11	Baker, J.	26.93	14.23	4.31	13.21	$58.68	$14.93	$1.00	
12	Smith, D.	20.32	9.14	0.00	6.35	$35.81	$13.79		
13	Flint, M.	28.96	11.43	0.25	8.89	$49.53	$14.48		
14	Brown, S.	4.32	14.74	12.70	7.61	$39.37	$13.97		
15	Vern, C.	15.24	27.44	27.95	20.83	$91.46	$16.57		
16	Marlow, I.	36.06	35.31	42.42	29.97	$143.76	$19.19		
17	Harper, L.	18.29	25.65	20.14	20.82	$84.90	$16.25		
18	Fleming, N.	14.73	30.12	57.63	49.79	$152.27	$19.61		
19	White, W.	23.12	26.67	27.18	25.40	$102.37	$17.12		
20	*Totals*	187.97	194.73	192.58	182.87	$758.15	$145.91		

Figure 5.5: Using the LOOKUP function

Now, before copying the bonus formula down column H, let's enter the formula for the total income:

1. Select cell I11.

2. Enter an equal sign to begin the formula.

3. Click cell G11 in the salary column.

4. Click cell H11, the newly calculated bonus. The formula bar appears as follows:

   = G11 + H11

5. Click the Enter box (or press the Enter key from the keyboard) to complete the formula entry.

Excel computes the total salary (base salary plus commission plus bonus) for the first salesperson as 15.93, representing $15,930.

Now you're ready to copy these two formulas—for the bonus and the total salary—down their respective columns.

Copying Two Formulas At Once

You have used the Fill Down command several times now to copy a single formula down its column. You have also used Fill Right to copy a formula across a row of the worksheet. Conveniently, you can use these same commands to copy multiple formulas at once. For example, the following steps copy both the bonus formula and the total salary formula in a single operation:

1. Select the range H11:I19.

2. Pull down the Edit menu and select the Fill Down command (or simply press ⌘-D from the keyboard).

You can see the result of this operation in Figure 5.6.

Press ⌘-S now to save this new version of your worksheet to disk. In our final exercise with the Sales Data worksheet, we'll discuss the use of date values in Excel worksheets.

Working with Date Values

You have mastered most of the tools available for entering and formatting text values and numeric values in a worksheet. In this section you'll begin learning about yet another kind of data value that Excel supports: dates. Excel has a convenient yet sophisticated facility for recognizing and handling dates in a worksheet. Consider the following features:

- Excel accepts—and correctly recognizes—dates that you enter into cells directly from the keyboard. (As you'll see shortly, Excel stores dates internally as numeric values.)

- The Number command in the Format menu gives you a variety of formats in which to display dates on the worksheet.

- A considerable group of built-in functions are available for working with dates.

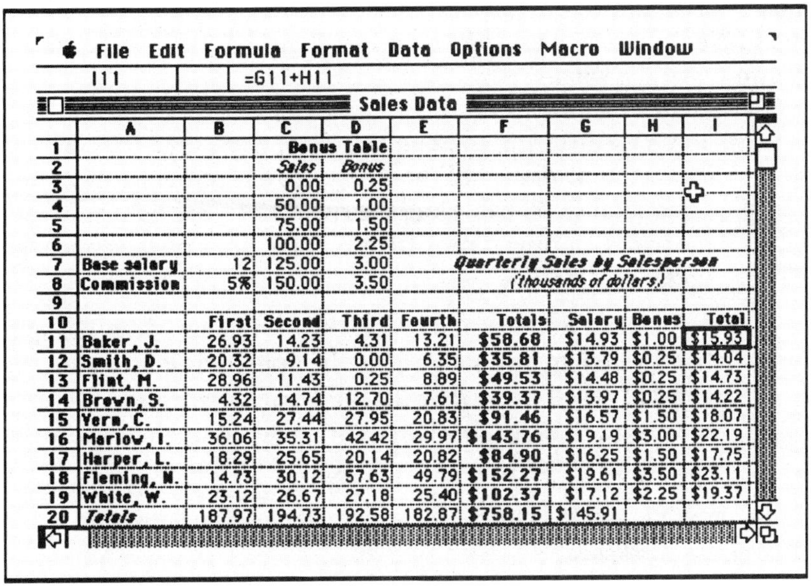

	A	B	C	D	E	F	G	H	I
1			Bonus Table						
2			*Sales*	*Bonus*					
3			0.00	0.25					
4			50.00	1.00					
5			75.00	1.50					
6			100.00	2.25					
7	Base salary	12	125.00	3.00		*Quarterly Sales by Salesperson*			
8	Commission	5%	150.00	3.50		*(thousands of dollars.)*			
9									
10		First	Second	Third	Fourth	Totals	Salary	Bonus	Total
11	Baker, J.	26.93	14.23	4.31	13.21	$58.68	$14.93	$1.00	$15.93
12	Smith, D.	20.32	9.14	0.00	6.35	$35.81	$13.79	$0.25	$14.04
13	Flint, M.	28.96	11.43	0.25	8.89	$49.53	$14.48	$0.25	$14.73
14	Brown, S.	4.32	14.74	12.70	7.61	$39.37	$13.97	$0.25	$14.22
15	Yern, C.	15.24	27.44	27.95	20.83	$91.46	$16.57	$1.50	$18.07
16	Marlow, I.	36.06	35.31	42.42	29.97	$143.76	$19.19	$3.00	$22.19
17	Harper, L.	18.29	25.65	20.14	20.82	$84.90	$16.25	$1.50	$17.75
18	Fleming, N.	14.73	30.12	57.63	49.79	$152.27	$19.61	$3.50	$23.11
19	White, W.	23.12	26.67	27.18	25.40	$102.37	$17.12	$2.25	$19.37
20	*Totals*	187.97	194.73	192.58	182.87	$758.15	$145.91		

Figure 5.6: *Copying two formulas at once*

- Excel supports two important *date-arithmetic* operations: you can subtract one date from another to find the number of days between the two dates, or you can add a number of days to a given date to produce a new date.

We'll explore some of these features in the following exercises.

Dividing the Window into Panes

We'll use columns J and K of the Sales Data worksheet for our experiments with dates. Unfortunately, there is no further room on the desktop to display additional columns of this worksheet. You can, of course, scroll the worksheet horizontally until columns J and K come into view; but then you can no longer see column A, which contains the names of your salespeople.

Excel provides a simple solution for this particular problem: you can divide the worksheet window into more than one *pane*. Panes are separate divisions of the worksheet window that you can scroll semi-independently. You can create two horizontal panes and two vertical panes—as many as four panes at once. To do so, you drag one of two small black bars, called *split bars* (see Figure 5.7), located in the perimeter of the window:

- To create a vertical division between panes, drag the split bar located immediately to the left of the left scroll arrow on the horizontal scroll bar. Drag the split bar to the right to create the panes, or drag it back to its original position to restore the undivided window.

- To create a horizontal division between panes, drag the split bar located immediately above the upper scroll arrow on the vertical scroll bar. Drag the split bar downward to create the panes, or drag it back to its original position to restore the undivided window.

For example, perform these steps to create a vertical division in the Sales Data worksheet:

1. Position the mouse pointer over the vertical split bar located at the left side of the horizontal scroll bar. (As you do so, the pointer is transformed into a pair of short vertical lines, with small arrows that point to the right and left.)

2. Press the mouse button and drag the split bar to the right, until the double-line pane division is located over the border between columns A and B.

3. Release the mouse button. Notice that the new panes have independent horizontal scroll bars.

4. Scroll the pane on the right side of the window until columns J and K are displayed next to column A in the other pane. Your worksheet should look like Figure 5.7. You can now view the salespeoples' names while you enter new data into columns J and K.

Entering Dates from the Keyboard

In column J you'll enter the date on which each sales person was hired. Then in column K you'll use these dates to compute the total

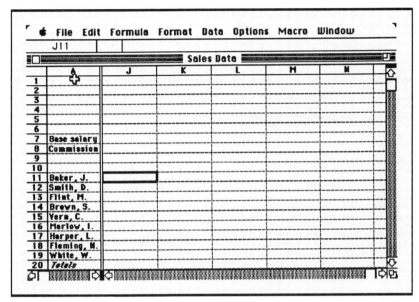

Figure 5.7: *Splitting the worksheet window into panes*

number of years each person has worked for the firm. Begin this exercise by entering the label **Date Hired** into cell J10, and **Years w/ Firm** into cell I10. Use the Style command in the Format menu to display these labels in boldface type.

You'll enter the dates in the following format:

month/day/year

For example, enter the following date for the first salesperson into cell J11:

1/5/85

When you press the Enter key to complete the date entry, you'll notice two rather subtle changes that take place on the desktop:

- Excel right-justifies the date value in its cell, suggesting that the entry will be treated as a numeric value.

- The formula bar displays the date value in a slightly expanded form:

1/5/1985

These two small changes are enough to show you that Excel has recognized your entry as a date value.

Enter the rest of the dates into column J, as shown in Figure 5.8. To facilitate the performance of arithmetic operations with dates, Excel actually stores dates internally as numeric values, although there is currently no indication on the Sales Data worksheet that this is the case. Let's explore this situation.

Understanding Serial Numbers

The following experiment reveals the way in which Excel handles dates:

1. Select the range of dates J11:J19.

2. Pull down the Format menu, and select the Numbers command.

3. Scroll up to the top of the list of formats, and select the General format.

4. Click the OK box to complete the operation.

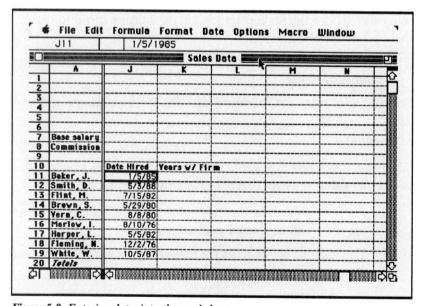

Figure 5.8: Entering dates into the worksheet

As a result of these steps, the date values are transformed into five-digit integer values, as you can see in Figure 5.9.

What is the relationship between these numbers and the dates that you originally entered into the worksheet? The answer is simple: Each of these values represents a count of the number of days forward from the starting date in Excel's chronological system, up to the date that you have entered. Specifically, the starting date in the system is January 1, 1904. Thus the number displayed in cell J11 shows you that the date January 5, 1985 is 29,590 days forward from January 1, 1904.

The Excel documentation refers to the numeric values that you see in column J as *serial numbers*. (Another term you may encounter in other contexts is *scalar dates*.) Here is the full range of serial numbers supported in Excel's date system:

- The number 0 represents January 1, 1904.

- The number 49710 represents February 6, 2040, the last date recognized in the system.

Consecutive numbers from 1 to 49709 therefore represent the dates from January 2, 1904 to February 5, 2040.

| | **File** | **Edit** | **Formula** | **Format** | **Data** | **Options** | **Macro** | **Window** |

| J11 | | 29590 |

Sales Data

	A	J	K	L	M	N
1						
2						
3						
4						
5						
6						
7	Base salary					
8	Commission					
9						
10		Date Hired	Years w/ Firm			
11	Baker, J.	29590				
12	Smith, D.	30804				
13	Flint, M.	28685				
14	Brown, S.	27908				
15	Vera, C.	27979				
16	Marlow, I.	26520				
17	Harper, L.	28614				
18	Fleming, N.	26634				
19	White, W.	30593				
20	*Totals*					

Figure 5.9: *Dates converted to integer values*

As you'll see shortly, this numeric system is very convenient when you want to find the difference, in days, between two dates. To perform this operation all you have to do is subtract one date from another; internally, Excel finds the difference between the serial number equivalents of the two dates.

Let's convert the serial numbers in the Sales Data worksheet back into a readable date format. The Number command in the Format menu offers a variety of predefined formats for displaying serial numbers as recognizable dates. To examine these formats, perform the following steps:

1. Select the range J11:J19.

2. Pull down the Format menu, and select the Number command.

3. Scroll about half-way down the list of formats to locate the predefined date formats. As shown in Figure 5.10, select the format that looks like this:

    d-mmm-yy

4. Click OK (or press the Return key) to complete the operation.

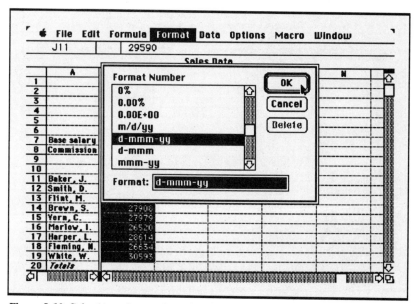

Figure 5.10: Selecting a format for a date value

The dates are now in a new format, in which the month is presented as a three-letter abbreviation. For example, the first date in the list now appears as follows:

5-Jan-85

You're now ready to use these dates in a calculation.

Performing Date Arithmetic

To find the number of *days* that a given salesperson has worked for the firm, you can subtract the date the person was hired from today's date. Dividing the result by 365 yields the number of years the person has worked for the firm.

Excel has a built-in function that supplies the serial equivalent of today's date. The function is named NOW; it reads today's date from the internal calendar built into the Macintosh computer. NOW requires no arguments.

The following expression gives the number of days that the first salesperson has worked for the firm:

= NOW( ) – J11

Consequently this formula gives the number of years:

= (NOW( ) – J11)/365

The parentheses in this second formula force Excel to perform the subtraction before the division, as discussed in Chapter 4. Also notice that the reference to the NOW function must be followed by a pair of empty parentheses, even though the function does not take arguments. This is the notation that Excel requires in order to recognize the name of a function.

Enter this formula into cell K11, and then perform the Fill Down command to copy the formula down the column. Use the Number command in the Format menu to display the numbers with two decimal places (the format represented by *0.00*). The result of your work is shown in Figure 5.11.

As a final exercise, you might want to create formulas to compute some simple statistics about the employees' length of service. Enter

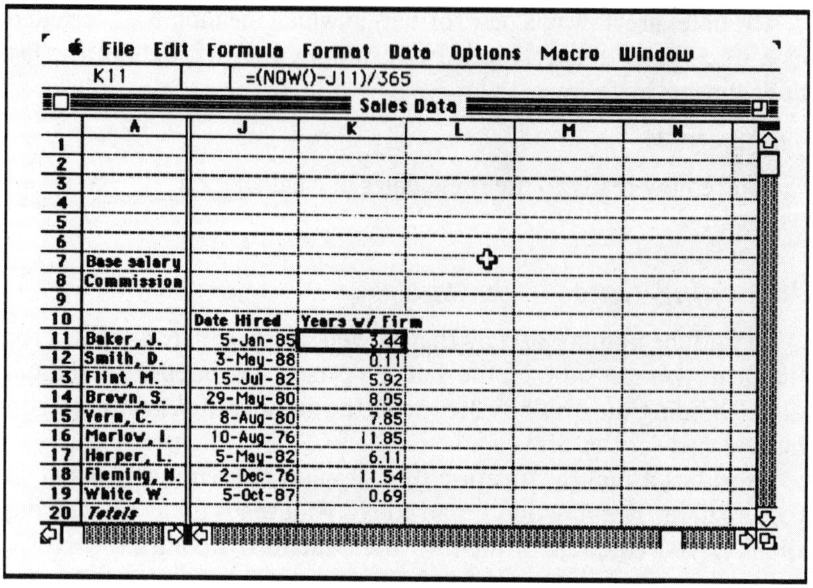

Figure 5.11: *The completed date-arithmetic calculations*

these formulas into cells K20 and K21, respectively:

> **= SUM(K11:K19)**
> **= AVERAGE(K11:K19)**

As its name indicates, the AVERAGE function computes the average of a range of values.

Now enter the following two labels into cells L20 and L21, respectively:

> **(total employee years)**
> **(average employee years)**

These labels describe the results of the two functions. Your worksheet now appears as shown in Figure 5.12.

You have now worked with four of Excel's built-in functions:

- SUM and AVERAGE are simple arithmetic functions that return simple values.

- LOOKUP is a somewhat more complex function that fetches a value from a lookup table that you have entered onto the worksheet.

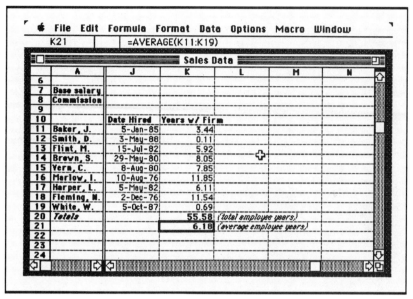

Figure 5.12: *Computing statistics on employees' lengths of service*

- NOW is a chronological function that supplies the serial equivalent of today's date.

We'll be discussing additional built-in functions as we explore the other components of the Excel program.

PART III

Enhancing Your Presentations with Charts

6

Creating Charts from Your Worksheet Data

Featuring:

Using the Gallery menu

Adding a legend and a title to a chart

Creating a chart from multiple worksheet selections

Printing and saving a chart

Once you have developed a worksheet application, Excel offers a seemingly endless variety of options for creating charts from the numeric values in your worksheet. Not only can you select among a large "gallery" of chart types, but you can also control almost every visual detail of the chart type you select. Excel gives you the tools to meet the requirements of your application, and to satisfy your own sense of graphic aesthetics. Furthermore, Excel's what-if facility extends efficiently to charts; if you make changes in the worksheet that supplies data to a given chart, Excel automatically redraws the chart to reflect changes in the data.

The first steps in creating a chart are remarkably simple, as you'll discover in this chapter. The general procedure is as follows:

1. Select the range of worksheet data for which you want to create a chart.

2. Open a new chart document onto the desktop. Excel quickly draws an initial version of your chart, according to the data you have selected.

3. Modify the initial chart in any way you wish: change the chart type, add new elements such as a legend and a title, and make any appropriate adjustments in the presentation.

This chapter guides you through these three basic steps in detail. You'll begin by inventing yet another worksheet application from the table of numbers that you've stored on disk under the name Data Table. The subject of this new application is far removed from the earlier applictions you've worked with; the worksheet's title is "Seasonal Precipitation in Major U.S. Cities." Once you've created this worksheet, you'll design two charts to illustrate different portions of the data.

Preparing the Seasonal Precipitation Worksheet

Figure 6.1 shows the application you'll develop for your work in this chapter. Begin by loading the basic Data Table worksheet onto the desktop from disk. Then follow these steps to create the precipitation worksheet:

1. Use the mouse to select the range containing the table of numbers—A1:D9.

2. Pull down the Format menu and select the Number command. Select the format represented simply as 0; this format displays numbers as rounded integers. Click the OK button to complete the formatting operation.

3. Drag the mouse to select rows 1 through 5, and then press ⌘-I to insert five blank rows at the top of the data table.

4. Likewise, select column A and press ⌘-I again to insert a blank column at the left side of the data table.

5. Enter the list of city names in the range A6:A14, in the following order:

   Honolulu
   Los Angeles
   San Francisco
   Denver
   St. Louis
   New Orleans
   Cleveland
   Miami
   New York

6. Enter the following two title lines into cells C1 and C2, respectively:

   Seasonal Precipitation in Major U.S. Cities
   (centimeters)

7. Select the range C1:C2, pull down the Format menu, and select the Alignment command. Activate the Center option, and click OK to complete the operation. This step centers the title text horizontally around column C.

8. Use the Style command in the format menu to display the first line of the title in boldface type and the second line in italics.

9. Enter the following four column labels into the range of cells from B5 to E5:

   Winter   Spring   Summer   Fall

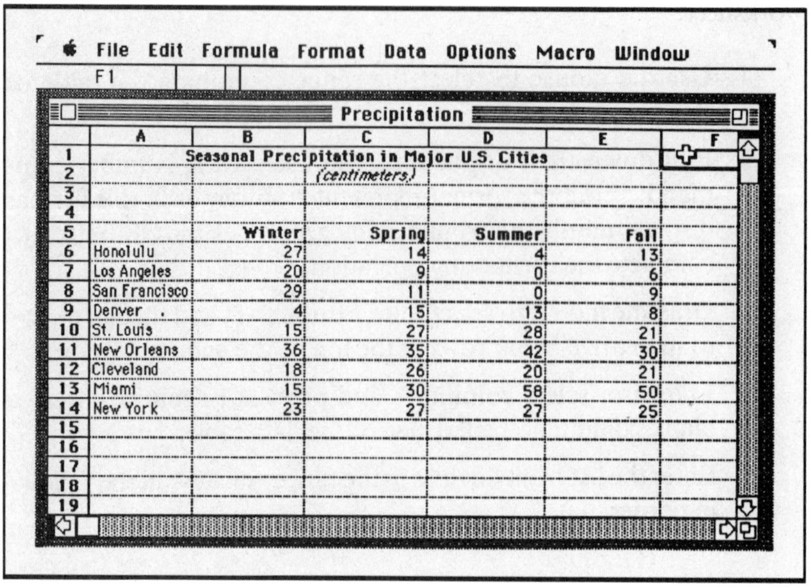

Figure 6.1: *Developing the precipitation worksheet*

10. Use the Style command to display these four column labels in boldface type, and the Alignment command to right-justify each label in its cell.

11. Use the Save As command to save the worksheet on disk under the name **Precipitation**.

Now you are ready to produce a chart from the precipitation worksheet. In the following exercise you'll create a *stacked-column chart*, in which the annual precipitation of each city in the worksheet is represented by a multipatterned vertical column. Each pattern in a given column represents one season's average precipitation for the corresponding city.

Creating Your First Chart

Conveniently, Excel can incorporate both numeric and text data from your worksheet into a chart. As you design a worksheet from which you intend eventually to create a chart, you should keep in mind that the row labels and column labels you write to identify your worksheet data can also become part of the chart. You'll see exactly how this happens as you work through this first exercise.

Use the range A5:E14 on the precipitation worksheet as the target data for the first chart. Note that this range includes the column of city names and the row of column labels, along with the nine-row by four-column range of numeric data. Follow these simple steps to create the initial version of your chart:

1. Select the target range, A5:E14.

2. Pull down the File menu and select the New command (or simply press ⌘-N from the keyboard). Then click the Chart option (as shown in Figure 6.2); this instructs Excel to open a new chart document onto the desktop. Click OK to complete the operation. Excel immediately opens a new chart document named Chart1, and draws a bar chart inside the window.

3. Click the zoom box (at the upper-right corner of the chart window) to expand the window over the entire available desktop space.

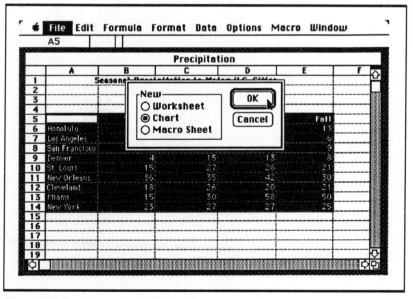

Figure 6.2: Creating a chart with the New command

Figure 6.3 shows the chart. At this point, there are two documents on the desktop relating to the precipitation application—the original worksheet and your new chart. We say that the chart is *linked* to the worksheet, because Excel has built the chart from references to data stored in the worksheet. If you change the worksheet data, a corresponding change occurs on the chart. We'll continue discussing this point in upcoming chapters.

By default, Excel initially draws a column chart, in which each value in the worksheet is represented by an individual column. The height of each column represents the relative magnitude of the corresponding numeric value from the worksheet, and the numbers displayed along the chart's vertical axis show how column heights translate into actual values from the worksheet.

The four seasonal columns for a given city are grouped together, and the name of the city appears just below the horizontal axis of the chart. (Later in this chapter you'll learn how to add a *legend* to the chart to identify the meaning of each distinct pattern on the chart.) In short, the juxtaposition of all these individual columns gives you an instant picture of the whole data set.

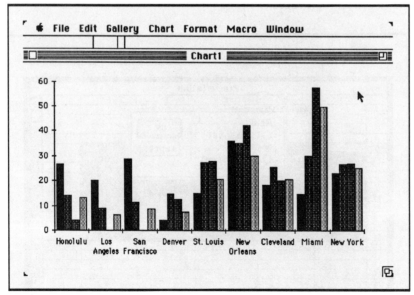

Figure 6.3: The chart created automatically from the precipitation worksheet

However, this is not the type of chart that you originally set out to create. For this particular application, a stacked column chart more clearly expresses the meaning of the data. Fortunately, Excel gives you a convenient set of menu commands to modify the chart type.

You may be surprised to notice that some changes have occurred in the menu line at the top of the desktop. Here is what the menu looks like now:

File   Edit   Gallery   Chart   Format   Macro   Window

This menu appears whenever the *active document* is a chart. (The active document is simply the window that you have selected on the desktop for your current work. As you first learned in Chapter 2, you can select and activate a window on the desktop by pulling down the window menu and selecting the corresponding window name. You can also simply click a document with the mouse to activate it.)

In the menu line for charts, the Formula, Data, and Options menus disappear, and two new menus—Gallery and Chart—take their place. (You return control of desktop activities to the worksheet menu by activating any worksheet.) The Gallery menu is the tool you use to change the format of the active chart document. Let's examine this menu.

Using the Gallery Menu

When you pull down the Gallery menu you'll see a list of the seven different chart types that Excel can produce. Each of these types uses a different graphic scheme to represent series of numbers from a worksheet. Here are brief general descriptions of the seven types:

- An *area* chart represents a set of data as a filled-in area on the chart. The top border of the area slants up or down the width of the chart, depicting the magnitude of the numeric data from the linked worksheet.

- A *bar* chart represents individual numbers as horizontal bars on the chart. The length of a given bar represents the relative magnitude of the corresponding numeric value.

- A *column* chart, as you have already seen, represents individual values as vertical columns on the chart.

- A *line* chart represents numbers as individual points on the chart. You can instruct Excel to connect the points representing a given series of numbers, creating a line that depicts upward or downward trends in the data.

- A *pie* chart represents individual numbers as wedges of a circle radiating from a common center, like slices of pie. The internal angle of each wedge indicates the magnitude of each numeric value in relation to the total of all the values.

- A *scatter* chart, perhaps the most complex of the seven types, represents *ordered pairs* of numbers as individual points on the chart. This means that the horizontal position of a given point represents one number (sometimes referred to as the X value), and the vertical position represents a second number (the Y value). A group of such points may depict a mathematically significant correlation between two sets of numbers.

- A *combination* chart uses two different graphic schemes to represent different sets of numbers from the worksheet. For example, one data set might appear as columns while another could be represented as lines superimposed over the columns.

When you select one of these chart types from the Gallery menu, Excel displays a dialog box giving you even more options. Each of the different chart types has several different formats; the dialog box for a given Gallery command shows you pictures representing the formats available. For example, the dialog box for the Column command appears in Figure 6.4. As you can see, Excel offers eight different column chart formats under this command. Initially the first of these is highlighted (that is, displayed with a dark background). You can change the format of the chart you are currently working on by selecting one of the other options.

Notice that the dialog box also has buttons labeled Next... and Previous... You can use these buttons to switch directly to the dialog box for one of Excel's other chart types. For example, from the Column dialog box you can click the Previous... button to view the dialog box for the Bar chart command, or the Next... button to view the dialog box for the Line chart command. This gives you an easy way to browse around the available types and formats if you are not exactly

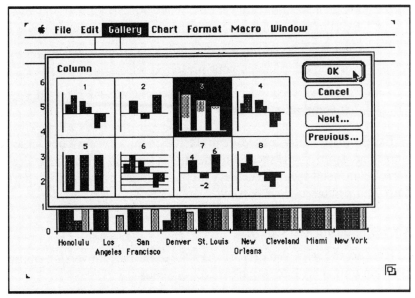

Figure 6.4: *The Column command from the Gallery menu*

sure how you want to display your chart. (You might want to use these buttons now to give yourself a quick tour of Excel's seven chart types.)

In the earlier versions of Excel, the Next... and Previous... buttons are not available; if you are working in one of these versions, you have to pull down the Gallery menu and select a chart command each time you want to view the dialog box for a given chart type.

Changing the Preferred Chart Format

By the way, you might notice that a check mark appears at the left of the Column command in the Gallery menu. The column chart is currently the default, or *preferred*, type of chart. When you first create a chart from a worksheet, Excel initially formats the chart according to the selected format in the preferred chart type. (You have seen this happen already in Figure 6.3.)

You can perform these steps to change the preferred chart type:

1. Pull down the Gallery menu, and select the chart type that you want to designate as the preferred type.

2. From the resulting dialog box, select the format that you want Excel to use as the preferred format for a new chart.

3. Click OK. Excel then redraws the chart you are currently working on to match your preferred selection.

4. Pull down the Chart menu and select the Set Preferred Format command.

Excel subsequently uses your preferred format for any new chart you create from a worksheet. Furthermore, you can perform the Preferred command from the Gallery menu to transform an active chart into your preferred chart format.

Creating a Stacked Column Chart

Here are the steps you perform to change the current version of the precipitation chart into a stacked column chart:

1. Pull down the Gallery menu and select the Column command.

2. Use the mouse to select the third format option in the Column dialog box. The graphic icon for this option represents a stacked column chart.

3. Click the OK button to complete the operation.

Figure 6.5 shows the resulting chart. Now the chart has one column representing each city in the precipitation worksheet. Each column is divided into differently patterned sections, depicting the four seasonal precipitation levels. (These divisions are stacked one on top of another, which explains the name of this particular chart format.) The total height of a given column shows the annual precipitation for the corresponding city. As before, you can read the value represented by a particular column height from the numbers displayed along the vertical axis at the left side of the chart.

Adding New Elements to the Chart

Once you have selected the chart format that you want to work with, Excel gives you a large variety of tools for customizing your chart. For example, you can add new graphics and text to the chart,

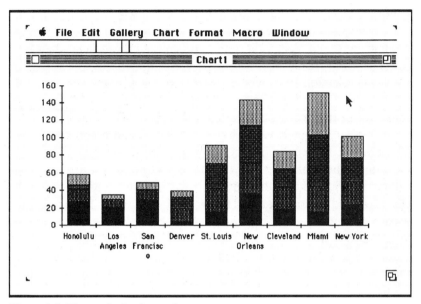

Figure 6.5: *The stacked column chart*

and you can reformat existing features. The commands for performing these operations are located in the Chart and Format menus. (Keep in mind that the Gallery and Chart menus appear on the menu line only when the active document is a chart. Furthermore, the Format menu for an active chart is very different from the Format menu for a worksheet.)

We'll explore many of these commands and options in Chapter 7. For now, your stacked bar chart seems incomplete without at least two more text features. Specifically, the chart needs

- A *legend* to explain the meaning of the differently patterned portions that make up each column
- A title to identify the application

Let's see how to add these two elements to the chart.

Adding a Legend

A legend is box of information that explains the patterns or symbols on the chart itself. Excel normally gets the text for a legend directly from the labels on your worksheet.

For example, a legend on your current chart will show the patterns that correspond to the four seasons of precipitation: Winter, Spring, Summer, and Fall. As you'll recall, you entered these four labels into row 5 of your original worksheet, and you included this row as part of the range selection from which Excel has created the chart. For this reason, the appropriate Legend labels are already available for the chart; to see them, all you have to do is activate the legend.

To display a legend, you select the Add Legend command in the Chart menu. You may subsequently want to move the legend to a new location in the chart area. By default, Excel places the legend vertically at the right side of the chart. Unfortunately, your precipitation chart is already a little cramped horizontally. (Notice in Figure 6.5 that there is not quite enough horizontal space to display all the city names in unbroken lines of text: the name *San Francisco* is split over three lines.) For this reason, you'll probably want to transform the shape of the legend to a horizontal format, and display it along the bottom of the chart.

Here are the steps for creating the legend and displaying it at the most convenient location for this chart:

1. Pull down the Chart menu and select the Add Legend command. The legend automatically appears at the right side of the chart area.

2. Use the mouse to select the legend: position the mouse pointer over any part of the legend itself, and click the mouse button. In response, Excel displays small circles around the legend's border to indicate that you have selected the legend for some further operation (see Figure 6.6).

3. Pull down the Format menu and select the Legend command.

4. Click the Bottom option, as shown in Figure 6.6. This option moves the legend to the bottom of the chart area.

5. Click OK to complete the operation.

6. Position the pointer in a blank portion of the chart area, and click the mouse button. This deselects the legend, removing the small circles from the legend's border.

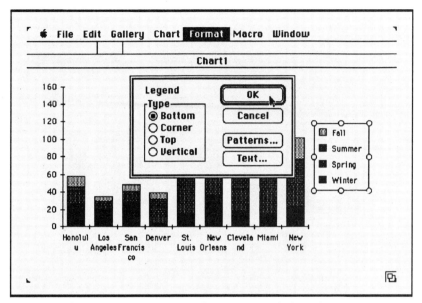

Figure 6.6: *Using the Legend command to reposition the legend*

The resulting chart appears in Figure 6.7. Notice that all of the city names are now displayed appropriately, and the legend box is located immediately below these names. Thanks to the legend, you can now easily see the meaning of each pattern in the stacked columns.

By the way, when a legend appears in the active chart, Excel changes the Add Legend command (in the Chart menu) to the Delete Legend command. You can use this new command if you should want to remove the legend from your chart.

Your next step is to add a title to the chart.

Adding a Title

The Attach Text command in the Chart menu allows you to add explanatory text to one of several fixed locations in the chart. For example, you can use this command to add a title or a label for the horizontal or vertical axis. When you use the Attach Text command, Excel determines the appropriate location for displaying the text. (In contrast, you can also place *unattached text* inside your chart, and display it at any location in the chart area. You'll learn how to do this in Chapter 7.)

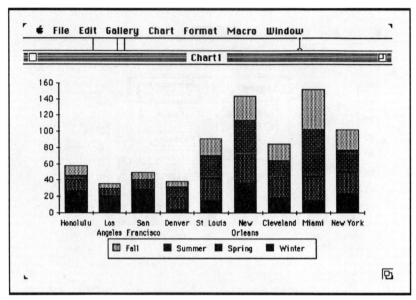

Figure 6.7: *The legend relocated at the bottom of the chart*

Adding a title requires several steps. First you invoke the Attach Text command, then you enter the actual title into the chart. Finally you perform any appropriate formatting operations to change the appearance of the title.

Here are the steps for adding a title to the precipitation chart:

1. Pull down the Chart menu and select the Attach Text command.

2. In the resulting dialog box, the default option selection is Chart Title, as shown in Figure 6.8. Click the OK button to accept this selection. At the top of the chart, Excel displays the word *Title*, surrounded by a border of small circles. The circles—and the appearance of the title in the formula bar at the top of the desktop—show you that this title text is selected for some further operation.

3. To change the title text, simply begin typing the actual title for the chart in the formula bar. Here are the three lines of text to

use for the precipitation chart:

**Seasonal Precipitation
in Major U.S. Cities
(centimeters)**

As you type these lines, the text appears inside the formula bar. Press the Return key after each of the first two lines. The formula bar expands to accommodate a multiple-line title (Figure 6.9).

4. After you have typed the third line of the title, press the Enter key to complete the text entry.

5. Click the mouse in any blank portion of the chart area to deselect the title text.

Note the important distinction between the Return key and the Enter key in the process of entering the title. The Return key expands the formula bar to make room for another line of text. The Enter key completes the text entry and displays the title on the chart.

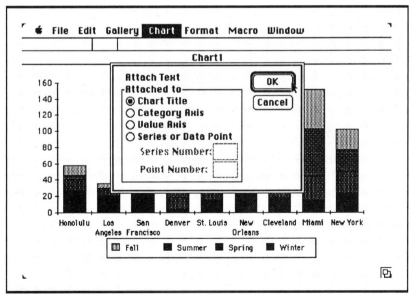

Figure 6.8: *Adding a title to the chart*

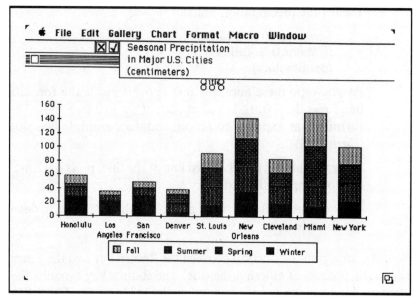

Figure 6.9: *Entering text for the title using the formula bar*

The resulting chart appears as shown in Figure 6.10. If you compare this chart closely with Figure 6.7, you'll notice that Excel has proportionally reduced the heights of the columns a bit to make room for the title.

Just as on a worksheet, you can reformat the text in a chart in boldface and italic type styles. You'll learn how to do this in the next section.

Formatting the Title Text

The Text command in the Format menu offers a variety of options for displaying text in a chart. You can use this command to change the font, the style, the orientation, and the alignment of the text. (You can even change the color of the text if you are working on a Macintosh with a color screen.)

However, the Text command is available only when you have actually selected some text on the chart. For this reason, you begin the following exercise by selecting the title again:

1. Click the title with the mouse. (Excel places the border of small circles around the title, and displays the title in the formula bar.)

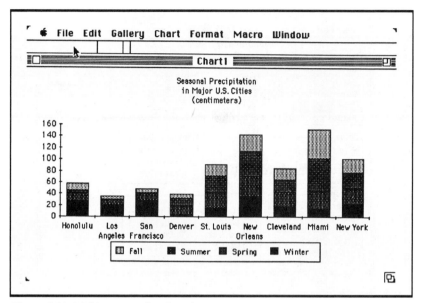

Figure 6.10: *Making room for the title*

2. Pull down the Format menu and select the Text command. The resulting dialog box is shown in Figure 6.11.

3. Click both the Bold and Italic options in the Style box.

4. Click the OK button to complete the operation.

5. Click the mouse at any blank portion in the chart area to deselect the title text.

The title now appears in boldface italics.

*S*aving the Chart

The process of saving a chart as a file on disk is essentially the same as saving a worksheet document. The first time you save the chart, you use the Save As command, which gives you the opportunity to supply a name for the file. Perform these steps to save the precipitation chart:

1. Pull down the File menu and select the Save As command.

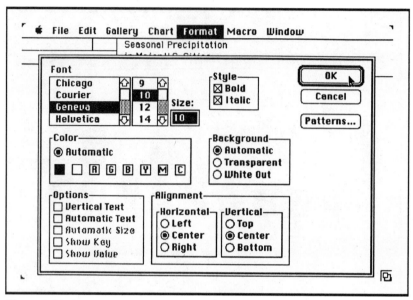

Figure 6.11: *The dialog box for the Text command*

2. Use the Drive and/or Eject buttons if necessary to select the appropriate drive and change the disk for the save operation.

3. Enter the text **Precipitation Chart** as the name of the chart.

4. Click the Save button (or press the Return key) to complete the save operation.

You can see in Figure 6.12 that the filename you supply becomes the new name of the chart window.

Whenever you create one document that is linked to another, Excel encourages you to save the supporting document before you save the dependent document. In an application using a worksheet and a chart, these documents can be defined as follows:

- The *supporting document* is the worksheet that supplies the data for building the chart.

- The *dependent document* is the chart that is linked to the worksheet.

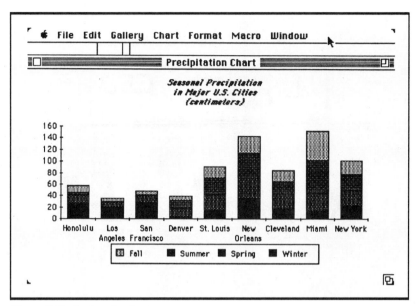

Figure 6.12: *Saving the chart*

In the precipitation application you have developed a supporting worksheet and a dependent column chart. You should therefore save the worksheet to disk before you attempt to save the chart.

If you attempt to save a chart before ever saving the supporting worksheet, Excel displays an alert box on the screen, asking you, in effect, if you are sure you want to proceed. If you see this question (as shown in Figure 6.13), you should click the Cancel box to terminate the current save operation. Then save the two documents in the suggested order. (You'll learn much more about the links between charts and worksheets in Chapter 8.)

Creating a Chart from Multiple Worksheet Selections

Version 1.5 of Excel allows you to create a chart from noncontiguous ranges on your worksheet. This means that you can select distant rows or columns of data to build a chart from a worksheet application. In this

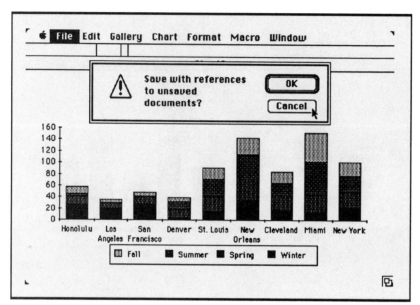

Figure 6.13: *The alert box when saving a dependent document before saving the supporting document*

section we'll explore this useful new feature by building a second chart from the precipitation worksheet.

Selecting More than One Range on the Worksheet

You have frequently used the mouse to select ranges on a worksheet, but up to now these ranges have always been contiguous selections of cells. Now you'll see how to use the Command key (⌘) along with the mouse to make selections that consist of more than one range.

Pull down the Window menu and activate the precipitation worksheet. Let's say that you now want to create a pie chart depicting the seasonal precipitation for one individual city—St. Louis, for example. Unlike the stacked column chart that you built earlier, a pie chart illustrates a single set of worksheet data—one row or one column of numbers. Along with this numeric data, Excel can incorporate a range of labels from the worksheet into a legend for the chart.

In short, to create a pie chart for the annual precipitation in St. Louis, you would like to select two rows of data from the precipitation worksheet:

- The labels displayed in the range A5:E5
- The label and numbers displayed in the range A10:E10

Here are the steps for making this selection:

1. Drag the mouse pointer over the range A5:E5 to select the row of labels.

2. Hold down the ⌘ key at the keyboard. At the same time, drag the mouse pointer over the range A10:E10 to select the row of data for St. Louis.

Figure 6.14 shows what your worksheet should look like at this point. This two-range selection includes the exact data set that you want to include in your pie chart for St. Louis. You are now ready to build that chart.

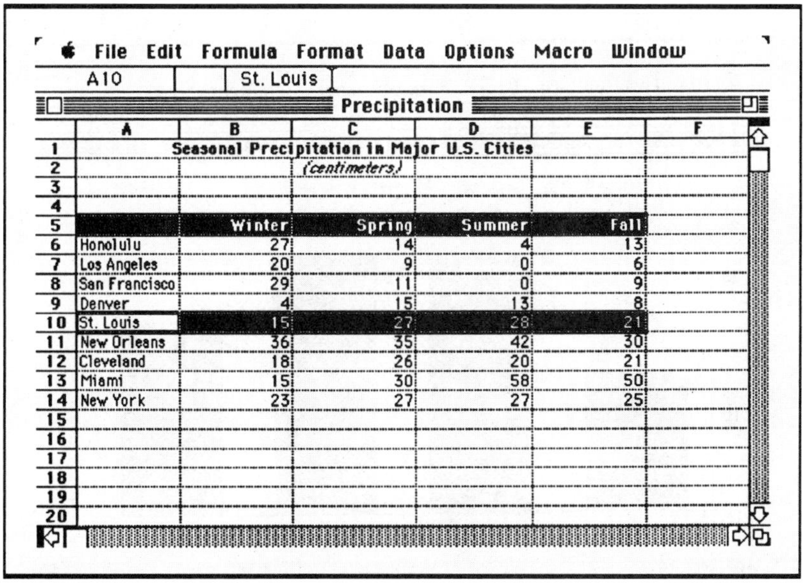

	A	B	C	D	E	F
1	Seasonal Precipitation in Major U.S. Cities					
2		(centimeters)				
3						
4						
5		Winter	Spring	Summer	Fall	
6	Honolulu	27	14	4	13	
7	Los Angeles	20	9	0	6	
8	San Francisco	29	11	0	9	
9	Denver	4	15	13	8	
10	St. Louis	15	27	28	21	
11	New Orleans	36	35	42	30	
12	Cleveland	18	26	20	21	
13	Miami	15	30	58	50	
14	New York	23	27	27	25	
15						
16						
17						
18						
19						
20						

Menu bar: ⌘ File Edit Formula Format Data Options Macro Window

A10   St. Louis

Precipitation

Figure 6.14: *Selecting two ranges at once*

Creating a Chart from the Selected Ranges

Here are the steps for creating the St. Louis chart:

1. Pull down the File menu and select the New command (or simply press ⌘-N from the keyboard).

2. Select the Chart option on the New command's dialog box, and click the OK button to create the new chart document. Excel initially creates a column chart (the current preferred format) for the selected data, as shown in Figure 6.15. Notice that the new chart window is named Chart2.

3. Pull down the Gallery menu and select the Pie command. Figure 6.16 shows the available pie chart formats in the resulting dialog box.

4. Select the sixth format (which displays the numeric percentage of each wedge in the chart), and click the OK button to complete the operation. Excel draws a pie chart in which each wedge represents St. Louis precipitation during one of the four seasons.

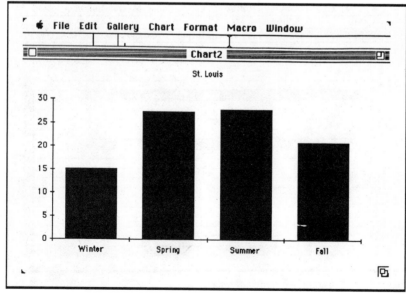

Figure 6.15: The preferred-format chart created from the two ranges

5. Pull down the Chart menu and select the Add Legend command. A legend appears at the right side of the chart area, identifying the four patterns displayed in the chart wedges.

Figure 6.17 shows the chart at this point in your work. Notice that Excel has automatically taken the label in cell A10 of your worksheet—*St. Louis*—as the chart's title. You'll probably want to expand this title a little, and then save your worksheet on disk. Here are the steps:

1. Position the mouse pointer over the title in the chart area, and click the mouse to select the title. A border of small circles appears around the selected title, and the text appears in the formula bar.

2. Position the mouse pointer at the end of the text in the formula bar and click the mouse button. Press the Return key to add a new line to the title. Type the following text as the second line:

Normal Precipitation

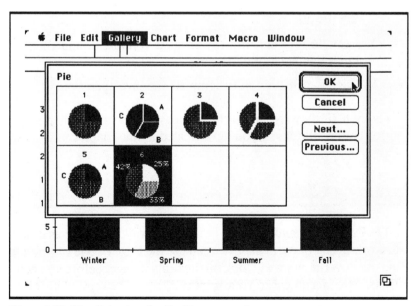

Figure 6.16: The dialog box for the Pie command

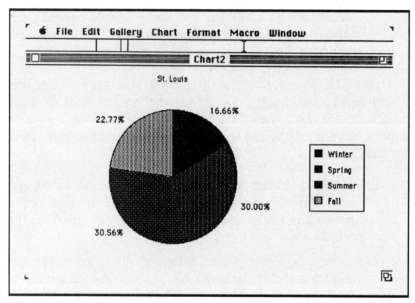

Figure 6.17: The pie chart created from the two ranges

3. Press the Enter key to complete the editing operation.

4. Click the mouse in a blank portion of the chart area to deselect the title.

5. Press ⌘-S to perform the Save As command, and enter **St.
   Louis Weather** as the filename.

6. Click the OK button to complete the save operation.

Figure 6.18 shows your chart. You may now want to try printing
one or both of the charts you have created in this chapter.

*P*rinting a Chart

The Print command operates in the same way for charts as it does
for worksheets. In particular, you can use the Page Preview option to
find out how the chart will look on the printed page, before you actually send the document to your printer.

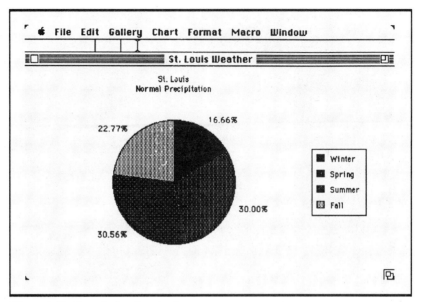

Figure 6.18: *Completing the pie chart*

Perform these steps to print a chart:

1. Use the Window menu, if necessary, to activate the chart that you want to print.

2. Pull down the File menu and select the Print command (or simply press ⌘-P).

3. Click Page Preview to activate this option. (An X appears in the small box located at the left of the option.)

4. Click OK to view the preview. The preview screen is shown in Figure 6.19.

5. If you are satisfied with the chart, click the Print button to send it to your printer.

As you examine your printed chart, review the basic charting skills you have mastered in this chapter:

• Performing the New command to create a chart from a worksheet selection.

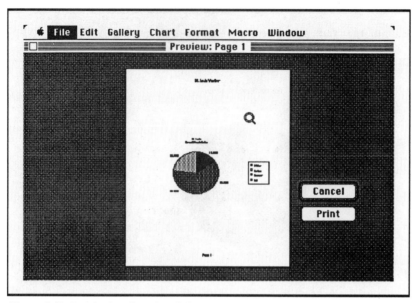

Figure 6.19: *Previewing the printed chart*

- Using the Gallery menu to change the chart type and format.
- Adding a legend to a chart using the Add Legend command, and a title using the Attach Text command.
- Creating a chart from a multiple-range selection.

These skills alone are enough to create an endless variety of useful charts from your worksheet applications. However, you have seen only a small portion of the features available in Excel's charting component. In Chapter 7 you'll learn to use a number of additional charting tools.

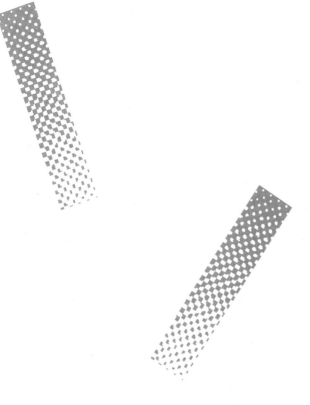

7

Customizing Your Charts

Featuring:

Adding unattached text and an arrow to a chart

Changing the presentation of text

Adding gridlines and changing patterns on the chart

Producing a combination chart

Excel's charting component allows you to develop your own distinctive style of presentation for each chart that you produce. Using the tools that Excel puts at your disposal, you can modify and customize almost every visual element of a chart. What's more, version 1.5 of Excel makes these changes extremely easy to perform; with a double-click of the mouse, you can instantly start defining the appearance of any chart element that you select.

This chapter guides you briskly through a series of exercises focusing on the tools available for modifying charts. You'll continue working with the two charts that you developed in the previous chapter: the pie chart depicting precipitation in St. Louis and the stacked column chart comparing precipitation in nine major U.S. cities. During the course of this chapter you'll make changes in the style—and to a lesser extent the content—of these two charts. If you want a quick preview of the work ahead of you, glance forward at Figures 7.7 and 7.17. As you can see, you'll make some rather dramatic changes in the appearance of these two charts.

Finally, in a slightly more advanced exercise at the end of this chapter, you'll learn to produce a combination chart. Specifically, you'll build a chart that represents three sets of data as columns and a fourth set as a line chart. This exercise will introduce you to some of the techniques and tools available for designing complex charts.

You have probably quit Excel since your work in the previous chapter. To prepare for the exercises in this chapter, begin by starting Excel again and reopening the documents that you created in Chapter 6. Open the precipitation worksheet from your disk, and then open both charts—the stacked column chart (Precipitation Chart) and the pie chart (St. Louis Weather).

Let's begin working with the pie chart. The purpose of your work on this first chart will be to draw special attention to a single wedge of the pie.

*A*dding New Graphic Elements to a Chart

You may sometimes want to place emphasis on one chart element that represents a particular value—a value that for one reason or another is more important than other values. Excel gives you two interesting ways to do this:

- You can write a short block of text describing the special element, and move the text to an appropriate location near the target element.

- You can write a block of text and then place an arrow on the chart that points from the text you have written to the special chart element.

Furthermore, in a pie chart you can pull a given wedge slightly away from the center of the pie, setting the wedge off from the remainder of the chart. You'll perform all of these tasks on the St. Louis Weather chart in the sections ahead.

*A*dding Unattached Text

Unattached text is a block of text that you enter into the formula bar for display on the active chart. Unlike the text elements that you incorporate into the chart with the Attach Text command, you can move unattached text to any location you choose in the chart area. In the following exercise you'll enter a block of unattached text into the St. Louis pie chart. The purpose of the text will be to describe and emphasize the smallest wedge in the pie—the wedge representing winter precipitation.

Activate the chart window named St. Louis Weather. To create a block of unattached text you simply begin typing the text into the formula bar. Here are the steps:

1. Type the following three-line message from the keyboard:

   Winter snows represent
   a sixth of the city's total
   annual precipitation.

   As you type, the text appears in the formula bar. After each of the first two lines, press the Return key to begin the next line. Then at the end of the third line, press the Enter key to complete the data entry. When you are finished, the unattached text appears inside the chart as shown in Figure 7.1. The small black squares displayed around the text are

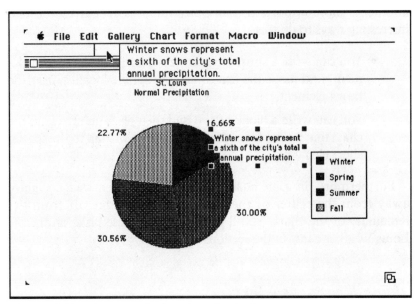

Figure 7.1: *Entering unattached text into the pie chart*

Excel's way of indicating that the block can be moved to any location you choose.

2. Use the mouse to drag the unattached text toward the upper-right corner of the chart area. As you drag, a moving border represents the new position of the text, as shown in Figure 7.2.

3. Release the mouse button to complete the move operation. The text moves to the position you selected.

4. Click in a blank area of the chart to deselect the unattached text.

Now that you have entered this block of text into your chart, you'll want to place an arrow in the chart to point from the text to the target wedge.

*A*dding an Arrow

Adding an arrow to your chart is simply a matter of performing the Add Arrow command in the Chart menu, and then using the mouse to

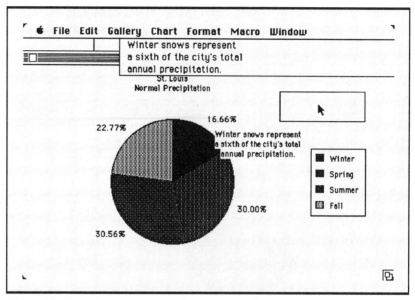

Figure 7.2: Dragging the unattached text to a new location

position the arrow where you want it. Here are the steps for adding an arrow to the St. Louis Weather chart:

1. Pull down the Chart menu and select the Add Arrow command. An arrow appears on the chart; initially this arrow begins near the upper-left corner of the chart area, and points down toward the center of the chart, as shown in Figure 7.3. (You can scarcely see the black arrow head in this figure, because the initial position of the arrow happens to be located directly in front of a black wedge. However, you'll be able to see the entire arrow as soon as you move it to a white background area.) At each end of the arrow is a small black box that you can drag to reposition the arrow.

2. Click the mouse on the tail of the arrow and drag it to its new position just below your block of unattached text. As shown in Figure 7.4, the shaft of the arrow pivots around the opposite end. The image of the arrow in its original position disappears when you release the mouse button.

3. Use the same method to drag the arrow head to a position just to the right of the target wedge.

4. Deselect the arrow by clicking the mouse in any blank section of the chart area. The small black squares disappear from both ends of the arrow.

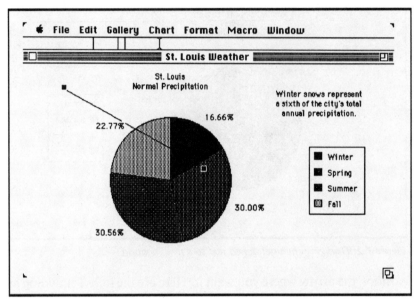

Figure 7.3: *Adding an arrow to the pie chart*

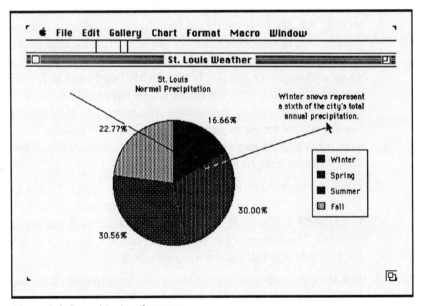

Figure 7.4: *Repositioning the arrow*

The arrow appears in your chart as shown in Figure 7.5. As you can see, the arrow helps to identify the wedge that is the subject of the unattached text. To make the emphasis even clearer, however, your next step will be to pull the target wedge slightly away from the center of the pie chart.

Pulling Out a Wedge of the Pie

You can use the mouse to drag any wedge of a pie chart slightly away from the center of the pie. As a side effect, this process results in a pie with a smaller radius; but the relationship between the sizes of the wedges does not change. The purpose of pulling a wedge out (*exploding* it) is to draw special attention to the value that the wedge represents.

The procedure for exploding a wedge is very simple, as you can see in the following steps:

1. Position the mouse pointer over the wedge that represents winter precipitation.

2. Press the mouse button and drag the wedge carefully away from the center of the pie. As you drag, a moving border of the wedge appears on the chart, as shown in Figure 7.6. Excel lets you drag the wedge as far away as you want (within the confines of the chart area), but the further you move it the smaller the pie chart will become. For this reason, try not to place the wedge more than about a quarter of an inch away.

3. Release the mouse button when you have reached the position where you want to display the wedge.

4. Click in a blank area of the chart to deselect the wedge.

The result of these steps is shown in Figure 7.7. In summary, you have used three elements to draw attention to the target wedge:

- Unattached text
- An arrow
- An exploded wedge

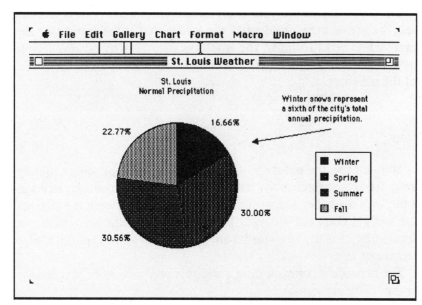

Figure 7.5: *The arrow positioned to emphasize a particular wedge*

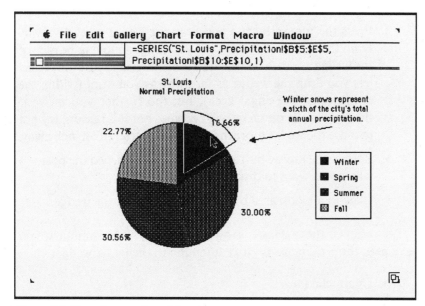

Figure 7.6: *Dragging a wedge of the pie*

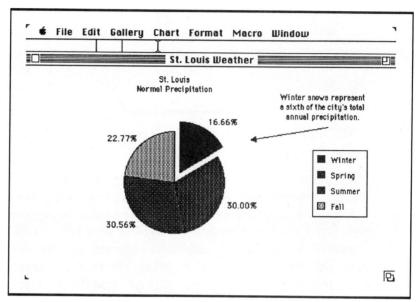

Figure 7.7: *Exploding the wedge*

Next we'll discuss a variety of operations that you can perform on existing chart elements. In a series of exercises, you'll use the stacked bar chart to explore the results of these operations. Begin now by activating this chart (Precipitation Chart) so you can see it on the desktop.

Modifying the Existing Format of a Chart

We'll concentrate here on several commands that are offered in the Format menu when the active document is a chart. You can use the commands in this menu to change patterns, positions, borders, backgrounds, type styles, alignments, and arrangements of individual chart elements. The commands apply in various ways to all of the following graphic and textual elements:

- Attached and unattached text
- The legend
- The axes

- The arrow (if one exists)
- The chart elements that represent numbers from the worksheet

Using the Format Menu

Here is a brief summary of the commands that you'll be working with in the Format menu:

- The Patterns command allows you to change patterns, backgrounds, borders, and line weights. If you are working on a Macintosh with a color monitor, the Patterns command also gives you control over colors displayed in your chart. This command is available for each of the text and graphic elements that can be selected on the chart. The Patterns dialog box offers various sets of options, depending on the chart element that you have selected.

- The Axis command gives you broad control over the organization of the vertical and horizontal axes in a chart. For example, you can modify the scale of the numeric values displayed along an axis; control the position at which the two axes cross; establish the order of values displayed along an axis; or specify the number of *tick labels* (the small cross lines and labels displayed along an axis). The Axis command is available only when you select one of the two axes in a chart. (Don't confuse it with the Axes command, located in the Chart menu; we'll discuss the Axes command later in this chapter.)

- The Legend command lets you change the shape and position of the legend in the chart area. As you saw in Chapter 6, you can move the legend to any of four positions; the shape of the legend box changes according to the position you choose. This command is available only when you select the legend.

- The Text command offers text display options, including font, style, and color. This command is available for any block of attached or unattached text.

In version 1.5 of Excel there are two techniques available for performing these commands. The first technique is one that you have used several times already:

1. Use the mouse to select the graphic or text that you want to change.

2. Pull down the Format menu and select a command.

For example, in Chapter 6 you changed the position of the legend in the stacked bar chart by first selecting the legend and then performing the Legend command. Likewise, you changed the type style of the title by selecting the text and then performing the Text command.

The second technique for performing these commands is generally simpler and more direct: move the mouse pointer over the chart element that you want to work with, and then double-click the mouse button. In response, Excel automatically brings up the dialog box for the Patterns command, presenting options that are relevant to the selected chart element. In addition, Excel provides one or more command buttons at the right side of the Patterns dialog box; you can click these buttons to move directly to other appropriate commands in the Format menu.

You'll practice this second technique in the following exercises. However, keep in mind that if you are working in an earlier version of Excel, you will have to use the first technique for performing a format operation: Select the target chart element, then pull down the Format menu and select the appropriate command.

Changing the Text Background

Returning now to the stacked bar chart, you'll begin by working with the title text and the legend. Using the Patterns command, you'll place a shadowed border around the title, and you'll fill the legend box with a pattern.

Here are the steps for accomplishing these tasks:

1. Position the mouse pointer over the three-line block of text you have supplied as the chart's title, and double-click the mouse button. This action invokes the Patterns command

from the Format menu, displaying the dialog box shown in Figure 7.8.

2. Click the Shadow option in the Border Pattern section of the dialog box. This option does two things: it supplies a border and produces a shadow effect "behind" the border.

3. Click the OK button to complete this portion of the operation.

4. Position the mouse pointer over the legend, and once again double-click the mouse button to invoke the Patterns command.

5. In the Border Pattern section of the the dialog box, click the Shadow option.

6. In the Background Pattern section of the dialog box, click the third square in the row of patterns.

7. Click the OK button to complete the operation.

8. Position the mouse pointer over a blank area of the chart, and click the mouse button to deselect the legend.

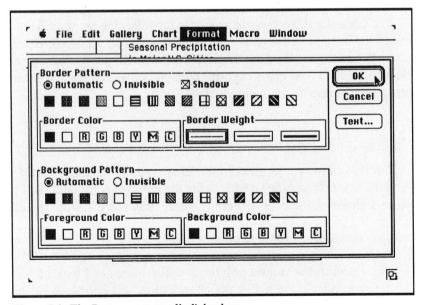

Figure 7.8: The Pattern command's dialog box

Figure 7.9 shows the result of these operations. Both the title and the legend now have borders and shadows, and the interior of the legend box is filled in with a light gray pattern.

*A*dding Gridlines

Now you'll add horizontal gridlines to improve the readability of the column chart. These gridlines should extend across the chart from the vertical axis, clearly marking levels in the numeric scale of values. You use the Axes command in the Chart menu to display gridlines. Once you've done this, the Axis command in the Format menu gives you control over the number of gridlines that actually appear on the chart. In the following exercise you'll work with both of these commands:

1. Pull down the Chart menu and select the Axes command. You can see the resulting dialog box in Figure 7.10.

2. Click the Major Grid Lines option in the Value Axis section of the dialog box. (An X appears in the small square located just to the left of the option.) The value axis is the vertical axis in

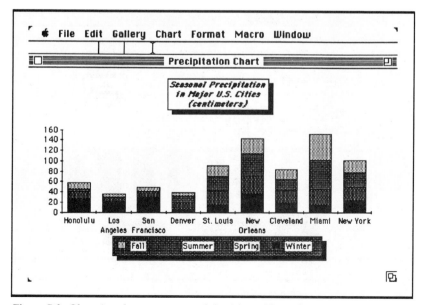

Figure 7.9: *Changing the appearance of the title and legend*

the precipitation chart—that is, the axis that displays the scale of numeric values.

3. Click the OK button to complete the operation. Excel draws the horizontal gridlines across the width of the chart, as shown in Figure 7.11.

4. Double-click the chart's vertical axis to invoke commands from the Format menu. The dialog box for the Patterns command appears on the screen.

5. Click the Axis button at the right side of the Patterns dialog box. As a result, the dialog box for the Axis command appears, as shown in Figure 7.12.

6. Use the mouse to select the value displayed in the Major Unit input box. This number controls the increment between values displayed on the chart's vertical axis. The default increment is 20, giving the current scale values: 0, 20, 40, 60, and so on.

7. Enter a new value of 40 for the Major Unit increment amount. As you will see shortly, the result of this operation is to decrease the number of gridlines by half.

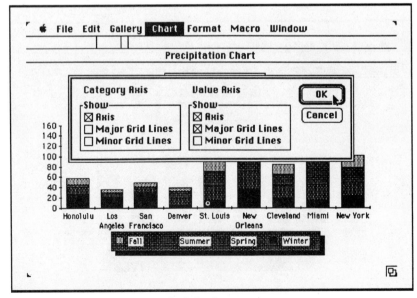

Figure 7.10: The Axes command's dialog box

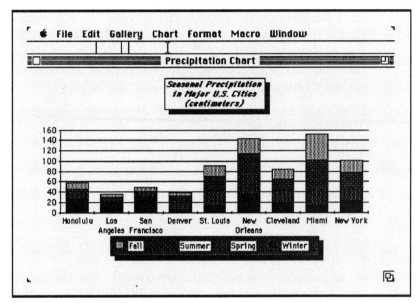

Figure 7.11: Adding horizontal gridlines to the chart

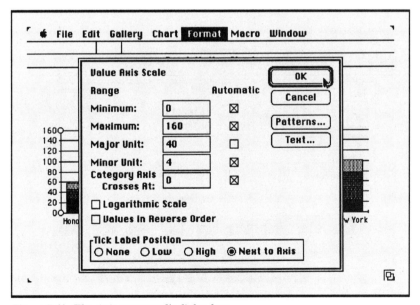

Figure 7.12: The Axis command's dialog box

8. Click the Text button located at the right side of the Axis dialog box; this action brings up the dialog box for the Text command, as shown in Figure 7.13. You can use the options of this command to change the font, style, and color of the numbers displayed along the vertical axis.

9. Click the Bold option in the Style section of the dialog box. This will display the numbers along the vertical axis in boldface type.

10. Click the OK button to complete the operation.

11. Position the mouse pointer in a blank area of the chart, and click the mouse button to deselect the vertical axis.

The new version of your chart is shown in Figure 7.14. Notice that the scale of numbers displayed along the vertical axis is now in multiples of 40; specifically, the numbers displayed are 0, 40, 80, 120, and 160. A horizontal gridline extends across the width of the chart to mark the level of each value in this scale. Finally, notice that the scale numbers are now displayed in boldface type.

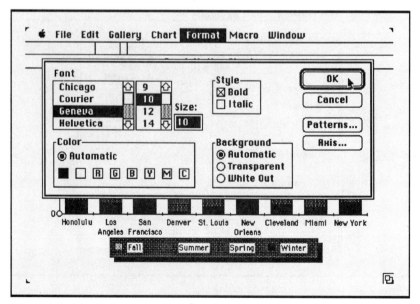

Figure 7.13: The Text command's dialog box

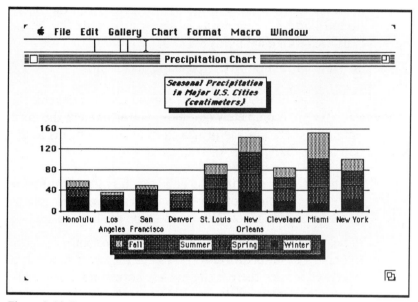

Figure 7.14: *Decreasing the number of horizontal gridlines*

Changing the Background of the Entire Chart

Some formatting operations affect the entire chart area. To work with this area, you first perform the Select Chart command in the Chart menu. In response, Excel places small circles around the entire perimeter of the chart area. Subsequently, the Patterns command is available in the Format menu to supply background and border patterns for the chart area. Let's experiment with these commands.

Perform the following steps to produce a border and background pattern for the chart:

1. Pull down the Chart menu and choose the Select Chart command (or press ⌘-A from the keyboard). As mentioned, small circles appear around the perimeter of the chart.

2. Pull down the Format menu and select the Patterns command (see Figure 7.8).

3. Click the Shadow option in the Border Pattern section of the Patterns dialog box. This supplies a shadowed border around the entire perimeter of the chart.

4. Click the fourth square in the row of patterns in the Background Patterns section of the dialog box. This fills in the chart area with a light gray pattern.

5. Click the OK button to complete the operation.

Figure 7.15 shows the resulting chart. As you can see, the chart is beginning to take on a completely new look. Unfortunately, the most recent formatting operation has produced two new problems in the presentation of the chart:

- The pattern representing the Fall season is identical to the background pattern of the entire chart area. As a result, the stacked sections for Fall precipitation are hard to see.

- Some of the city names displayed along the horizontal axis are broken up in unfortunate ways. (Since the chart now has a shadowed border, there is slightly less horizontal space available for the content of the chart. As a result, Excel has had to split some of the city names over two or three lines.)

We'll find solutions for these two problems in the next two exercises.

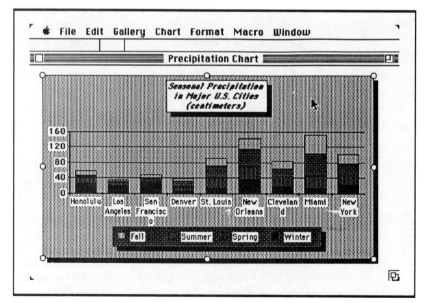

Figure 7.15: Adding a border and background pattern for the chart

Changing Individual Patterns on the Chart

When you create a stacked column chart, Excel supplies a default sequence of patterns for the stacked divisions appearing in each column. You can use the Patterns command to change any or all of these patterns individually. To do so, select an existing pattern that you want to change and then double-click the pattern in any one of the columns. In response, Excel displays the dialog box for the Patterns command on the screen.

For example, follow these steps to change the pattern representing Fall precipitation:

1. Position the mouse pointer over the stacked division representing Fall precipitation in Miami, and click the mouse button. (The Miami column has the largest division in this category, and therefore is the easiest column to click.) Excel displays the dialog box for the Patterns command.

2. Click the fifth square in the row of patterns located inside the Area Pattern section of the dialog box. The "pattern" in this square is white.

3. Click the OK button to complete the operation. As you can see in Figure 7.16, the white pattern stands out much more sharply against the patterned background of the chart.

Before you move on to the next exercise, notice the contents of the formula bar in Figure 7.16. When you select one of the divisions of a column on the chart, Excel displays one of the special formulas that actually control the contents of the chart itself. This formula consists of the SERIES function, and contains references to specific ranges on the supporting worksheet for the chart. In Chapter 8 we'll discuss the SERIES function in some detail, and you'll learn more about how Excel builds charts from worksheet data.

You can now click the mouse pointer in a blank area of the chart to deselect the column division. In the next section of this chapter, you'll turn your attention once again to the precipitation worksheet. You'll find out what happens to the chart when you make changes on the supporting worksheet.

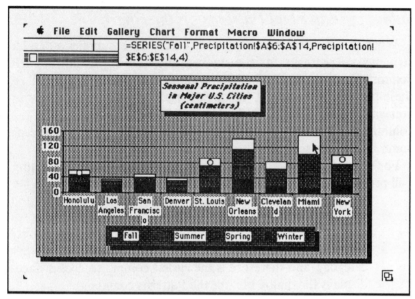

Figure 7.16: Changing one of the patterns in the stacked column

Modifying Entries on the Supporting Worksheet

You need to find a way to fix the broken labels displayed along the horizontal axis. One solution is to abbreviate the longest names, so that each city can be displayed in a single line along the axis. The best place to make this change is on the supporting worksheet.

Pull down the Window menu and activate the precipitation worksheet. (When you do so, you'll notice that the original worksheet menu line returns to the top of the desktop.) In column A of the worksheet, enter the list of city names in an abbreviated form, as follows:

Honolulu
L.A.
S.F.
Denver
St.Louis
N.Orlns
Clvlnd
Miami
N.Y.

Press ⌘-S to save the new version of your worksheet to disk.

Now pull down the Window menu again and activate the precipitation chart. As you can see in Figure 7.17, Excel has automatically transferred your worksheet changes to the linked chart. The abbreviated city names have solved the problem of broken labels along the horizontal axis. Press ⌘-S again to save this version of the chart to disk.

So far you have worked with only two types of charts: a pie chart and a stacked column chart. Keep in mind that all of the formatting tools you have studied in this chapter are available for all of Excel's chart types. In some cases the dialog boxes offer different options than those you have seen, corresponding to the characteristics of a particular chart type.

In this chapter's final exercise, you'll learn to create a combination chart.

Producing a Combination Chart

A combination chart uses two different chart types to depict rows or columns of numeric data from a worksheet. We refer to the two chart types in such an arrangement as the *main chart type* and

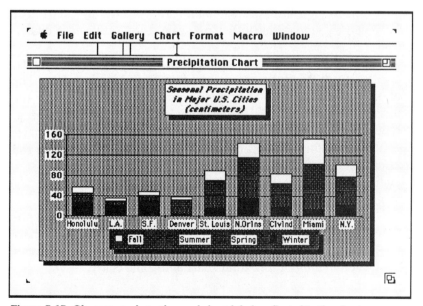

Figure 7.17: *Changes made to the worksheet labels reflected in the chart*

the *overlay chart type*. Here are some reasons for creating a combination chart:

- To depict different sets of data values as visually distinct components of the chart

- To plot groups of data against two different numeric scales on the same chart

- To place special emphasis on one particular set of values in the chart

You use the Combination command in the Gallery menu to transform the active chart into one of several available combination chart formats. Then you can take advantage of the following commands in the Chart and Format menus to define the chart's characteristics:

- The Main Chart Type and Overlay Chart Type commands in the Chart menu allow you to select among all the available chart types for the main chart and the overlay chart.

- The Overlay Chart command in the Format menu gives you control over the allocation of data sets between the two chart types.

- The Main Chart Axis command and the Overlay Chart Axis allow you to define individual scales for plotting each chart.

The following exercise is a brief introduction to combination charts. You'll transform the precipitation chart into a combination chart. The goal of your work will be to devise a special visual treatment for the values of the Fall season. The precipitation levels for the Winter, Spring, and Summer seasons will appear as individual columns on the chart; but the Fall season will appear as a line chart, superimposed over the columns for the other seasons.

Activate the precipitation chart, and perform these steps:

1. Pull down the Gallery menu and select the Combination command. In the resulting dialog box, the first combination chart format is selected by default (Figure 7.18). This format gives a combination of a column chart and a line chart.

2. Click the OK button to accept this format. In the resulting chart, Excel divides the data sets in half between the two chart types; the first two columns of worksheet data (Winter and Spring) are depicted in the column-chart format, and the second two columns of worksheet data (Summer and Fall) are depicted in the line-chart format.

3. Pull down the Format menu and select the Overlay Chart command.   .

4. In the resulting dialog box (Figure 7.19), enter a value of 4 into the input box labeled *First Series in Overlay Chart*. This option controls the division between the main chart and the overlay chart. Entering a value of 4 means that the first three columns of worksheet data (Winter, Spring, and Summer) become the main chart and the fourth column (Fall) becomes the overlay chart. Press the Enter key or click the OK button to complete this operation.

5. Position the mouse pointer over the chart's vertical axis and click the mouse button. Excel displays a circle at both ends of the axis to indicate the selection.

6. Pull down the Format menu and select the Main Chart Axis command.

7. In the resulting dialog box, use the mouse to select the contents of the input box labeled Maximum, and enter a value of **60** from the keyboard. Then select the input box labeled Major Unit and enter a value of **10**. This creates a scale from 0 to 60 along the vertical axis, with tick labels at increments of 10. Click the OK button to complete this operation.

8. Double-click one of the columns representing summer precipitation. Excel displays the dialog box for the Patterns command on the screen.

9. Click the fifth square (white) in the row of patterns displayed in the Area Pattern section of the dialog box. Click OK to complete the operation.

10. Click the mouse in a blank area of the chart to deselect the column.

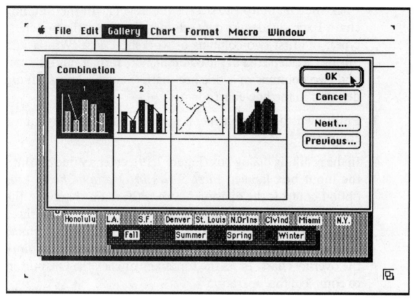

Figure 7.18: *The Combination command's dialog box*

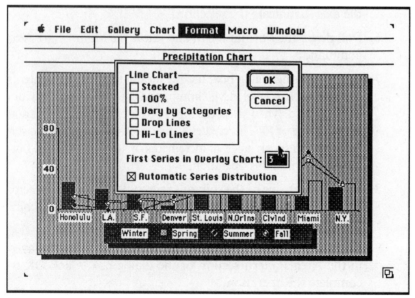

Figure 7.19: *The Overlay Chart command's dialog box*

11. Pull down the File menu and select the Save As command. Enter **Combination Chart** as the name for this new version of the chart. Click the OK button to complete the save operation.

Figure 7.20 shows the result of your work. The overlay line chart now clearly distinguishes the Fall precipitation data from the other three sets of data. As you can see, a carefully prepared combination format can be an excellent tool for emphasizing one particular part of the data in a chart.

You have now seen several different ways to change the style and content of charts in Excel. The best way to continue learning about chart formats is simply to experiment with as many different charts as possible. The more you practice with the various tools Excel puts at your disposal, the more adept you will become at producing chart presentations exactly as you want them to appear.

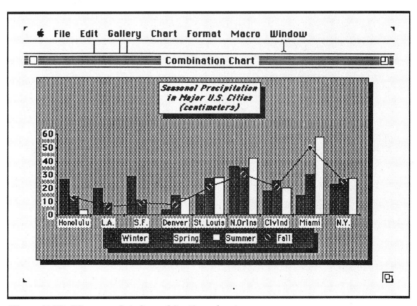

Figure 7.20: *The completed combination chart*

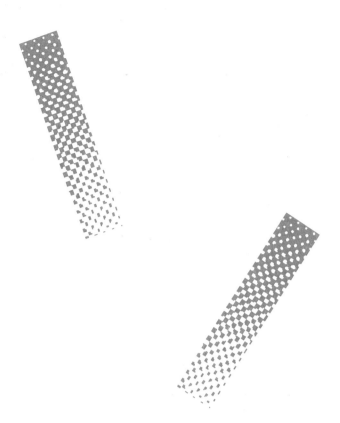

8

Understanding the SERIES Function

Featuring:

Understanding the meaning of the SERIES function

Editing series names and the order of series in a chart

Near the end of Chapter 7 you had a first brief look at the SERIES function. This is the function that appears in the formula bar when you select a stacked pattern in the bar chart, as you can see back in Figure 7.16. Excel builds SERIES functions to define the contents of a chart.

Compared to the straightforward charting techniques you have been studying in the last two chapters, the SERIES function may initially seem somewhat difficult and esoteric. In fact, you have come a long way in your work with charts—and you could continue even further—without knowing anything specific about SERIES. However, in some cases it is useful and important to understand how Excel expresses the underlying definition of a chart. To a great extent, Excel allows you to modify the contents of a chart by working with the chart's SERIES formulas. Furthermore, the process of examining these formulas inevitably leads to a better understanding of a chart's logical structure.

In this short chapter you'll examine the format and purpose of the SERIES function. Along the way, you'll learn the meanings of several important charting terms—notably, *series*, *category*, and *data point*. And finally, in an exercise at the end of the chapter, you'll find out how to produce specific changes in a chart by revising the chart's SERIES functions.

How Excel Organizes a Chart

Look again at the precipitation worksheet and the stacked column chart that you have developed from it. (You should open these two documents onto the desktop for your work in this chapter; they are shown in Figures 8.1 and 8.2.) Think back to the very first steps you took to create the chart; you originally selected the ten-row, five-column range A5:E14 on the precipitation worksheet and then used the New command to open the new chart window. You subsequently transformed the format into a stacked column chart, and you added a legend.

In response to these steps, here is how Excel has automatically organized your chart:

- Each row of worksheet data is represented by a single stacked column in the chart.

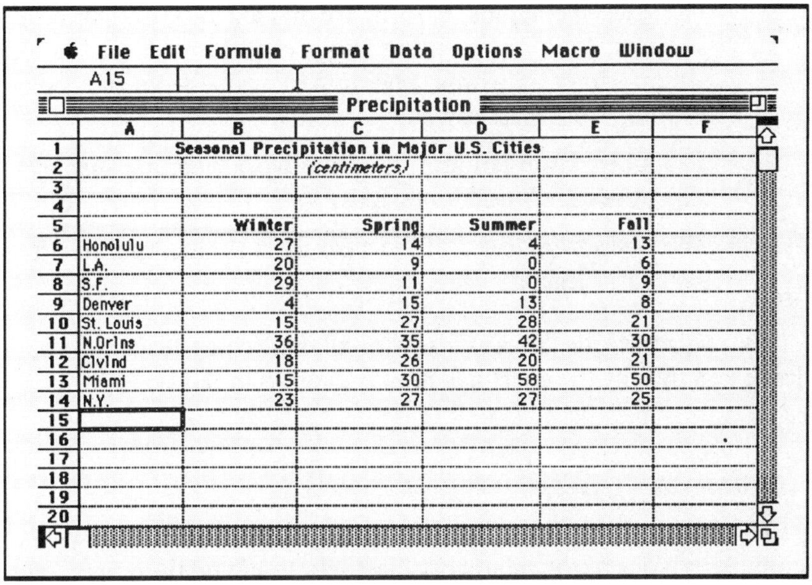

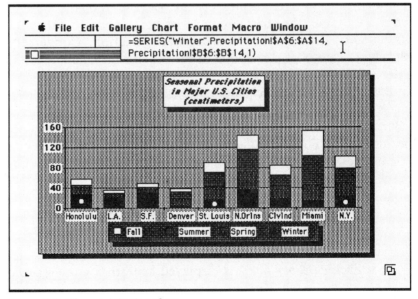

Figure 8.1: *The precipitation worksheet*

Figure 8.2: *The precipitation chart*

- The stacked columns, in turn, are divided into four patterned sections, each representing the precipitation level for one season—in other words, one numeric value from the corresponding worksheet row.

- The labels from column A of the worksheet are displayed along the chart's horizontal axis.

- The labels from row 5 of the worksheet are incorporated into the chart's legend.

As we discuss Excel's vocabulary for all these chart elements, you'll learn exactly why the chart has been organized in this way.

Understanding Series and Categories

To build a chart, Excel establishes a link between the rows and columns of your rectangular worksheet selection, and the corresponding chart elements called *data series* and *categories*. In order to predict the organization of the chart that Excel will produce, you have to know exactly how Excel defines this link. Depending on the shape of your data table, the chart's data series correspond to either the columns or the rows of the worksheet selection. Conversely, the chart's categories correspond to the rows or the columns of the selection.

For example, in the precipitation worksheet, Excel by default designates each worksheet column of seasonal data as one data series in the chart. The rows within each worksheet column become the categories in each series. Following Excel's internal rules for creating charts, these series/category definitions automatically determine how the resulting stacked column chart is organized:

- A given data series is represented by one patterned section in each of the stacked columns, and the *series name* appears as a label in the chart's legend.

- Each *category name* is displayed beneath a given stacked column in the chart.

- The *data points* in the chart—the individual chart elements that represent numbers from the worksheet—appear as patterned divisions in the stacked columns.

As you can see, the series/category definitions are essential to the final result of a charting operation. Accordingly, Excel follows specific and consistent rules for deciding how to designate series and categories from a given worksheet selection. The default criterion for this decision is the shape of the selection—specifically, whether the selection has more rows than columns, or more columns than rows:

- If the worksheet selection has more rows than columns, Excel defines the columns of worksheet data as the series of the chart, and the rows of data as the category elements of each series. (This is the case in the precipitation worksheet.)

- Conversely, if the worksheet selection has more columns than rows, or the same number of columns and rows, Excel defines the rows of worksheet data as the series of the chart, and the columns of data as the category elements of each series.

*P*redicting the Orientation of a Chart

Why is it important for you to understand these rules? First of all, you can use this knowledge to predict the kind of chart Excel will draw from a given worksheet table.

For example, imagine transposing the rows and columns of the precipitation worksheet, producing a data table like the one shown in Figure 8.3. The columns in this table represent the precipitation data for each city, and the rows represent the four seasons.

	Honolulu	L.A.	S.F.	Denver	St.Louis	N.Orlns	Clvlnd	Miami	N.Y.
Winter	27	20	29	4	15	36	18	15	23
Spring	14	9	11	15	27	35	26	30	27
Summer	4	0	0	13	28	42	20	58	27
Fall	13	6	9	8	21	30	21	50	25

Seasonal Precipitation in Major U.S. Cities
(centimeters)

Figure 8.3: *Transposing the rows and columns of the precipitation worksheet*

You might initially be surprised to learn that Excel will produce the same chart from this transposed table as from the original. Since the table has more columns than rows, the data series in the resulting chart will correspond to the rows of data from the worksheet (the seasons) and the categories will correspond to the worksheet columns (the cities). Given these links, Excel builds the same stacked column chart as before. In short, transposing the data does *not* reverse Excel's standard rules for defining the orientation of a chart. The shape of the data table still ultimately determines the series and categories.

In some applications you may actually want to reverse the default charting rules. For example, your goal might be to produce a chart in which the nine city names appear in the legend, and the four season names appear along the horizontal axis. To accomplish this, you must use special techniques for controlling the selection of series and categories. These techniques are the subject of Chapter 9.

There is another reason why you should know Excel's standard rules for distinguishing between series and categories: you need this knowledge to work successfully with the SERIES function.

Excel builds a SERIES function for each data series in a chart. This function specifies four characteristics about the data series:

- The series name

- The range of data values that make up the series

- The range of category labels

- The order of the series inside the chart

Master the syntax of the SERIES function, and you will be able to control and modify the resulting chart in some important ways. Let's see how SERIES works.

The SERIES Function

To look at an example of the SERIES function on the desktop, perform these steps:

1. Pull down the Window menu and activate the precipitation chart.

2. Position the mouse pointer over the black patterned section at the bottom of any one of the stacked columns.

3. Click the mouse button. The formula for this data series appears in the formula bar as shown in Figure 8.2.

This particular SERIES function represents the data for Winter precipitation in the nine cities:

= SERIES("Winter",Precipitation!$A$6:$A$14,
Precipitation!$B$6:$B$14,1)

(Note that the SERIES function is a single formula; Excel breaks the function into two lines only if the formula happens to be too long to fit into one line of the formula bar.)

As you can see, the SERIES function has four arguments. Two of the arguments are *external references*—that is, references to ranges of values on the supporting worksheet. Since this is the first time you've encountered external references, let's pause to examine their meaning and format.

External References

An external reference is the address of a particular cell or range of cells located on another named worksheet document. Like any other reference, an external reference represents the value or range of values stored at a specified worksheet address. The essential distinction is that this kind of reference creates a link between two different Excel documents. In terms that you have already learned, a chart or worksheet that contains an external reference is a *dependent document*; the worksheet named in the the external reference is thus the *supporting document*.

In a SERIES function, an external reference has the following form:

WorksheetName!RangeReference

As you can see, the reference has three parts:

- The name of the supporting worksheet

- An exclamation point, which serves simply as a separator

- An absolute reference to a range of data on the worksheet

For example, the following external reference identifies the location of the nine city names on the precipitation worksheet:

Precipitation!$A$6:$A$14

The external references in a SERIES function create the link between a chart and its supporting worksheet.

The Arguments of the SERIES Function

We can express the general format of the SERIES function as follows:

= SERIES(*SeriesName, CategoryRange, DataRange, SeriesOrder*)

Here are the four arguments of the function:

- *SeriesName* is the name of the series as labeled in the worksheet. This is always a text value, enclosed in quotation marks; for example, "Winter".

- *CategoryRange* is an external reference to the category names; for example, Precipitation!$A$6:$A$14.

- *DataRange* is an external reference to the series data; for example, Precipitation!$B$6:$B$14.

- *SeriesOrder* is an integer giving the place of the series in the chart; for example, 1 designates the first series in a chart.

Excel generates a SERIES function for each data series depicted in the chart. You can demonstrate this fact by clicking each of the four patterned sections of a given stacked column in turn, from bottom to top. Here are the four SERIES functions you'll see in the formula bar:

= SERIES("Winter",Precipitation!$A$6:$A$14, Precipitation!$B$6:$B$14,1)

= SERIES("Spring",Precipitation!$A$6:$A$14, Precipitation!$C$6:$C$14,2)

= SERIES("Summer",Precipitation!$A$6:$A$14, Precipitation!$D$6:$D$14,3)

**=SERIES("Fall",Precipitation!$A$6:$A$14,
Precipitation!$E$6:$E$14,4)**

Notice that all four functions contain the same external reference for the category names: the city names in column A of the worksheet. Each function then has a different external reference for the actual data series: the seasonal precipitation data from column B, C, D, and E of the worksheet. Finally, the fourth argument of each function gives the consecutive order of the four series in the chart: 1, 2, 3, or 4.

Excel uses these functions to define the contents of the chart itself. Knowing this, you can carefully edit the SERIES formulas to produce certain changes in the content and appearance of the chart. You'll learn how to do this in the next exercise.

Modifying the SERIES Function

Near the end of Chapter 7 you needed to abbreviate the city names displayed along the chart's horizontal axis. The approach you took to accomplish this was to edit the names on the supporting worksheet. Now you know why this approach works: each SERIES formula in the chart contains an external reference to the category names on the precipitation worksheet. When you change these names on the worksheet, Excel automatically changes them on the chart as well.

Unlike the category names, the series names are represented in the SERIES functions as literal text values enclosed in quotes: "Winter", "Spring", "Summer", and "Fall". Changing these labels on the precipitation worksheet has no effect at all on the chart, because there is no external reference to link these values between the two documents. If you want to modify the series names in the chart, thus changing the labels that appear in the legend, you have to edit them directly in their respective SERIES functions.

Another chart characteristic that is easy to change is the order of the data series. You can change the fourth argument of any SERIES formula to give the corresponding data series a new position in the order of series in the chart. When you do so, Excel automatically adjusts the orders of the other series accordingly. You'll see how this happens as you observe the changes in the SERIES formulas in the upcoming exercises.

Changing the Series Names and the Order of the Series

Let's say you've decided to be more precise about the seasons represented on the chart. Instead of Winter, Spring, Summer, and Fall, you want to insert the following four labels into the chart's legend:

Dec/Jan/Feb   Mar/Apr/May   Jun/Jul/Aug   Sep/Oct/Nov

Furthermore, you'd like the labels to appear in chronological order in the legend, rather than the reverse order that Excel has initially supplied.

You'll accomplish both of these changes by editing each of the chart's four SERIES formulas in turn. Here are the steps for changing the first formula:

1. If you have not already done so, click the bottom patterned section in any one of the stacked columns, so that your chart looks like Figure 8.2.

2. In the formula bar, select the word *Winter* by dragging the mouse pointer from left to right over the word so that it is highlighted, as shown in Figure 8.4. Don't include the quotation marks in the selection.

3. From the keyboard, enter the new series name: **Dec/Jan/Feb**. This label takes the place of the selected text in the formula bar (Figure 8.5).

4. Edit the fourth argument—currently the value 1—in the SERIES formula: position the mouse pointer just to the right of the number, click the mouse button, and press the Backspace key. Then enter a new value of **4** for the argument (Figure 8.5).

5. Press the Enter key to complete the editing operation.

6. Click in a blank area of the chart to deselect the series.

As a result of these steps, your worksheet now looks like Figure 8.6. The following changes have taken place in the chart:

- The series label displayed in the legend is now *Dec/Jan/Feb*.

- This label is the first entry in the legend rather than the last.

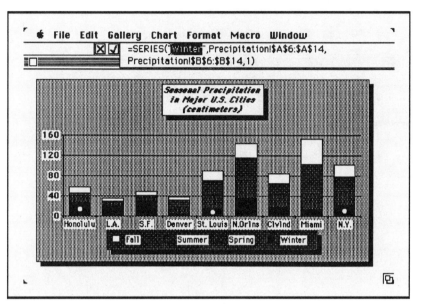

Figure 8.4: Editing a series name

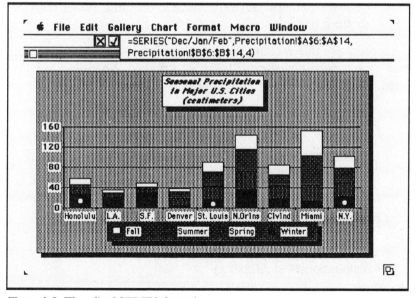

Figure 8.5: The edited SERIES formula

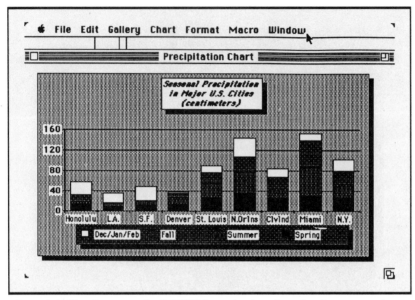

Figure 8.6: *The changes to the SERIES formula viewed on the chart*

- The corresponding data series is represented by the top patterned section (white) in the stacked columns, rather than the bottom one.

To complete this exercise, perform similar editing operations on each of the remaining three SERIES formulas. When you are finished, the four formulas should appear as follows:

   **=SERIES("Dec/Jan/Feb",Precipitation!$A$6:$A$14,
Precipitation!$B$6:$B$14,4)**

   **=SERIES("Mar/Apr/May",Precipitation!$A$6:$A$14,
Precipitation!$C$6:$C$14,3)**

   **=SERIES("Jun/Jul/Aug",Precipitation!$A$6:$A$14,
Precipitation!$D$6:$D$14,2)**

   **=SERIES("Sep/Oct/Nov",Precipitation!$A$6:$A$14,
Precipitation!$E$6:$E$14,1)**

The final version of your worksheet is shown in Figure 8.7. Note that you have accomplished the two changes that you wanted to make: the

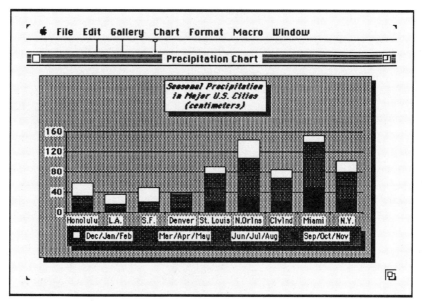

Figure 8.7: The final edited version of the precipitation chart

legend is now in chronological order, and the series names are displayed as month labels rather than season labels.

Now that you know the distinctions between series and categories, you are ready to explore techniques for controlling the orientation of charts. This is the subject of Chapter 9, our final chapter on charting.

9

Changing the Orientation of Charts

Featuring:

Using the Paste Special command to create a chart

Selecting multiple worksheets to build a chart

Using the Page Setup command for charts

Opening a chart without its supporting worksheet

For some applications you may need to produce charts that are oriented differently from the way Excel normally builds them. To do this, you'll need to override Excel's default series/category designations. As an example, consider the chart in Figure 9.1, created from the precipitation worksheet. Unlike the precipitation charts you've created in previous chapters, this new chart has nine individual patterns representing the cities. Notice the other characteristics of this chart:

- The nine city names are displayed in the chart's legend.

- The columns in the chart are grouped together in four seasonal categories.

- The season names are displayed along the horizontal axis.

- The chart contains nine SERIES formulas—one for each city's data. (You can see one of these formulas in the formula bar in Figure 9.1.)

In short, the nine rows of city data from the precipitation worksheet have become the data series in this chart, and the four columns

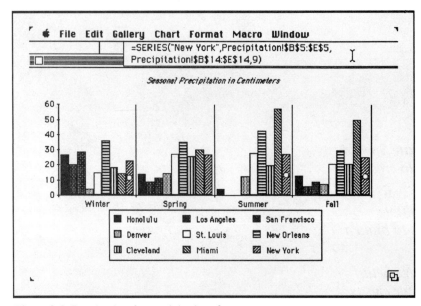

Figure 9.1: *Reorienting the precipitation chart*

of seasons are the categories in each series. This arrangement is the converse of Excel's default chart orientation that we looked at in Chapter 8.

There are two different techniques that you can use to change a chart's orientation. One technique involves using the Paste Special command (in the Edit menu) to control the way Excel builds the SERIES functions for the chart. This technique is rather detailed, but is available with any version of Excel from 1.0 on.

The other technique is a bit simpler, but requires Excel version 1.5. In this second technique, you begin by making multiple selections on the supporting worksheet and then use the New command to create your chart. This technique is similar to the steps you performed in Chapter 6 to create the pie chart depicting St. Louis precipitation.

This chapter presents a pair of exercises that will guide you through both of these techniques. In each case, the end result of your work will be a chart like the one shown in Figure 9.1.

We'll begin with the Paste Special command. Open the precipitation worksheet onto the desktop if you haven't done so already. For purposes of this chapter, you can replace the abbreviations in column A of the worksheet with the complete city names, since the new chart will have plenty of space to display the city names in full.

Using the Paste Special Command

The Paste Special command gives you enhanced control over the way Excel builds data series for a chart. To use this command, you first perform the following three steps:

1. Select the range of worksheet data from which you want to develop a chart.

2. Perform the Edit menu's Copy command, placing a marquee around the selected range.

3. While the worksheet marquee is still active, use the New command (from the File menu) to open a new chart document.

As a result of this sequence of steps, Excel opens an *empty* chart window onto the desktop, and waits for you to perform a paste operation to transfer information from the worksheet to the chart. At this point, you can use the Paste Special command to select one of the following options, regardless of the shape of the worksheet selection:

- You can designate worksheet columns as the data series and rows as the categories

- You can designate rows as the data series and worksheet columns as the categories

In short, this technique gives you control over the series/category orientation of the resulting chart. Let's look at a specific example of the technique. In the following exercise you'll create the chart displayed in Figure 9.1.

Creating the Chart

Activate the precipitation worksheet on the desktop, and perform the following sequence of steps:

1. Use the mouse to select the range A5:E14, which includes the numeric precipitation data along with the column and row labels.

2. Pull down the Edit menu and select the Copy command (or simply press ⌘-C from the keyboard), preparing to copy the worksheet data to a chart. At this point the worksheet appears as shown in Figure 9.2.

3. Pull down the File menu and select the New command (or press ⌘-N from the keyboard).

4. On the New dialog box, select the Chart option, as shown in Figure 9.3.

5. Click the OK button to open a new chart document onto the desktop. The new window is empty, as shown in Figure 9.4.

6. Pull down the Edit menu and select the Paste Special command. The dialog box appears as shown in Figure 9.5. The Rows and Columns options are currently the focus of your attention. The Columns option is selected initially; if you were to accept this option, Excel would create data series from the columns of the worksheet table.

7. Click the Rows option, as shown in Figure 9.6. As a result of this option, Excel will create data series from the rows of the worksheet table. Notice that Excel now expects to read series names from the first column of the worksheet selection, and category names from the first row.

8. Click OK to complete the Paste Special operation. Excel draws a bar chart into the previously empty chart window.

9. Click the chart's zoom box to expand the chart window over the entire available desktop area.

10. Pull down the Chart menu and select the Add Legend command.

The resulting chart is shown in Figure 9.7. As you can see, you've successfully created data series for the chart from the rows of worksheet data. Each city is represented as a distinct data series with its own unique pattern on the chart.

Now you'll perform several more operations to make the chart easier to read.

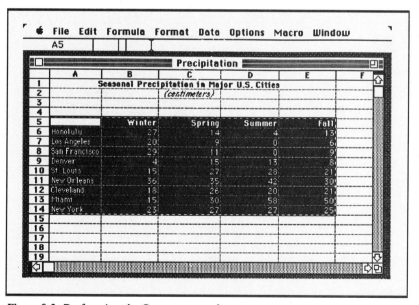

Figure 9.2: *Performing the Copy command*

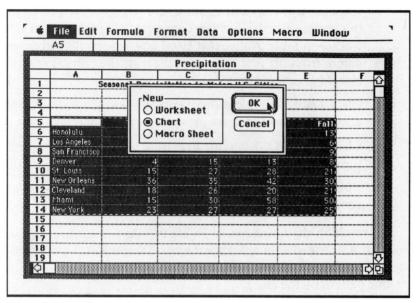

Figure 9.3: *Performing the New command*

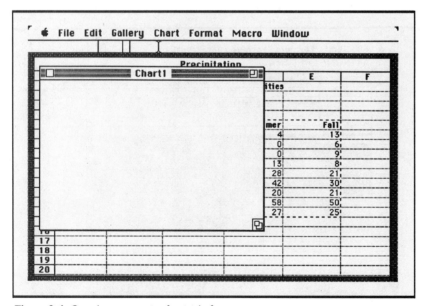

Figure 9.4: *Opening an empty chart window*

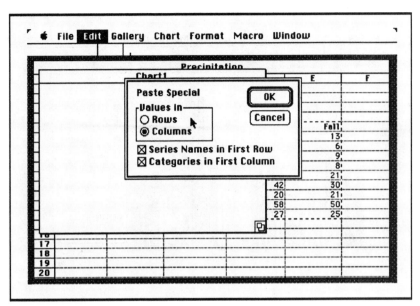

Figure 9.5: *The Paste Special command's dialog box*

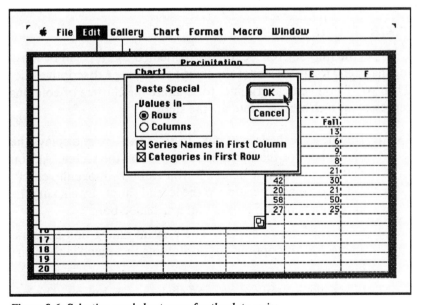

Figure 9.6: *Selecting worksheet rows for the data series*

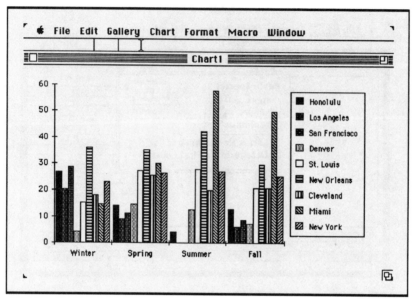

Figure 9.7: The reoriented precipitation chart

Completing the Chart

To put the finishing touches on the reoriented chart, begin by moving the legend to the bottom of the chart and adding a descriptive title. Then you'll add vertical gridlines to separate the clusters of columns representing each season. Here are the steps:

1. Double-click the legend box. In response, Excel displays the dialog box for the Patterns command on the screen. As you first discovered in Chapter 7, you can now move directly to other commands relating to the legend simply by clicking the appropriate button on the Patterns dialog box.

2. Click the Legend button. The Legend dialog box appears, giving you four options for positioning the legend in the chart area.

3. Select the Bottom option, and click the OK button. The legend moves to the bottom of the chart area.

4. Pull down the Chart menu and select the Attach Text command. Click OK to accept the selected Chart Title option. The text that appears initially at the top of the chart area is simply *Title*.

5. Enter the following one-line title from the keyboard:

Seasonal Precipitation in Centimeters

Press the Enter key to complete the text entry.

6. Pull down the Format menu and select the Text command. On the resulting dialog box, select the Italic option, and click OK. As a result of this operation, the chart title appears in italic type.

7. Pull down the Chart menu and select the Axes command. Click the Major Grid Lines option in the Category Axis section of the dialog box, as shown in Figure 9.8. This option displays vertical gridlines between each cluster of columns on the chart.

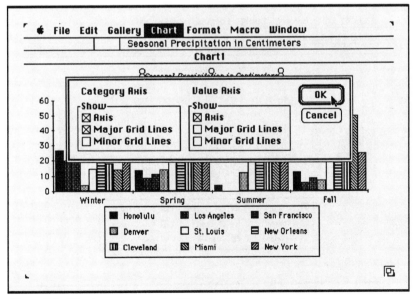

Figure 9.8: *The Axes command settings for the reoriented chart*

8. Pull down the File menu and select the Save As command (or press ⌘-S). Enter the following text as the filename:

   Precipitation by City

   Click the Save key (or press Return) to complete the save operation.

Figure 9.9 shows the final result of your work. To examine one of the SERIES formulas, click any one of the columns in the chart. For example, here is the formula for the final data series:

= SERIES("New York",Precipitation!$B$5:$E$5, Precipitation!$B$14:$E$14,9)

The first argument gives the series name, "New York", from column A of the worksheet. The second and third arguments are external references—to the category names in row 5 of the worksheet and to the actual series data in row 14. Finally, the fourth argument indicates that this is the ninth series in the chart.

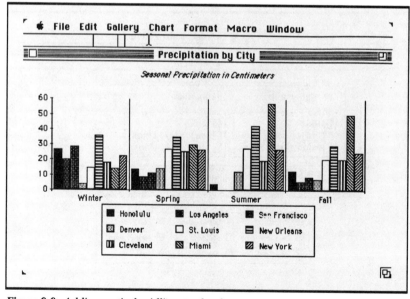

Figure 9.9: Adding vertical gridlines to the chart

In the next exercise you'll learn another way to control the selection of data series for the chart. Keep in mind, however, that this next technique cannot be used in early versions of Excel.

Making Multiple Selections to Control Chart Orientation

As you learned in Chapter 6, Excel 1.5 permits you to make a chart from a multiple-range selection on the worksheet. You have used this technique once to build a pie chart from noncontiguous rows. Now you'll select the entire range from A5 to E14 on the precipitation worksheet, but in two consecutive groups of rows. Excel reads this multiple-range selection as an instruction to build data series for the chart from rows rather than columns of worksheet data.

You can actually divide the worksheet table into any two groups of rows for this operation. In the following steps you'll start with a one-row range at the top of the table, and then you'll select the rest of the rows as the second range:

1. Use the mouse to select the one-row range A5:E5. Your worksheet is shown in Figure 9.10.

2. Hold down the Command key (⌘) while you select the second range, A6:E14, as shown in Figure 9.11.

3. Pull down the File menu and select the New command (or press ⌘-N from the keyboard).

4. Select the Chart option and click OK.

5. Pull down the Chart menu and select the Add Legend command.

At this point in your work, the new chart should be identical to the one that you produced using the Paste Special command (Figure 9.7). To complete the chart now, you can follow the same sequence of steps you performed before: move the legend to the bottom of the chart, add a title, display the title in italics, and add vertical gridlines to separate the clusters of columns.

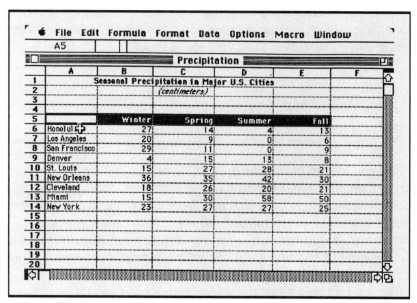

Figure 9.10: *Selecting the one-row range*

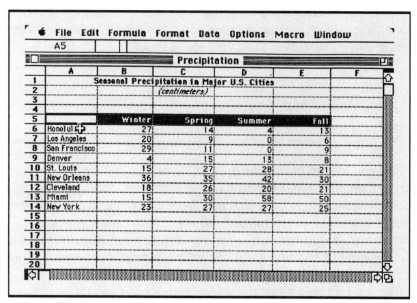

Figure 9.11: *Selecting the second range*

Before we end our discussion of Excel's charting component, we'll briefly discuss two final topics, involving printer and disk operations. First, we'll examine the features of the Page Setup command for printing charts. Then we'll see how Excel reacts when you open a chart document alone from disk, without first opening the supporting worksheet.

Using the Page Setup Command

You have seen how to use the Page Setup command to control the format of a printed worksheet. This command's dialog box is only slightly modified for a chart document. One difference is that the Page Setup offers you a choice between the following two options for printing a chart:

- The Screen Size option produces a chart that is the same size as it appears on the screen.

- The Fit to Page option retains the original proportions of the chart, but uses as much of the available page area as possible.

In effect, you can use the Fit to Page option to enlarge the chart on the printed page.

Like most charts, the precipitation chart is wider than it is tall. For this reason, you'll probably want to rotate the chart 90 degrees, printing it sideways on the paper. In the following exercise you'll print the precipitation chart in as large a format as possible on a 8½-by-11 sheet of paper. Begin by activating the chart on the desktop, then perform these steps:

1. Pull down the File menu and select the Page Setup command.

2. In the resulting dialog box, click the sideways icon under the Orientation heading.

3. Use the mouse to select the contents of the Page Header input box, and press the Backspace key to delete the default code for this option.

4. Likewise, select the contents of the Page Footer input box, and press the Backspace key.

5. Enter the following new values into the Margin, Width, and Height input boxes:

Left Margin: 0   **Print Width: 11**
Top Margin: 0   **Print Height: 8.5**

Since the chart is to be printed sideways, the Print Width option now refers to the length of the paper, and Print Height refers to the width of the paper. Figure 9.12 shows the final form of the Page Setup dialog box.

6. Click OK to complete the Page Setup operation. (Note that you have retained the default selection of the Fit to Page option.)

7. Pull down the File menu and select the Print command (or press **⌘-P** from the keyboard), and click OK to print the chart.

Looking at the result of this printing operation, you can see how a larger print format provides greater clarity of detail in the final result.

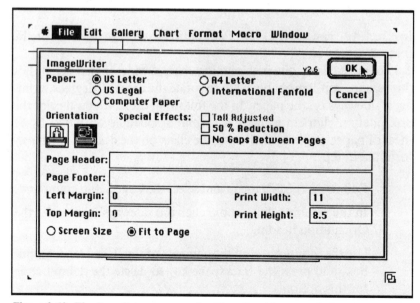

Figure 9.12: The Page Setup command settings for sideways printing

Opening a Chart onto the Desktop

Finally, a brief note on the process of opening a chart onto the desktop from disk. As you have seen, a chart is normally a dependent document, linked to the worksheet that supplies the original data to the chart. For this reason, you'll usually want to have the supporting worksheet on the desktop along with a given chart. The typical sequence of operations for opening a chart onto the desktop involves opening the supporting worksheet from disk and then opening the dependent chart.

Excel will allow you to open a dependent document onto the desktop alone, without its supporting document. However, when you do so, Excel anticipates the possibility that some changes may have occurred on the supporting document since the last time you opened the dependent document. For this reason, Excel needs to elicit special instructions from you before opening the dependent document.

Specifically, Figure 9.13 shows the question that Excel asks you if you attempt to open a chart onto the desktop without first opening the chart's supporting worksheet:

Update references to non-resident sheets?

This question asks you whether you want Excel to look on disk for the supporting worksheet (the "non-resident sheet" in this case) and update the chart with any new information that may be stored on the worksheet. You have two choices in response to this question:

- Click OK; in response, Excel locates the supporting worksheet on disk and redraws the chart from the data currently stored in the worksheet. (Excel does not open the worksheet onto the desktop.)

- Click Cancel; Excel displays the chart exactly as it appeared when you last saved it to disk, regardless of any changes that might have occurred on the supporting worksheet.

In either event, the full chart appears on the desktop. But the first option gives you the opportunity to update the chart according to the most recent data in the worksheet. Of course, if you are sure that you

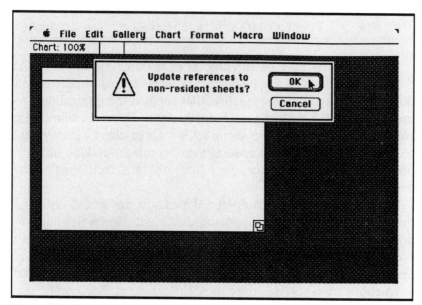

Figure 9.13: Opening a chart without its supporting worksheet

have not changed the supporting worksheet in any way since the last time you viewed the chart, clicking the Cancel button is the appropriate response to Excel's question.

PART IV

Managing Data with Excel Databases

10

Working with Databases in Excel

Featuring:

Using the Sort
command

Defining a database
range

Establishing selection
criteria

Performing the Find
command

Excel's third component is *database management*. As you learned in Chapter 1, a *database* in Excel is a table of records that you enter into a worksheet. Some common examples of business database applications are employee records, address lists, production records, invoice records, inventory, product-line information, and expense records. Imagine any one of these applications displayed in the rows and columns of a worksheet, and you have an example of an Excel database.

Excel offers a variety of operations that you can perform on the information in a database:

- Searches for records that match conditions you express

- Extracting a group of selected records, forming a separate data table

- Deleting selected records from the database

- Statistical calculations with selected records

- Rearranging the entire database in ascending or descending order

Excel 1.5 cannot be called a "complete" database-management program; it is not designed to handle very large or very complex database applications. For most Excel users, the database component is third in importance after worksheets and charts. Nonetheless, in the context of an appropriately chosen application, Excel's database operations are useful and impressive.

In essence, a database is a table of numers, text, or any combination of the two, arranged in rows and columns on a worksheet. The rows in the data table are called the *records* of the database, and the columns are called the *fields*. In order to perform database operations, you must first organize and define your database according to Excel's simple requirements:

1. Format your database in a consistent record structure, with a fixed number of identified fields.

2. Use the Set Database command in the Data menu to define the database range on the worksheet.

3. Create a range of *criteria* on the same worksheet, expressing conditions for selecting certain records in the database.

4. Use the Set Criteria command in the Data menu to define the criteria range on the worksheet.

This chapter guides you through the basic steps for setting up a database in Excel. In a series of short exercises, you'll define the database range, prepare some criteria for record selection, and then perform the simplest of the database operations—the Find command. In Chapter 11 you'll study the other database operations, Extract and Delete, and you'll learn more about selection criteria. Finally, in Chapter 12 you'll examine Excel's built-in functions that perform statistical operations on databases. Together, these three chapters introduce you to the major database capabilities available in Excel.

This chapter also covers a subject that does not belong exclusively to database applications—sorting. Excel has a quick and powerful Sort command that you can use to rearrange a database or any other table of information. While sorting is a topic that we commonly associate with database applications, Excel's Sort command is actually available for sorting any data that you store on a worksheet.

Organizing a Database

Your first tasks in this chapter will be to create a simple database and to perform a variety of sorting operations on the information. You'll develop a quarterly sales application similar to the worksheet you last worked on in Chapter 5. But here you'll organize and define the information formally as a database. The new version of this application appears in Figure 10.1. The table lists the names of nine salespeople, along with the familiar numeric information about quarterly sales. In addition, there is a new column labeled Region, identifying the sales region in which each person works.

Each record in this database describes the activities of one person in your sales force. As you can see, the records appear as rows in the data table, and the worksheet columns are the fields of the database. There are seven fields in this database, supplying the name, region, four quarterly sales figures, and total sales for each salesperson. The final column is a *calculated field*, the sum of the four quarterly sales.

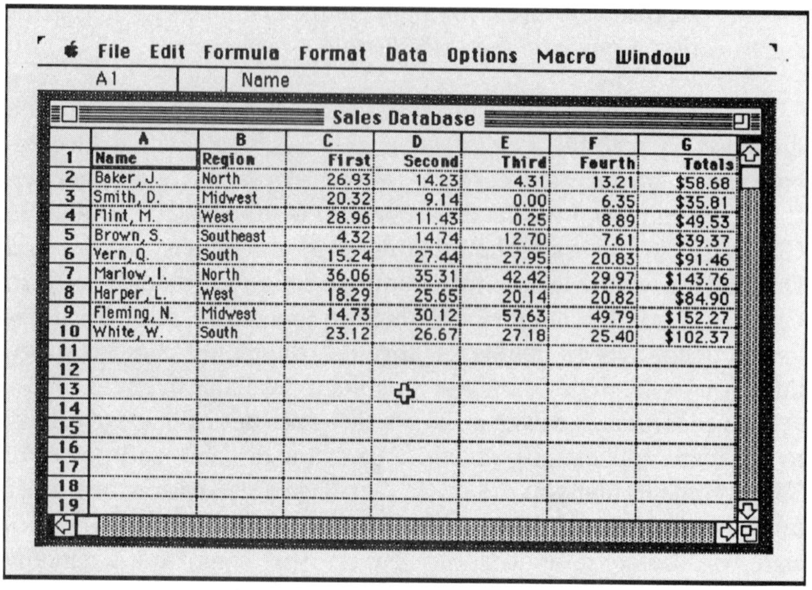

	A	B	C	D	E	F	G
1	Name	Region	First	Second	Third	Fourth	Totals
2	Baker, J.	North	26.93	14.23	4.31	13.21	$58.68
3	Smith, D.	Midwest	20.32	9.14	0.00	6.35	$35.81
4	Flint, M.	West	28.96	11.43	0.25	8.89	$49.53
5	Brown, S.	Southeast	4.32	14.74	12.70	7.61	$39.37
6	Yern, Q.	South	15.24	27.44	27.95	20.83	$91.46
7	Marlow, I.	North	36.06	35.31	42.42	29.97	$143.76
8	Harper, L.	West	18.29	25.65	20.14	20.82	$84.90
9	Fleming, N.	Midwest	14.73	30.12	57.63	49.79	$152.27
10	White, W.	South	23.12	26.67	27.18	25.40	$102.37

Figure 10.1: *Developing a sales database*

The *field names* are the labels at the top of the columns. Field names are very important in a database application; they have a functional role in identifying both individual data entries and entire columns of information in the data table. Excel requires that you enter a complete row of field names at the top of a defined database. Each column must have a unique name.

Your first task is to reproduce this database on your own computer. By now you should be able to do so without detailed instructions. Here, then, is a broad outline of the steps:

1. Open the Data Table worksheet onto the desktop from disk.
2. Use the Number command in the Format menu to display all the numbers consistantly, with two digits after the decimal point. (As before, these numbers represent units of $1,000 in the sales application. For example, the entry 35.31 represents $35,310.)
3. Insert two blank columns at the left of the data table and one blank row at the top of the table. Use the Column Width command in the Format menu to decrease the width of columns B

through F to 8 and the width of column G to 9. This allows
you to view columns A through G on one screen.

4. Enter the field names into row 1. Use the Style command to
   display them in boldface type. Then use the Alignment command to right-justify the field names that identify numeric
   fields.

5. Enter the column of names into column A and the regions
   into column B.

6. Enter the following formula into cell G2:

   = C2 + D2 + E2 + F2

   Then perform the Fill Down command to copy this formula
   down column G. Use the Numbers command to display the
   values in the Totals field in the dollar-and-cent format.

7. Perform the Save As command to save the database under the
   filename **Sales Database**.

Your worksheet should now be identical to Figure 10.1. Note that
this is a very small database, designed for the purpose of illustrating
Excel's database operations. Most real-life databases are larger than
this; in fact, Excel can work efficiently with databases that contain
hundreds of records and dozens of fields. But, as you'll soon discover,
Excel's database commands can prove as useful with small databases
as with large ones.

As a first exercise with the sales database, let's begin discussing
Excel's powerful Sort command.

Sorting Database Records

In the initial version of the sales database, the records are not
arranged in any particular order. To satisfy the requirements of particular applications, you might want to rearrange a database table alphabetically or numerically by a selected field. For example, you could
arrange the records of the sales database in alphabetical order by the
salespeople's names. The process of rearranging the database is called
sorting.

Sorting is easy and fast in Excel. The Sort command is located in the Data menu. When you select this command, the resulting dialog box gives you a versatile group of options, as you can see in Figure 10.2. You sort a data table either by rows or by columns. In a database application you'll typically sort by rows, rearranging the order of the records in the database.

You also select one or more columns to serve as *keys* in a database sort. For example, to arrange the database alphabetically by the salespeople's names, you would choose the Name field as the key to the sort. Excel allows you to select as many as three sorting keys. A secondary key determines the sorting order in the event that any two records have identical data entries for the first key field. Likewise, a third key governs the order of any records that match in the first and second key fields.

In the following exercises, you'll first sort the database by a single key, then you'll sort by multiple keys.

Sorting by One Key

To sort a database, you begin by selecting all the records that you want to rearrange. Then you pull down the Data menu and invoke the

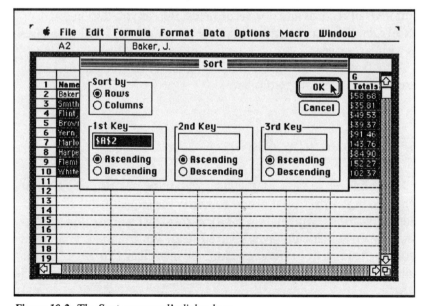

Figure 10.2: The Sort command's dialog box

Sort command. When you select the database records, you have to be very careful *not* to include the field names in your selection. If you were to include the row of field names, Excel would alphabetize each field name in with the rest of the records in the column. The field names must always remain at the top of the database table.

Follow these steps to sort the sales database alphabetically by the salespeople's names:

1. Select the database records in the range A2:G10. A2 should be the active cell in this range selection.

2. Pull down the Data menu and select the Sort command. Figure 10.2 shows the resulting dialog box. Notice that Excel has entered an absolute reference to the active worksheet cell into the 1st Key input box: $A$2. This single cell in column A is sufficient to select the first column—the Name field—as the key for sorting the database. You can simply accept Excel's suggested options for your first sort operation, since you want to sort the database by rows and use the Name field as the key to the sort. Furthermore, you want the sort to be performed in *ascending* order, alphabetically from A to Z.

3. Click the OK button (or press Return) to accept the default selections on the dialog box and to begin the sort operation.

4. Select cell A1 so that you can view the sorted database clearly.

As you can see in Figure 10.3, the database records are now arranged in alphabetical order by the Name field. The sort occurs instantaneously for a database this small. (However, Excel's Sort command is also very fast for larger databases.)

In the following exercises, you'll sort the database by two keys.

Sorting by More than One Key

Let's say that you would next like to rearrange the database alphabetically by the Region field. Then, within each Region, you want to sort the records alphabetically by the salespeople's names. Here are the steps for accomplishing this task:

1. Select the range of cells that contain the database records, A2:G10.

	A	B	C	D	E	F	G
	File Edit Formula Format Data Options Macro Window						
	A1		Name				
	Sales Database						
1	**Name**	**Region**	**First**	**Second**	**Third**	**Fourth**	**Totals**
2	Baker, J.	North	26.93	14.23	4.31	13.21	$58.68
3	Brown, S.	Southeast	4.32	14.74	12.70	7.61	$39.37
4	Fleming, N.	Midwest	14.73	30.12	57.63	49.79	$152.27
5	Flint, M.	West	28.96	11.43	0.25	8.89	$49.53
6	Harper, L.	West	18.29	25.65	20.14	20.82	$84.90
7	Marlow, I.	North	36.06	35.31	42.42	29.97	$143.76
8	Smith, D.	Midwest	20.32	9.14	0.00	6.35	$35.81
9	Yern, Q.	South	15.24	27.44	27.95	20.83	$91.46
10	White, W.	South	23.12	26.67	27.18	25.40	$102.37

Figure 10.3: The database sorted alphabetically by name

2. Pull down the Data menu and select the Sort command.

3. Move the Sort dialog box further down the desktop, so that you can see the fields of your database. (To accomplish this, position the mouse pointer over the title bar at the top of the dialog box, hold down the mouse button, and drag the box down. Release the mouse button when you have placed the dialog box where you want it, as shown in Figure 10.4.)

4. The 1st Key input box is currently highlighted, ready for you to enter the primary sorting key. To select the Region field as the first sorting key, click the mouse in cell B1 of the worksheet. An absolute reference to this cell appears in the 1st Key input box, and a marquee appears around the cell itself in the worksheet.

5. Activate the 2nd Key input box by clicking the mouse inside the box.

6. To select the Name field as the second sorting key, click the mouse in cell A1 of the worksheet. An absolute reference to this cell appears in the 2nd Key input box. Your desktop now looks like Figure 10.4.

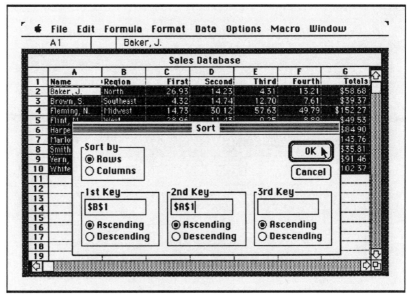

Figure 10.4: *Selecting two keys for a sort*

7. Click the OK button (or press Return) to complete the sort operation.

Figure 10.5 shows the result of the sort. The records are now arranged alphabetically by the sales regions. Within each region, the records appear in alphabetical order by the salespeople's names.

Now try a final sorting exercise on your own. Select the Region field as the primary sorting key, and the Totals field as the secondary sorting key. (While the Sort dialog box is on the screen, select a given sort key by clicking any cell inside the appropriate worksheet column, just as you did in the previous exercise.) Within each region, sort the records in *descending* order by the total sales; click the Descending option in the 2nd Key box to accomplish this, as shown in Figure 10.6. The result of this sort appears in Figure 10.7.

Keep in mind that the Sort command is not reserved exclusively for database applications. You can use the command to sort any information in a worksheet.

Next you'll define your sales application formally as a database. This is a required step in the process of preparing for Excel's database operations.

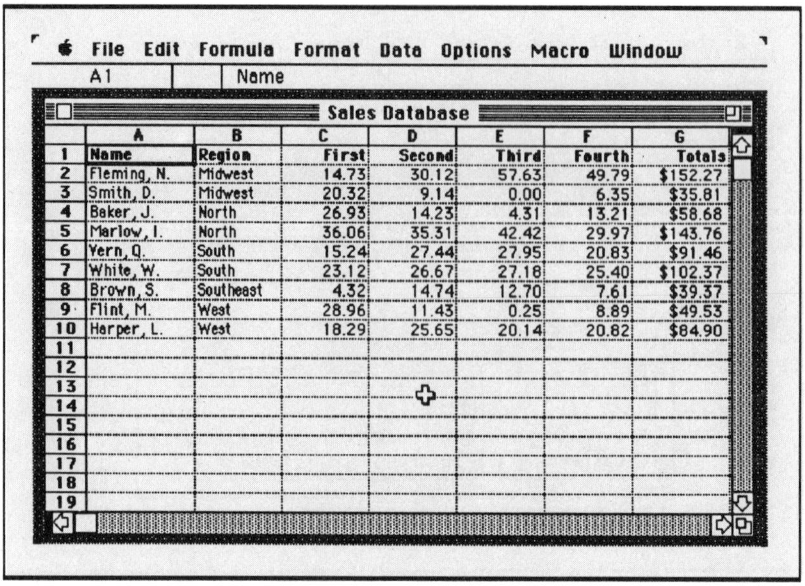

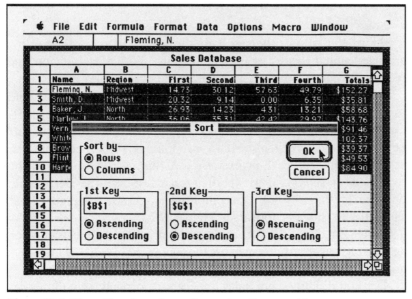

Figure 10.5: The database sorted by two keys—the Region and Name fields

Figure 10.6: *The settings for a descending sort on the second key*

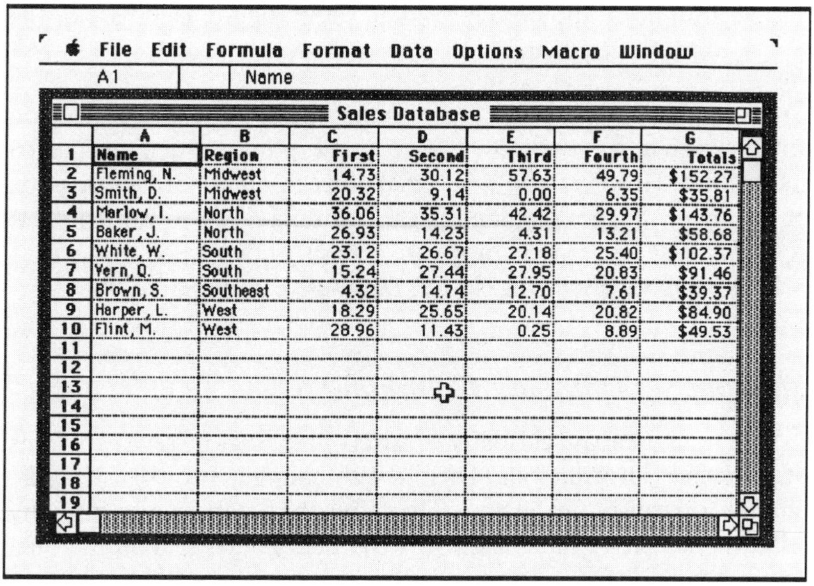

	A	B	C	D	E	F	G
1	Name	Region	First	Second	Third	Fourth	Totals
2	Fleming, N.	Midwest	14.73	30.12	57.63	49.79	$152.27
3	Smith, D.	Midwest	20.32	9.14	0.00	6.35	$35.81
4	Marlow, I.	North	36.06	35.31	42.42	29.97	$143.76
5	Baker, J.	North	26.93	14.23	4.31	13.21	$58.68
6	White, W.	South	23.12	26.67	27.18	25.40	$102.37
7	Yern, Q.	South	15.24	27.44	27.95	20.83	$91.46
8	Brown, S.	Southeast	4.32	14.74	12.70	7.61	$39.37
9	Harper, L.	West	18.29	25.65	20.14	20.82	$84.90
10	Flint, M.	West	28.96	11.43	0.25	8.89	$49.53

Figure 10.7: The database sorted by two keys—the Region and Totals fields

Defining a Database

Pull down the Data menu, and examine the first five options in the menu list:

Find ⌘**F**
Extract... ⌘**E**
Delete
Set Database
Set Criteria

These are Excel's database operations. The first three commands, Find, Extract, and Delete, all depend on explicitly defined database and criteria ranges on the active worksheet. If these definitions do not exist as specific range names on the worksheet, you cannot perform the database commands.

Fortunately, Excel makes it very easy for you to define database and criteria ranges, using the Set Database and Set Criteria commands. You use both of these commands in the same way:

1. Select the worksheet range that you want to define as the database or the criteria.

2. Pull down the Data menu and select the Set Database or Set Criteria command.

No dialog box results from these commands, nor does Excel give you any message to let you know that the operation has been performed successfully. However, you'll find that you can examine the dialog box of the Define Name command in the Formula menu to confirm that your database and criteria range are correctly established.

Let's begin by discussing the Set Database command.

Using the Set Database Command

Your sales database currently consists of ten rows by seven columns of worksheet information. (There are actually nine rows of records, plus the top row of field names.) To define the database, you begin by selecting this entire table, including the field names and all the field columns.

Here are the steps for defining the sales database:

1. Select the range A1:G10.

2. Pull down the Data menu and select the Set Database command, as shown in Figure 10.8.

Next you may want to confirm that the database has been defined. To do so, follow these steps:

1. Pull down the Formula menu and select the Define Name command (or press ⌘-L from the keyboard). The name *Database* appears in the list of names presented in the dialog box.

2. Click this name with the mouse. The dialog box appears as shown in Figure 10.9.

The Set Database command has created the name Database for the worksheet range identified as $A$1:$G$10. This is the range that contains the row of field names and the nine rows of records. Once you have examined the definition of Database, you can click the Cancel button on the Define Name dialog box to continue with your work on the desktop.

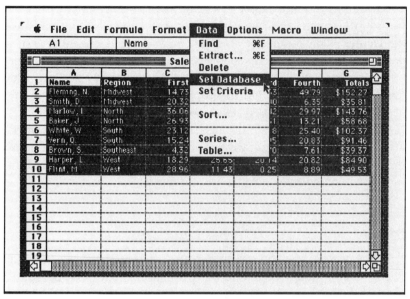

Figure 10.8: Defining the database with the Set Database command

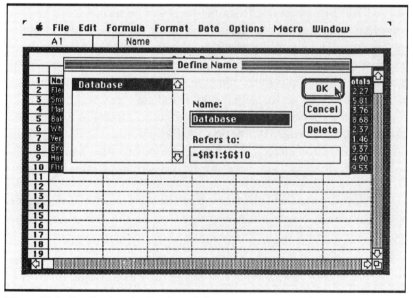

Figure 10.9: Confirming the database definition

As you learned in Chapter 5, a range name is normally just a convenient way to refer to a range of cells on a worksheet. You usually use the Define Name command to create such a name. In the case of a database, however, the range name is no mere convenience: it is essential for performing database operations. Accordingly, Excel provides the Set Database command to simplify the process of defining this name on your worksheet.

Only one database definition can exist at a time on a given worksheet. However, the exact range of the database might change many times during your work. For example, you might want to expand the range by adding new records to the database.

*I*nserting New Records in the Database

Let's say a salesperson has been transferred to the sales staff that you supervise. You need to add this person's name to your database, along with the person's quarterly sales records for the last year.

There are two ways you can approach the process of adding a new record to your database, depending on where you want to insert the record. The first approach is simply to enter the record into the first empty row after the last record currently in the database—row 11 in the sales database. However, if you append the new record in this way, Excel has no way of knowing that your database has expanded. Consequently, the next required step is to redefine the database range, by selecting the entire database and performing the Set Database command again.

A simpler approach is to insert a new record somewhere inside the current database range. If you do this, Excel automatically redefines the database range correctly for you. Let's see how this happens.

Follow these steps to insert a new record into your sales database:

1. Use the mouse to select row 6 on the worksheet. (Click 6 in the column of row numbers located at the left side of the worksheet.)

2. Press ⌘-I to insert a new row at this location. Row 6 becomes an empty row, and the rest of the records move down by one row, as shown in Figure 10.10.

3. Enter the following field entries into cells A6 to F6:

   Jackson, A.   North   21.88   13.15   5.02   9.18

4. Enter the following formula into cell G6, to calculate the total annual sales for this person:

= C6 + D6 + E6 + F6

Now, to confirm that Excel has adjusted your database definition, pull down the Formula menu and select the Define Name command. Highlight the Database name in the list box, as shown in Figure 10.11. You can see that your database is now defined for the range $A$1:$G$11, one row more than before. Excel automatically expands the database range if you use the Insert command to add records inside the current range.

After you have examined the new database range, click the Cancel button on the Define Name dialog box so you can continue your work. For the purposes of the upcoming exercises, you'll now rearrange the database in alphabetical order by the salespeople's names. Select the ten rows of records (not including the row of field names), and perform the Sort command. When the operation is complete, the order of your database will be similar to Figure 10.3, except that there is now one additional record. If you want, you can examine the Define

	A	B	C	D	E	F	G
	Name	**Region**	**First**	**Second**	**Third**	**Fourth**	**Totals**
2	Fleming, N.	Midwest	14.73	30.12	57.63	49.79	$152.27
3	Smith, D.	Midwest	20.32	9.14	0.00	6.35	$35.81
4	Marlow, I.	North	36.06	35.31	42.42	29.97	$143.76
5	Baker, J.	North	26.93	14.23	4.31	13.21	$58.68
6							
7	White, W.	South	23.12	26.67	27.18	25.40	$102.37
8	Vern, Q.	South	15.24	27.44	27.95	20.83	$91.46
9	Brown, S.	Southeast	4.32	14.74	12.70	7.61	$39.37
10	Harper, L.	West	18.29	25.65	20.14	20.82	$84.90
11	Flint, M.	West	28.96	11.43	0.25	8.89	$49.53

Figure 10.10: Inserting a new record into the database

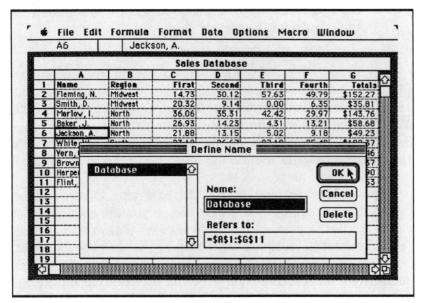

Figure 10.11: *Confirming the expanded database definition*

Name dialog box one more time to check the database range; you'll find that the sorting operation has not affected the definition of the database.

Now you're ready to begin establishing selection criteria for performing specific database operations.

Defining Selection Criteria

The tools that you'll be working with throughout the remainder of this chapter—and in the next two chapters—all operate on *selected* groups of records in a database. The success of these operations depends on Excel's ability to select individual records that match the conditions you specify.

The conditions for selecting records are referred to as *criteria* in Excel. You can express criteria in a variety of prescribed formats, but you must always enter these expressions directly onto the same worksheet that contains your database. The range of cells into which you enter these expressions is called the *criteria range*.

Here are the general steps for establishing a criteria range for a given database operation:

1. Find a convenient blank area on your database worksheet where you can store the criteria.

2. Enter a group of conditions into this area, in one of the formats that Excel recognizes for expressing selection criteria.

3. Select the range of cells that contain the criteria.

4. Perform the Set Criteria command in the Data menu, formally defining the criteria range.

Once you have taken these steps—and you have also defined your database range properly—you can perform any of Excel's database operations.

There are two general types of criteria in Excel, called *comparison criteria* and *computed criteria*. Each of these has its own prescribed format. In a comparison criterion, you identify a value (or range of values) that you wish to search for in a particular field of the database. In response to this criterion, Excel searches through the target field for the value you specify. A record is selected if it contains the value. You'll experiment with a variety of comparison criteria in the upcoming exercises.

A computed criterion is slightly more complicated. To define such a criterion, you write an expression that Excel can evaluate as either true or false for any given record in the database. This expression typically contains references to specific fields in the database. In a subsequent operation, Excel selects any record for which the expression is true. We'll discuss computed criteria further in Chapter 11.

For now, let's look at some examples of comparison criteria.

Comparison Criteria

Expressions defining critera are placed directly in a column of your database worksheet. Normally you should select an area that is adjacent to your database—rather than below it—for storing your selection criteria. This way the criteria will not be in the way if your database expands in length—that is, if you append additional records. For convenience in the following exercises, however, you'll simply use the area located directly below the sales database for entering your selection criteria. This location allows you to view the criteria and the database at the same time.

The simplest form of a comparison criterion contains two entries: a field name in one cell, and a field value in the cell immediately below. For example, let's say you want to examine all your salespeople who work in the North sales region. The criterion for selecting these records appears in cells A14 and A15 in Figure 10.12:

Region
North

You can think of this criterion as an instruction to Excel: "Select all the database records in which the Region field contains the word *North*."

Enter these two values into your own database worksheet. Next you need to establish this range formally as a criteria range. To do so, perform these steps:

1. Select the range A14:A15.

2. Pull down the Data menu and select the Set Criteria command, as shown in Figure 10.12.

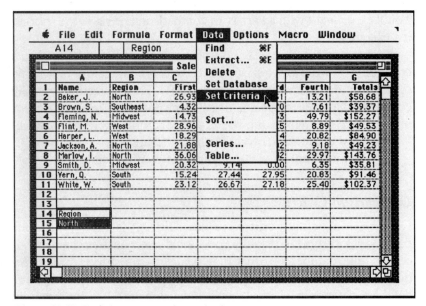

Figure 10.12: Defining a comparison criterion

Again, you will see no change in the worksheet after this operation. To confirm that Excel has defined the criteria range, you can consult the Define Name dialog box:

1. Pull down the Formula menu and select the Define Name command.

2. Click Criteria in the list of names presented in the resulting dialog box, as shown in Figure 10.13. Note the reference of the criteria range—$A$14:$A$15.

3. Click the Cancel button when you are satisfied that the criteria range is correctly defined.

Now you have formally defined both your database and a criteria range, and you are ready to perform a database operation. You'll learn to use the Find command in the upcoming exercises.

Performing a Find Operation

The Find command in the Data menu is designed to help you locate all the database records that match your expressed selection criteria.

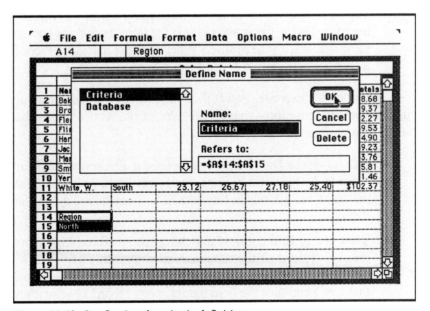

Figure 10.13: Confirming the criteria definition

In response to this command, Excel makes some special visual changes in the worksheet window, to remind you that you are in the Find mode. Specifically, the following changes occur when you select the Find command:

- Excel immediately highlights the first record in the database that matches your selection criteria. (Alternatively, if the active cell is located inside the database range at the time you invoke the Find command, Excel highlights the *next* record that matches the criteria, moving down the database from the active cell.)

- The scroll boxes are filled in with diagonal stripes, to indicate a temporary new scrolling mode. When you click the down scroll arrow in this mode, Excel scrolls from one matching record to the next. (Click the up scroll arrow to highlight the previous matching record.)

- You can now press ⌘-F repeatedly from the keyboard to highlight each matching record in sequence, down the length of the database. (This is the same as clicking the down scroll arrow with the mouse.) When the last matching record is highlighted, you'll hear a beep if you press ⌘-F again.

- You can also press Shift-⌘-F to highlight the *previous* matching record in the database. (This is the same as clicking the up scroll arrow with the mouse.) When the first matching record is highlighted, Shift-⌘-F produces a beep.

In the following exercise, you'll find the records that match your current selection criterion—that is, all salespeople who work in the North sales region:

1. Pull down the Data menu and select the Find command (or press ⌘-F from the keyboard). Excel highlights the first matching record, which happens to be the first record in the database.

2. Press ⌘-F to find the next matching record. Excel highlights the sixth record of the database, as shown in Figure 10.14. (The sixth record is in row 7 of the worksheet; keep in mind that row 1 contains the field names, not a record.) Notice that

a 6 appears in the display area just to the left of the formula bar; this number identifies the current record during a Find operation.

3. Click the down scroll arrow to find the next matching record. Excel highlights the seventh record.

4. Press ⌘-F or click the down scroll arrow again. This time the highlight does not change; instead you hear a beep, indicating that the current record is the last one in the database that matches your selection criterion.

5. Now try pressing Shift-⌘-F (or clicking the up scroll arrow) to move the highlight to the previous matching record. Excel once again selects the sixth database record.

To exit from the Find mode, you can perform either of two actions:

• Pull down the Data menu, and select the first command in the menu list. As you can see in Figure 10.15, this command becomes Exit Find when the Find mode is active.

• Activate a cell that is outside the database range.

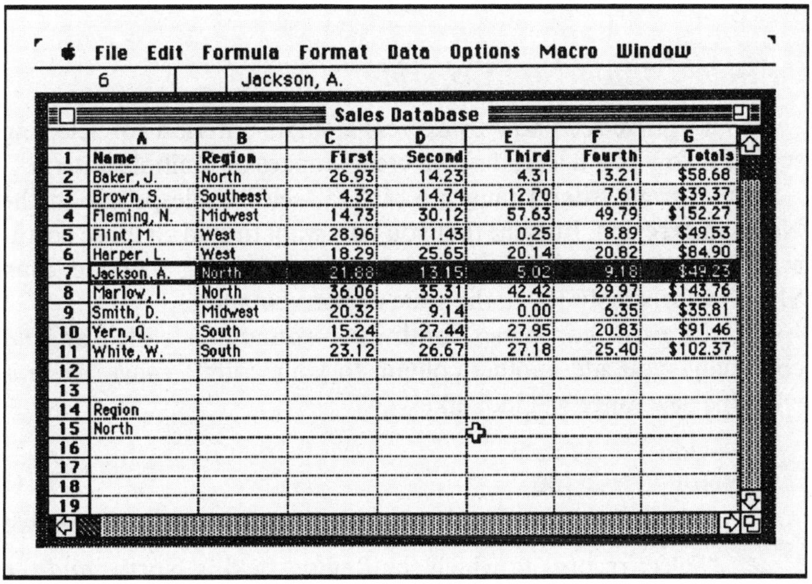

Figure 10.14: Using the Find command

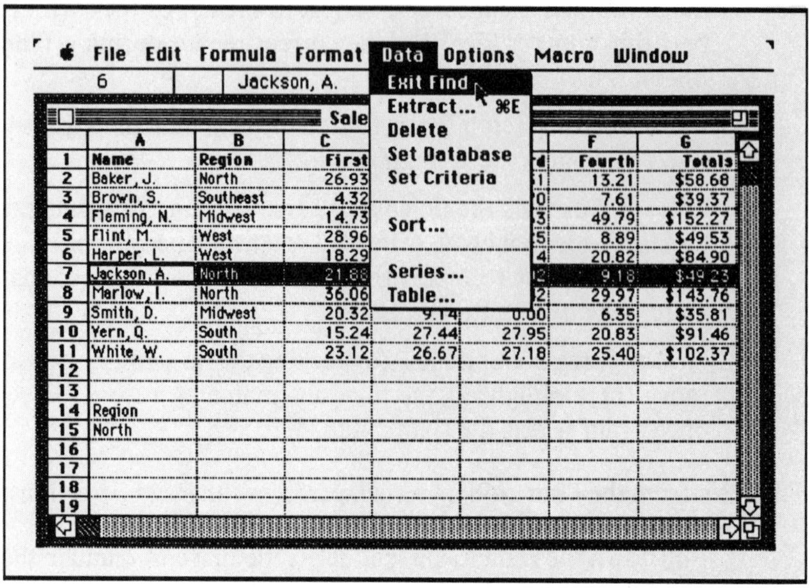

Figure 10.15: *Using the Exit Find command*

In the final two exercises of this chapter, you'll experiment further with comparison criteria.

Multiple Comparison Criteria

So far you've seen how to express a single criterion for selecting records. Now you'll learn how to create ranges of multiple criteria.

Your current criteria range, A14:A15, selects salespeople in the North sales region. Imagine that you now want to find all those northern salespeople who have an annual sales record that is greater than $100,000 (or simply 100 in the scale of your database).

To create this combined condition—sometimes called an *and* condition—you add another column to your criteria range. Here is what the new range will look like:

Region	Totals
North	>100

Paraphrased, these two columns give the following instruction to Excel: "Select records in which the Region field is North, *and* the Totals field contains a value that is greater than 100."

As you can see, the > symbol represents "greater than" in an Excel criterion expression. Here is a summary of all the *inequality* symbols you can use in a criterion:

>   Greater than

<   Less than

> =   Greater than or equal to

< =   Less than or equal to

Enter the new criterion into cells B14 and B15 of your database worksheet. Since the criteria range now consists of two columns, you have to redefine the range formally:

1. Select the range A14:B15.

2. Pull down the Data menu and select the Set Criteria command.

To test these criteria, pull down the Data menu and select the Find command. Excel immediately highlights the seventh record in the database, as you can see in Figure 10.16. Interestingly enough, this is

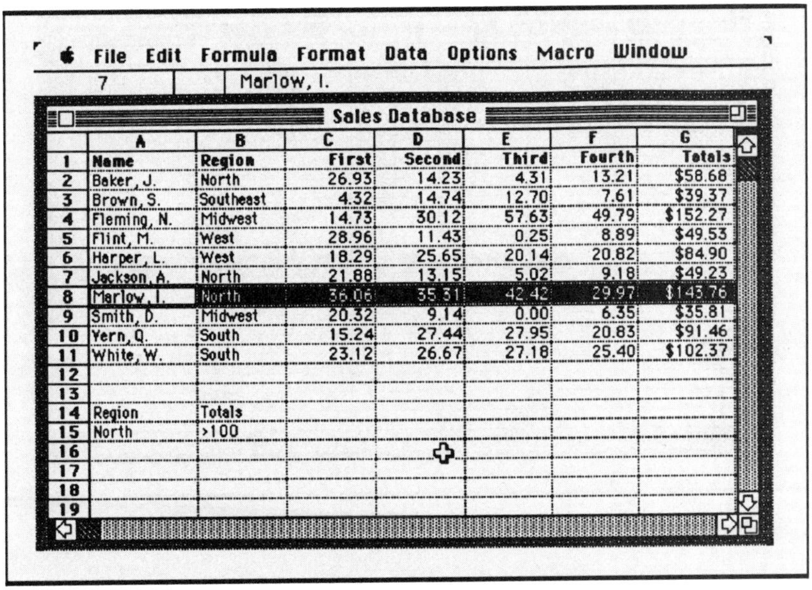

Figure 10.16: Selecting records that match multiple criteria

the only record in the database that matches the criteria you have established—a Region field of North and a Totals field that is greater than 100. If you press ⌘-F to find the next matching record, you will hear a beep.

Finally, in the following exercise you'll append another row to the criteria range. You have seen that two columns of criteria result in *and* conditions—a record must match both criteria to be selected. In contrast, multiple *rows* in the criteria range produce *or* conditions; to be selected, a given record needs to match the criteria in only one of the rows. You'll see how this works in the following exercise:

1. Enter the following entries in cells A16 and B16, respectively:

   South   >100

   Your criteria are now located in the range A14:B16, as shown in Figure 10.17.

2. Select the range A14:B16.

♦ File Edit Formula Format Data Options Macro Window
10	White, W.

Sales Database

	A	B	C	D	E	F	G
1	Name	Region	First	Second	Third	Fourth	Totals
2	Baker, J.	North	26.93	14.23	4.31	13.21	$58.68
3	Brown, S.	Southeast	4.32	14.74	12.70	7.61	$39.37
4	Fleming, N.	Midwest	14.73	30.12	57.63	49.79	$152.27
5	Flint, M.	West	28.96	11.43	0.25	8.89	$49.53
6	Harper, L.	West	18.29	25.65	20.14	20.82	$84.90
7	Jackson, A.	North	21.88	13.15	5.02	9.18	$49.23
8	Marlow, I.	North	36.06	35.31	42.42	29.97	$143.76
9	Smith, D.	Midwest	20.32	9.14	0.00	6.35	$35.81
10	Yern, Q.	South	15.24	27.44	27.95	20.83	$91.46
11	White, W.	South	23.12	26.67	27.18	25.40	$102.37
12							
13							
14	Region	Totals					
15	North	>100					
16	South	>100					
17							
18							
19							

Figure 10.17: Adding a row to the criteria range

3. Pull down the Data menu and select the Set Criteria command.

4. Pull down the Data menu and select the Find command (or press ⌘-F from the keyboard). The first record that matches the criteria is record 7.

5. Press ⌘-F (or click the down scoll arrow with the mouse) to find the next matching record. Excel highlights the last record in the database, number 10 (see Figure 10.17).

You've found the two records that match these criteria—the salespeople in the North and South sales regions whose total annual sales exceeded $100,000.

You'll continue working with database operations in the next chapter. Press ⌘-S to save the current version of the database worksheet to disk. You'll use these same criteria to experiment with the Extract command.

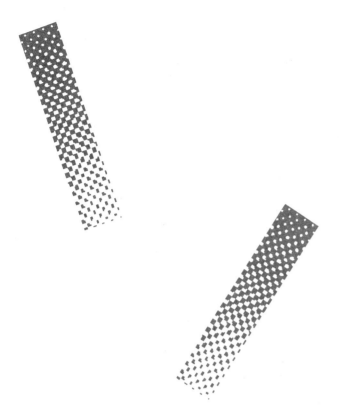

11

Performing Database Operations

Featuring:

Performing the Extract command

Using computed criteria

Performing the Delete command

This chapter shows you how to use two more of Excel's database operations, the Extract and Delete commands. Let's begin with a brief review of what you've already learned about databases.

All three of Excel's basic database operations—Find, Extract, and Delete—depend on precise definitions of a database range and a criteria range. A database is a collection of records stored in a worksheet range, where rows correspond to records and columns are fields. The top row of the database contains a complete set of field names. A criteria range contains one or more columns of expressions that Excel can use to select records from the database.

Here is an outline of the steps you follow to set up a database:

1. Enter the database into a range of rows and columns on your worksheet.

2. Perform the Set Database command to define the database range. This command creates the range name Database.

3. Create a range of criteria on the same worksheet.

4. Perform the Set Criteria command to define the criteria range. This command creates the range name Criteria.

You can create two categories of criteria: comparison and computed. We looked at comparison criteria in Chapter 10; you'll learn more about computed criteria in this chapter. Given these criteria, each of Excel's three database commands performs a different operation on the selected records:

• The Find command highlights each selected record in turn.

• The Extract command copies all or part of each selected record into a separate range on the database worksheet.

• The Delete command removes the selected records permanently from the database.

You've already performed several exercises with the Find command. Now let's move on to the other two commands, starting with Extract. You'll continue using the sales database that you developed in Chapter 10. Open it onto the desktop if it is not there already. The database contains ten records, arranged in alphabetical order by the salespeople's names. The current criteria range (A14:B16) selects all salespeople in the North and South sales regions who achieved annual sales of over $100,000.

Using the Extract Command

The Data menu's Extract command is perhaps the most useful and powerful of Excel's three database operations. This command creates a smaller data table of information, copied from your database. To prepare for this table, you perform two operations:

- Create a criteria range to select records from the database.

- Enter a row of field names—identifying the information that Excel is to copy from the database—at the top of the range where you want the extract table to appear.

In the upcoming exercise you'll use the current criteria of the sales database to create an extract table. For convenience, you'll position the extract table just to the right of the criteria range, below the database itself. (As noted in Chapter 10, you'll normally want to avoid placing the criteria range—or an extract table—below the database, unless you are certain that the database already contains all the records it will ever have.)

Setting Up an Extract Range

Before using the Extract command, you must designate the range on the worksheet where Excel will copy the selected information. There are three basic steps in setting up the extract range:

1. Decide where you want to place the extracted information.

2. Enter a row of field names corresponding to each column of data that you want to extract from the main database. These field names become the top row of the extract table.

3. Use the mouse to select the range of field names.

Note that you do not have to extract information from all the database fields; you can select the fields that interest you for a particular application. For example, Figure 11.1 shows the three fields you'll extract from the sales database. Cells C14, D14, and E14 contain the following field names:

Name   Region   Totals

Enter these three names into your own database in the same range of cells. You can either enter them manually from the keyboard, or you can use the Cut and Copy commands to copy them from the top row of the database. (If you use the Cut-and-Copy technique, Excel also copies the type styles and alignments that you have established in the original row of field names.)

Figure 11.1 also contains the following label in cell D13:

Extract Table

This optional title simply draws attention to the extract table; unlike the field names, this entry serves no functional role in the process of creating the table.

Your next step is to use the mouse to select the range of cells that contain the field names for the extract table. This selection tells Excel

	A	B	C	D	E	F	G
1	Name	Region	First	Second	Third	Fourth	Totals
2	Baker, J.	North	26.93	14.23	4.31	13.21	$58.68
3	Brown, S.	Southeast	4.32	14.74	12.70	7.61	$39.37
4	Fleming, N.	Midwest	14.73	30.12	57.63	49.79	$152.27
5	Flint, M.	West	28.96	11.43	0.25	8.89	$49.53
6	Harper., L.	West	18.29	25.65	20.14	20.82	$84.90
7	Jackson, A.	North	21.88	13.15	5.02	9.18	$49.23
8	Marlow, I.	North	36.06	35.31	42.42	29.97	$143.76
9	Smith, D.	Midwest	20.32	9.14	0.00	6.35	$35.81
10	Yern, Q.	South	15.24	27.44	27.95	20.83	$91.46
11	White, W.	South	23.12	26.67	27.18	25.40	$102.37
12							
13				*Extract Table*			
14	Region	Totals	Name	Region	Totals		
15	North	>100					
16	South	>100					
17							
18							
19							

Figure 11.1: Preparing the extract range

where to place the extract table and which fields to copy from the original database. Excel expects the selected range to contain at least one field name from the database. If it does not, an error message appears on the desktop when you try to perform the Extract command, as you can see in Figure 11.2. (Notice the error in this figure: The range of field names has not been selected.)

Here is one cautionary note about the Extract command: Before performing the command, Excel clears away any existing data below the row of field names you have entered for the extract table. For this reason, you should not place the extract table above any worksheet data that you want to keep.

Creating an Extract Table

Here are the steps for creating the extract table on the sales database:

1. Use the mouse to select the range C14:E14. This is the range of field names for the extract table.

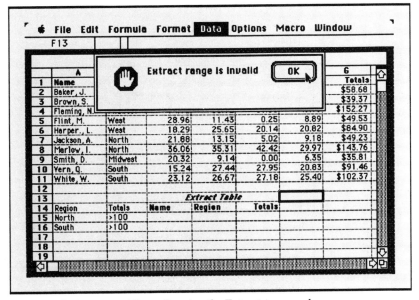

Figure 11.2: An error while performing the Extract command

2. Pull down the Data menu and select the Extract command. The resulting dialog box appears in Figure 11.3.

3. Click OK to perform the extract operation.

In response to these steps, Excel immediately copies the information that meets the criteria from the database to the extract table. You can see the result in Figure 11.4. Excel has copied the two records that match the conditions expressed in the criteria range. Following your instructions, Excel has extracted only the three designated fields: the salesperson's name, the region, and the total annual sales.

You may have noticed the single option that Excel offers on the Extract dialog box (Figure 11.3):

Unique Records Only

You can activate this option in applications where you want to avoid possible repetitive entries in the extract table. Repetitive entries occur when the original database contains multiple records that have identical information in all of the fields you have chosen for the extract table. Click Unique Records Only, and Excel copies only one representative record from each group of identical records in the database.

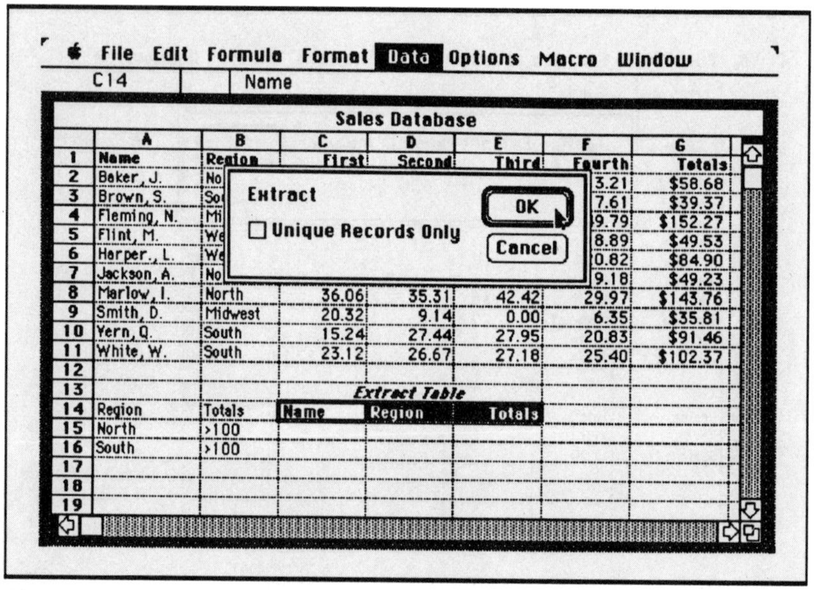

Figure 11.3: The Extract command's dialog box

File   Edit   Formula   Format   Data   Options   Macro   Window

	A	B	C	D	E	F	G
1	**Name**	**Region**	**First**	**Second**	**Third**	**Fourth**	**Totals**
2	Baker, J.	North	26.93	14.23	4.31	13.21	$58.68
3	Brown, S.	Southeast	4.32	14.74	12.70	7.61	$39.37
4	Fleming, N.	Midwest	14.73	30.12	57.63	49.79	$152.27
5	Flint, M.	West	28.96	11.43	0.25	8.89	$49.53
6	Harper., L.	West	18.29	25.65	20.14	20.82	$84.90
7	Jackson, A.	North	21.88	13.15	5.02	9.18	$49.23
8	Marlow, I.	North	36.06	35.31	42.42	29.97	$143.76
9	Smith, D.	Midwest	20.32	9.14	0.00	6.35	$35.81
10	Yern, Q.	South	15.24	27.44	27.95	20.83	$91.46
11	White, W.	South	23.12	26.67	27.18	25.40	$102.37
12							
13				*Extract Table*			
14	Region	Totals	**Name**	**Region**	**Totals**		
15	North	>100	Marlow, I.	North	$143.76		
16	South	>100	White, W.	South	$102.37		
17							
18							
19							

Figure 11.4: Three fields extracted from the main database

Excel offers a keyboard shortcut for performing the Extract command: ⌘-E. When given this keyboard command, Excel skips the Extract dialog box and immediately creates the extract table.

In the next exercise you'll create a new criteria range, resulting in a completely different extract table. To prepare for this new table, you might want to begin by clearing away the information from the previous exercise. You can use the Clear command from the Edit menu to do so:

1. Select the current criteria range, A14:B16.

2. Pull down the Edit menu and select the Clear command, then click the OK button in the resulting dialog box. Excel erases the contents of the criteria range.

3. Select the current extract table, C15:E16. (Keep the field names where they are, for use in the next exercise.)

4. This time, simply press ⌘-**B** to perform the Clear command. Excel erases the extract table.

In the next exercise you'll create a computed criterion for selecting records from the database. Specifically, you'll select all the records in which the total annual sales figure is below the average for the group as a whole. To prepare for this exercise, begin by entering a formula into the worksheet to find the average annual sales, using the following steps:

1. Enter the following label into cell F12:

   average =

   Use the Style command to display this label in italics, and the Alignment command to right-justify the label in its cell.

2. Select cell G12.

3. Pull down the Formula menu and select the Paste Function command. Select the AVERAGE function from the list of functions (after scrolling the list), and click OK. The AVERAGE function appears in the formula bar.

4. Use the mouse to select the range G2:G11. This range becomes the argument of the AVERAGE function in the formula bar, as shown in Figure 11.5.

5. Press Enter to complete the formula entry. Excel calculates the average annual sales figure as 80.74 (representing $80,740).

6. Use the Number command in the Format menu to display this figure in the dollar-and-cent format.

Now you are ready for the next extract exercise.

*W*riting a Computed Criterion

A computed criterion is a formula that results in a *logical value* of true or false for each record in the database. When you use such a criterion as a tool for extracting records, Excel selects all records for which the formula is true.

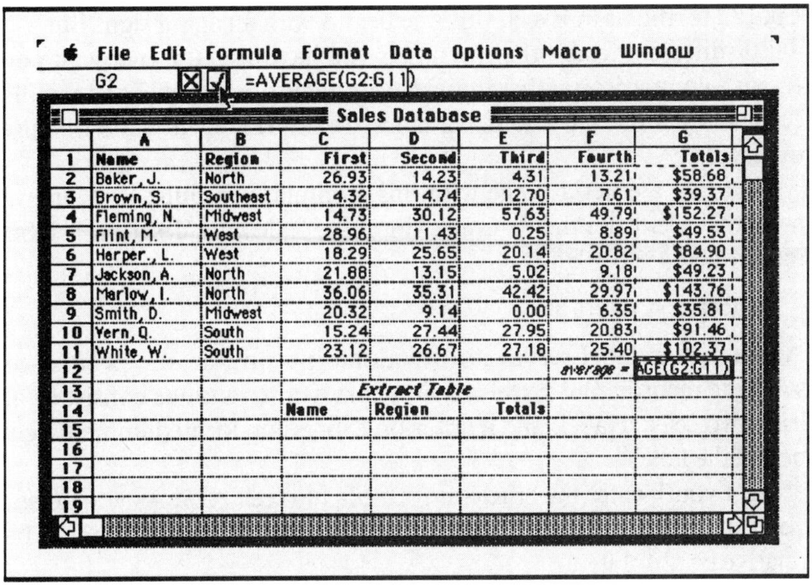

	A	B	C	D	E	F	G
1	Name	Region	First	Second	Third	Fourth	Totals
2	Baker, J.	North	26.93	14.23	4.31	13.21	$58.68
3	Brown, S.	Southeast	4.32	14.74	12.70	7.61	$39.37
4	Fleming, N.	Midwest	14.73	30.12	57.63	49.79	$152.27
5	Flint, M.	West	28.96	11.43	0.25	8.89	$49.53
6	Harper., L.	West	18.29	25.65	20.14	20.82	$84.90
7	Jackson, A.	North	21.88	13.15	5.02	9.18	$49.23
8	Marlow, I.	North	36.06	35.31	42.42	29.97	$143.76
9	Smith, D.	Midwest	20.32	9.14	0.00	6.35	$35.81
10	Vern, Q.	South	15.24	27.44	27.95	20.83	$91.46
11	White, W.	South	23.12	26.67	27.18	25.40	$102.37
12						average =	AGE(G2:G11)
13			Extract Table				
14			Name	Region	Totals		
15							
16							
17							
18							
19							

***Figure 11.5:** Entering the AVERAGE function*

The formula for a computed criterion typically compares specific field values in the database with other values. The following six relational operators are available for expressing such comparisons:

=	Equals
<>	Not equal to
<	Less than
>	Greater than
<=	Less than or equal to
>=	Greater than or equal to

For example, you now want to find all the salespeople who achieved less than average total sales for the year. You have already entered a formula for computing the average annual sales in cell G12. Accordingly, the following formula determines whether the total sales for the first record is below average:

=G2<G12

Like all formulas in Excel, this one begins with an equal sign. But it is a little different from other formulas you have seen up to now; it performs a comparison rather than an arithmetic operation. The formula results in a value of true if G2 is less than G12, or a value of false otherwise.

To create a criteria range with this formula, you must first enter a label that identifies the formula. Enter the following descriptive label into cell A14:

Totals < Average

Actually, this label serves no functional purpose in the process of selecting records. But Excel requires that a criteria range consist of at least two cells: a label, and a criterion expression located immediately below the label.

Next you'll enter the criterion formula into cell A15. As you do so, you'll have to decide whether each reference in the formula should be relative or absolute:

1. Activate cell A15, and enter an equal sign to begin the formula.

2. Click cell G2, the total sales figure in the first record. A relative reference to G2 appears in the formula bar. This reference represents the entire Totals field, and should therefore remain a relative reference. As Excel examines each record in turn, this reference will become G3, G4, G5, and so on.

3. Enter the comparison operator < (less than).

4. Click cell G12, the location of the AVERAGE formula. This reference should not change as Excel applies the comparison formula to each record in the database; in other words, it should be an absolute reference.

5. Pull down the formula menu and select the Reference command (or press ⌘-T from the keyboard). This operation changes the reference G12 to an absolute reference, $G$12.

6. Press the Enter key to complete the formula entry.

After these steps, your worksheet appears as shown in Figure 11.6. You can see the criterion formula in the formula bar. The formula has produced a value of TRUE for the first record in the database, indicating that the first salesperson had below-average sales for the year.

With this formula in place, you are ready to perform another extract operation. This time you'll build a data table that displays all the salespeople who had below average sales.

Using the Computed Criterion

You must begin the new extract operation by redefining the criteria range, since you have created a new criterion formula. Follow these steps to perform the extract operation:

1. Select the new criteria range, A14:A15.

2. Pull down the Data menu and select the Set Criteria command.

3. Select the row of field names for the extract table, C14:E14.

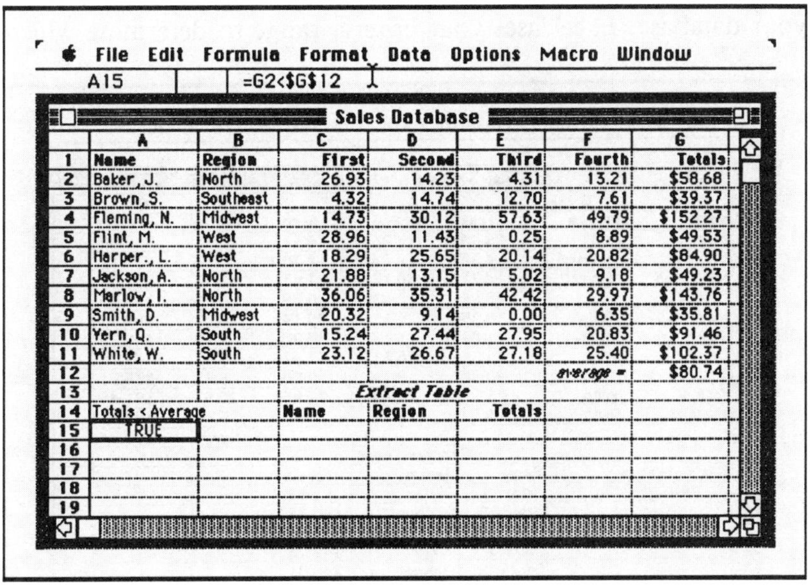

Figure 11.6: Creating a computed criterion

4. Press ⌘-E to perform the Extract command.

5. Activate cell A1 and click the window's zoom box so you can view the entire extract table that Excel has created.

Your worksheet should now look like Figure 11.7. As you can see, there are five salespeople who have recorded below-average annual sales. The extract table gives you their names, regions, and total sales.

In summary, the Extract command offers a simple and powerful technique for copying selected information from a larger database. You use a criteria range and a row of field names to define the exact information that Excel will extract for you. Although you can have only one database range and one criteria range on the worksheet at a time, you can build as many extract tables as you wish, each containing a different selection of information.

Next you'll learn to perform the Delete command.

Using the Delete Command

The Delete command permanently deletes selected records from your database. Excel uses your criteria range to determine which

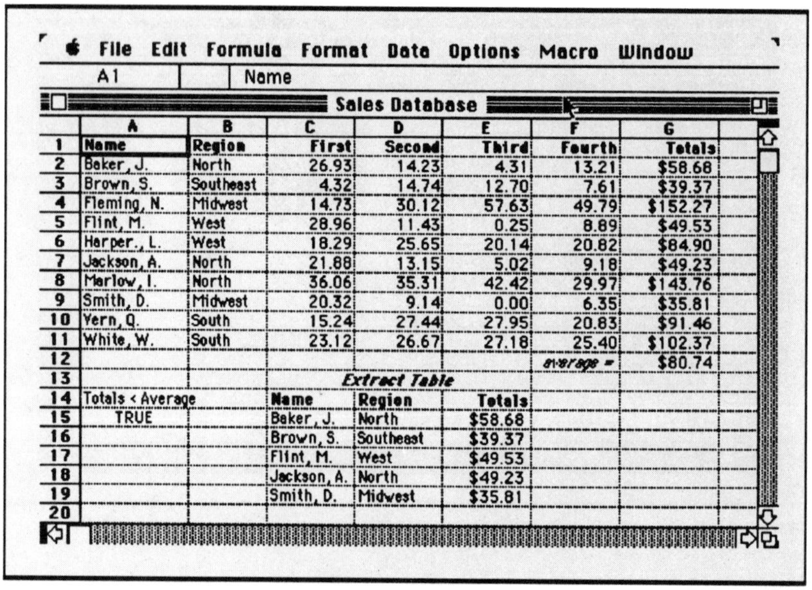

Figure 11.7: Extracting data with the computed criterion

records to delete. After deleting the records, Excel completes the operation by closing up any blank rows in the database.

There is no way to undo a delete operation. Once the records have been deleted, they are gone for good. For this reason, you should always take appropriate measures to save a backup copy of the current version of your database on disk before you perform the Delete command. In other words, you should keep two versions of the database on disk after a delete operation: the original database and the newly shortened database.

Delete is a powerful command, and can be quite useful if performed correctly. However, a small error in establishing criteria for the deletion can cause serious damage to your database, deleting many records that you intended to keep. For this reason you should use Delete carefully, especially if you are working with a long and valuable database.

Planning Ahead for a Delete Operation

In this exercise you'll create a new database document, containing only the salespeople who achieved below-average annual sales during the year. Your first task will be to perform the appropriate save operations—first to save the current version of the database to disk, and then to create a new file for the shortened database.

Here are the steps for beginning this exercise:

1. Press ⌘-S to save the current complete version of the sales database to disk.

2. Pull down the File menu and select the Save As command. Enter the following text as the name for the new version of the database you are about to create:

   Below Average Sales

   Click the OK button to complete the save operation. On the desktop, this becomes the new name of the database worksheet. (Keep in mind that the original Sales Database worksheet is safely stored on disk.)

3. Select the range of the extract table, C13:E19. You don't need this table any more in the current application, so press ⌘-B to erase it from the worksheet.

4. Enter the following new label into cell A14:

   Totals > = Average

   Notice the new comparison operator. You are going to delete all the records with average or better than average total annual sales, leaving behind the records that are below average.

5. Select cell A15, which contains the current criterion formula.

6. Use the mouse to click the formula bar just after the existing comparison operator, <. This click activates the formula bar, and places the flashing vertical cursor at the point that you clicked.

7. Press the Backspace key to erase the comparison operator, and enter the following operator in its place:

   >=

Press the Enter key to complete the formula edit. Figure 11.8 shows what your database worksheet should look like at this point.

This new criterion formula will delete salespeople who have average or better sales. You are now ready to perform the Delete command.

	File	**Edit**	**Formula**	**Format**	**Data**	**Options**	**Macro**	**Window**

A15		=G2>=$G$12	

Below Average Sales

	A	B	C	D	E	F	G
1	Name	Region	First	Second	Third	Fourth	Totals
2	Baker, J.	North	26.93	14.23	4.31	13.21	$58.68
3	Brown, S.	Southeast	4.32	14.74	12.70	7.61	$39.37
4	Fleming, N.	Midwest	14.73	30.12	57.63	49.79	$152.27
5	Flint, M.	West	28.96	11.43	0.25	8.89	$49.53
6	Harper., L.	West	18.29	25.65	20.14	20.82	$84.90
7	Jackson, A.	North	21.88	13.15	5.02	9.18	$49.23
8	Marlow, I.	North	36.06	35.31	42.42	29.97	$143.76
9	Smith, D.	Midwest	20.32	9.14	0.00	6.35	$35.81
10	Yern, Q.	South	15.24	27.44	27.95	20.83	$91.46
11	White, W.	South	23.12	26.67	27.18	25.40	$102.37
12						average =	$80.74
13							
14	Totals >= Average						
15	FALSE						
16							
17							
18							
19							
20							

Figure 11.8: Preparing to delete data

*C*ompleting the Delete Operation

You don't need to redefine the criteria range in this particular example, since you are using the same range as in the last exercise. However, keep in mind that an incorrectly established criteria range can be very dangerous in a Delete operation. For this reason, you might want to use the Define Name command to check the criteria range before you perform the Delete command.

Once you are certain that both the database range and the criteria range are defined correctly, here are the steps for the delete operation:

1. Pull down the data menu and select the Delete command. Excel displays a warning message on the screen, explaining that the step you are about to take is permanent. You can see this message in Figure 11.9.

2. Click OK if you are ready to complete the operation.

3. Press ⌘-S to save this new version of the database to disk. (You can perform this save operation safely at this moment, because you have saved the old database under its original name, and you have changed the name of the new database.)

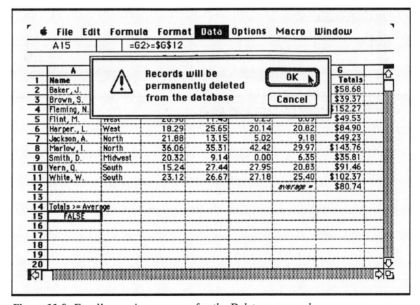

Figure 11.9: Excel's warning message for the Delete command

Figure 11.10 shows the new database. Only five records remain, and Excel has closed up the empty spaces from the deleted records. Also notice that the average formula has been recalculated; it now gives the average sales of the new shortened group of records.

This concludes your introduction to Excel's three database operations: Find, Extract, and Delete. In Chapter 12, you'll return to the original version of the sales database to explore Excel's special built-in database functions.

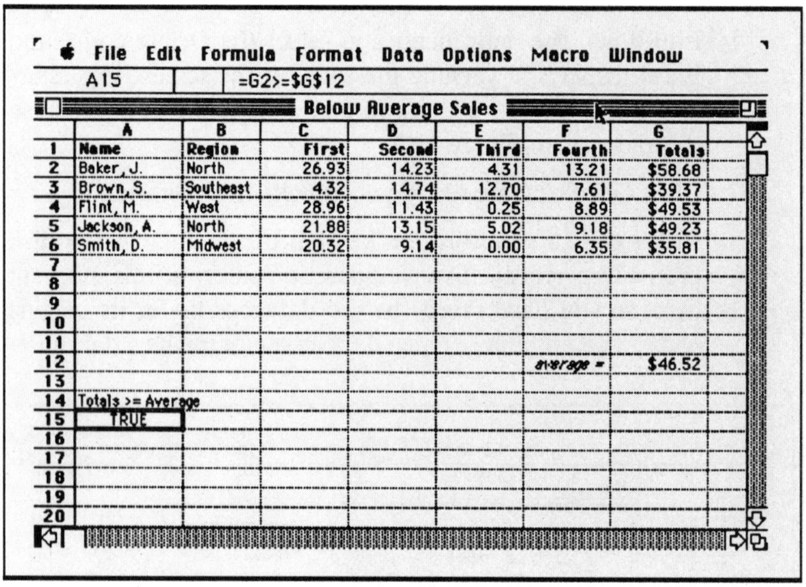

	A	B	C	D	E	F	G	
1	Name	Region	First	Second	Third	Fourth	Totals	
2	Baker, J.	North	26.93	14.23	4.31	13.21	$58.68	
3	Brown, S.	Southeast	4.32	14.74	12.70	7.61	$39.37	
4	Flint, M.	West	28.96	11.43	0.25	8.89	$49.53	
5	Jackson, A.	North	21.88	13.15	5.02	9.18	$49.23	
6	Smith, D.	Midwest	20.32	9.14	0.00	6.35	$35.81	
7								
8								
9								
10								
11								
12						average =	$46.52	
13								
14	Totals >= Average							
15	TRUE							
16								
17								
18								
19								
20								

A15 | =G2>=$G$12

Below Average Sales

Figure 11.10: The new database after the deletions

12

Using the Built-in Database Functions

Featuring:

*Using the database
statistical functions*

*Specifying exact
matches in
comparison criteria*

You have seen examples of Excel's built-in functions in several different contexts now. For instance, in Chapter 11 you used the following formula to compute the average of a column of numbers in the sales database:

= AVERAGE(G2:G11)

The AVERAGE function takes a range of numeric values as its argument and returns the average of the values. The result of this particular function is based on a calculation involving *all* of the numeric values in the range G2:G11.

In contrast, Excel's built-in *database functions* compute statistical values from *selected* values in a database field. Like the Data menu commands that you have been working with in the last two chapters, these functions are designed for use in a worksheet that contains both a database and a criteria range. The values that these database functions operate on are determined by the conditions you express in the criteria range.

The names of all the database functions begin with the letter D. For example, the DAVERAGE function returns the average of a selected group of numbers from a particular database field. In this chapter you'll learn how to use DAVERAGE, along with several other valuable functions available in Excel's collection of built-in database tools.

Understanding Database Functions

Excel has eleven database functions in all. Perhaps the most commonly used among these are the following five:

- DAVERAGE calculates the average of a selected group of record values in one database field.

- DCOUNT returns the number of numeric values in one field of a selected group of records.

- DMAX finds the largest field value in a selected group of records.

- DMIN finds the smallest field value in a selected group of records.

- DSUM computes the sum of the selected record values in a given field.

These are the five functions we'll concentrate on in this chapter. Along with these, Excel provides several other database functions: DSTDEV, DSTDEVP, DVAR, and DVARP compute various statistical values from selected numbers in a database (specifically, these functions calculate different versions of the standard deviation and the variance); DPRODUCT multiplies selected database values together; and DCOUNTA counts the number of non-blank cells in selected records of a database field.

The Arguments of the Database Functions

All of the database functions take the same types of arguments. For example, here is the general format of the DAVERAGE function:

= DAVERAGE(*Database, FieldName, Criteria***)**

The first argument represents the database range on the current worksheet; the second argument identifies a target field in the database; and the third argument is the criteria range on the worksheet. You can use the actual names Database and Criteria as the first and third arguments, respectively, assuming that you have performed the Set Database and Set Criteria commands on your database worksheet.

The second argument in the database functions can appear in either of two formats:

- A text value (enclosed in quotes), supplying the name of the database field that you want the function to work on.

- An integer, representing the position of the target field in the database—1 represents the first field; 2, the second; 3, the third; and so on.

For example, the following two formulas both supply the average of selected values in the Totals field of the sales database:

= DAVERAGE(Database,"Totals",Criteria)
= DAVERAGE(Database,7,Criteria)

In the next section you'll return once again to the sales database for some exercises with the database functions.

Setting Up a Statistical Table for the Database

Open the sales database onto the desktop, and use the Clear command (⌘-B) to erase any values currently stored in the area below the database. To prepare for the work ahead, begin by entering the following criterion into cells A14 and A15:

Region
North

This comparison criterion selects records of salespeople in the North sales region. Use the Set Criteria command to establish these two cells as the criteria range.

Now enter the following labels into cells B13 through B19:

Annual Regional Statistics:
Count:
Total:
Average:
Best:
Worst:

Use the Style command to display the labels in boldface type, and the Alignment command to right-justify the five short labels in their respective cells. Your worksheet should look like Figure 12.1.

You are now ready to build a table of statistical formulas that will supply information about any selected region in the database. Depending on the region displayed in the criteria range, this table will give you the following information:

- The number of salespeople in the region

- The total annual sales in the region

- The average annual sales of the salespeople in the region

- The best annual sales by any salesperson in the region

- The smallest annual sales by any salesperson in the region

In the next section you'll see how to create the formulas for computing these statistics.

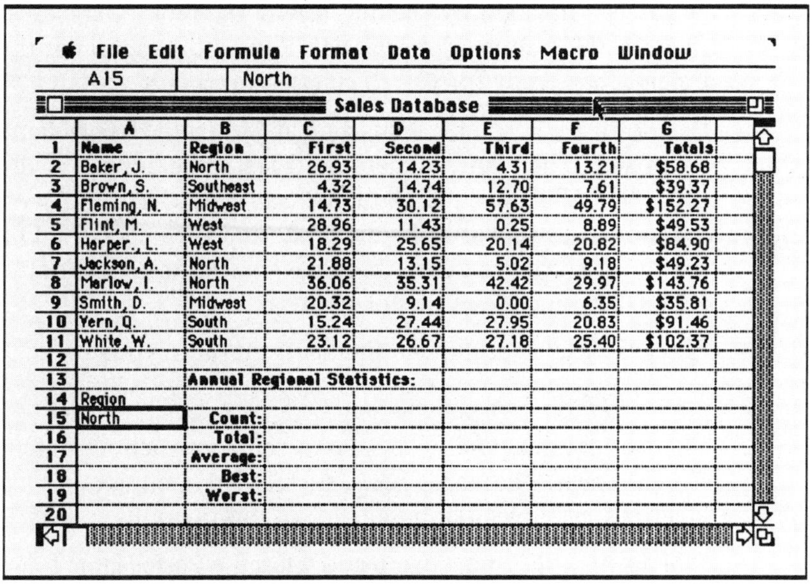

	A	B	C	D	E	F	G
1	Name	Region	First	Second	Third	Fourth	Totals
2	Baker, J.	North	26.93	14.23	4.31	13.21	$58.68
3	Brown, S.	Southeast	4.32	14.74	12.70	7.61	$39.37
4	Fleming, N.	Midwest	14.73	30.12	57.63	49.79	$152.27
5	Flint, M.	West	28.96	11.43	0.25	8.89	$49.53
6	Harper., L.	West	18.29	25.65	20.14	20.82	$84.90
7	Jackson, A.	North	21.88	13.15	5.02	9.18	$49.23
8	Marlow, I.	North	36.06	35.31	42.42	29.97	$143.76
9	Smith, D.	Midwest	20.32	9.14	0.00	6.35	$35.81
10	Yern, Q.	South	15.24	27.44	27.95	20.83	$91.46
11	White, W.	South	23.12	26.67	27.18	25.40	$102.37
12							
13		Annual Regional Statistics:					
14	Region						
15	North	Count:					
16		Total:					
17		Average:					
18		Best:					
19		Worst:					
20							

Figure 12.1: *Setting up a statistical table on the database worksheet*

Entering the Functions

As always, you can either enter the name of a built-in function directly from the keyboard, or you can select it from the dialog box of the Paste Function command (in the Formula menu). Paste Function lists the special database functions along with all the rest of Excel's built-in functions. Likewise, the Paste Name command (also in the Formula menu) contains a list of all the range names that are currently defined for the active worksheet. You can use this list to paste the Database and Criteria names into a database function.

You might argue that it is easier just to type the entire formula directly into the formula bar from the keyboard. Perhaps so, but just for practice, follow these steps to enter the DCOUNT function into cell C15:

1. Activate cell C15.
2. Pull down the Formula menu and select the Paste Function command. Press the **D** key to scroll the function list down to the first function beginning with the letter D. Highlight the

DCOUNT function by clicking it with the mouse, and then click the OK button. The DCOUNT function appears in the formula bar, ready for you to enter arguments.

3. Pull down the Formula menu again and select the Paste Name command. The names Criteria and Database appear in the name list. Highlight the Database name by clicking it with the mouse, as shown in Figure 12.2, and then click the OK button. The Database name becomes the first argument of the DCOUNT function in the formula bar.

4. Enter the second argument directly from the keyboard:

   ,"Totals",

   The two commas are necessary to separate each argument from the next. The word *Totals*, enclosed in quotation marks, identifies the target database field for this operation.

5. Pull down the Formula menu and select the Paste Name function. Click the Criteria name, and then click OK. The name appears as the final argument of the DCOUNT function.

6. Press the Enter key to complete the formula entry.

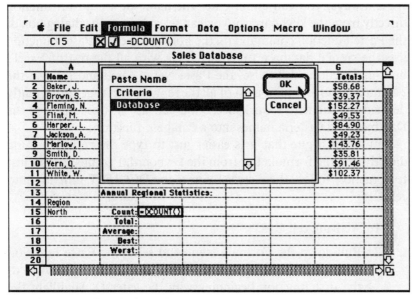

Figure 12.2: Building the formula using the Paste Name command

Your worksheet appears as shown in Figure 12.3. The formula you just entered has counted the number of salespeople who work in the North sales region; the result of the operation is 3. (Looking at the database itself, you can see that this is indeed the case. Of course, if this database were several hundred records long, you would be much more grateful for the result returned by the DCOUNT function.)

You still have four more database functions to enter into the worksheet, in cells C16, C17, C18, and C19. You can enter these formulas directly from the keyboard, or you can use the Paste Function and Paste Name commands as you did for the DCOUNT function. Here are the four formulas:

> = DSUM(Database,"Totals",Criteria)
> = DAVERAGE(Database,"Totals",Criteria)
> = DMAX(Database,"Totals",Criteria)
> = DMIN(Database,"Totals",Criteria)

When you have entered all four functions, use the Number command from the Formula menu to display the results in dollar-and-cent format. Your worksheet will then look like Figure 12.4.

File Edit Formula Format Data Options Macro Window

| C15 | | =DCOUNT(Database,"Totals",Criteria) | | | | | |

Sales Database

	A	B	C	D	E	F	G
1	Name	Region	First	Second	Third	Fourth	Totals
2	Baker, J.	North	26.93	14.23	4.31	13.21	$58.68
3	Brown, S.	Southeast	4.32	14.74	12.70	7.61	$39.37
4	Fleming, N.	Midwest	14.73	30.12	57.63	49.79	$152.27
5	Flint, M.	West	28.96	11.43	0.25	8.89	$49.53
6	Harper., L.	West	18.29	25.65	20.14	20.82	$84.90
7	Jackson, A.	North	21.88	13.15	5.02	9.18	$49.23
8	Marlow, I.	North	36.06	35.31	42.42	29.97	$143.76
9	Smith, D.	Midwest	20.32	9.14	0.00	6.35	$35.81
10	Yern, Q.	South	15.24	27.44	27.95	20.83	$91.46
11	White, W.	South	23.12	26.67	27.18	25.40	$102.37
12							
13		Annual Regional Statistics:					
14	Region						
15	North	Count:	3				
16		Total:					
17		Average:					
18		Best:					
19		Worst:					
20							

Figure 12.3: The completed DCOUNT formula

🍎 File   Edit   Formula   Format   Data   Options   Macro   Window

| C15 | =DCOUNT(Database,"Totals",Criteria) |

Sales Database

	A	B	C	D	E	F	G
1	Name	Region	First	Second	Third	Fourth	Totals
2	Baker, J.	North	26.93	14.23	4.31	13.21	$58.68
3	Brown, S.	Southeast	4.32	14.74	12.70	7.61	$39.37
4	Fleming, N.	Midwest	14.73	30.12	57.63	49.79	$152.27
5	Flint, M.	West	28.96	11.43	0.25	8.89	$49.53
6	Harper., L.	West	18.29	25.65	20.14	20.82	$84.90
7	Jackson, A.	North	21.88	13.15	5.02	9.18	$49.23
8	Marlow, I.	North	36.06	35.31	42.42	29.97	$143.76
9	Smith, D.	Midwest	20.32	9.14	0.00	6.35	$35.81
10	Yern, Q.	South	15.24	27.44	27.95	20.83	$91.46
11	White, W.	South	23.12	26.67	27.18	25.40	$102.37
12							
13		Annual Regional Statistics:					
14	Region						
15	North	Count:	3				
16		Total:	$251.67				
17		Average:	$83.89				
18		Best:	$143.76				
19		Worst:	$49.23				
20							

Figure 12.4: Entering the other database functions

Examine the results that these functions have supplied. You can see that the total annual sales for all the salespeople in the North sales region was $251,670. The average sales per salesperson was $83,890. And the best and worst performance levels were $143,760 and $49,230, respectively.

All of these are interesting statistical values that you can use to judge the activities of your salespeople in this region. To arrive at these values yourself, you would have had to look carefully through the database for the North region records, isolate the correct total sales figures, and then perform the calculations. While this might have been a straightforward—if time-consuming—exercise with our ten-record sample database, imagine the work involved if your database contained hundreds of records. Excel has done all this for you automatically, thanks to the built-in database functions.

But there's more. Now that you have set up this table of database statistics, you can use the same worksheet as a tool to analyze all of your sales regions. As you know, the results of the database functions depend on the criterion that you have written to select records from the database. If you change the value that controls the record selection—that is, the region name in cell A15—Excel instantly recalculates the entire statistics table for the new selected records. Let's see how this works.

Changing the Selection Criterion

Activate cell A15, and enter the following region name from the keyboard:

West

As soon as you press the Enter key to complete this data entry, Excel recalculates all the formulas that depend on this value—specifically, the five database formulas in the range C15:C19. You can see the results of the recalculation in Figure 12.5. The statistics table now describes the annual sales activities of the West sales region.

Now try entering the following region in cell A15:

South

Once again Excel instantly recalculates the entire statistics table; but this time the results are confusing. As you can see in Figure 12.6, the

```
 ⌘  File  Edit  Formula  Format  Data  Options  Macro  Window
    A15              |    West
```

	A	B	C	D	E	F	G
							Sales Database
	A	**B**	**C**	**D**	**E**	**F**	**G**
1	Name	Region	First	Second	Third	Fourth	Totals
2	Baker, J.	North	26.93	14.23	4.31	13.21	$58.68
3	Brown, S.	Southeast	4.32	14.74	12.70	7.61	$39.37
4	Fleming, N.	Midwest	14.73	30.12	57.63	49.79	$152.27
5	Flint, M.	West	28.96	11.43	0.25	8.89	$49.53
6	Harper., L.	West	18.29	25.65	20.14	20.82	$84.90
7	Jackson, A.	North	21.88	13.15	5.02	9.18	$49.23
8	Marlow, I.	North	36.06	35.31	42.42	29.97	$143.76
9	Smith, D.	Midwest	20.32	9.14	0.00	6.35	$35.81
10	Yern, Q.	South	15.24	27.44	27.95	20.83	$91.46
11	White, W.	South	23.12	26.67	27.18	25.40	$102.37
12							
13		Annual Regional Statistics:					
14	Region						
15	West	Count:	2				
16		Total:	$134.43				
17		Average:	$67.22				
18		Best:	$84.90				
19		Worst:	$49.53				
20							

Figure 12.5: Changing the selection value in the criteria range

table reports a total of three salespeople in the South region, with a annual total of $233,200 in sales. But as you scan the database, you can find only two salespeople in the South region, and their combined annual sales amount appears to be somewhat less than $200,000. What has gone wrong?

The answer to this problem lies in the way Excel matches text values from a criterion expression. When you enter the word *South* as the selection value in the criteria range, Excel actually searches through the database for all values in the Region field that *begin* with the letters *S o u t h*. The two South records are selected, as you would expect. But another field value in the database also begins with these letters: the second record contains the Region entry *Southeast*. Excel reads this value as a match with *South* and duly selects the record.

If you really want to calculate statistics from the South region alone, you have to use a slightly unusual technique for entering the criterion text.

Specifying an Exact-Match Criterion

To indicate to Excel that you want to select *only* the records that have the word *South* their region field values, you have to enter the

	A	B	C	D	E	F	G
	Name	Region	First	Second	Third	Fourth	Totals
2	Baker, J.	North	26.93	14.23	4.31	13.21	$58.68
3	Brown, S.	Southeast	4.32	14.74	12.70	7.61	$39.37
4	Fleming, N.	Midwest	14.73	30.12	57.63	49.79	$152.27
5	Flint, M.	West	28.96	11.43	0.25	8.89	$49.53
6	Harper., L.	West	18.29	25.65	20.14	20.82	$84.90
7	Jackson, A.	North	21.88	13.15	5.02	9.18	$49.23
8	Marlow, I.	North	36.06	35.31	42.42	29.97	$143.76
9	Smith, D.	Midwest	20.32	9.14	0.00	6.35	$35.81
10	Vern, Q.	South	15.24	27.44	27.95	20.83	$91.46
11	White, W.	South	23.12	26.67	27.18	25.40	$102.37
12							
13		Annual Regional Statistics:					
14	Region						
15	South		Count:	3			
16			Total:	$233.20			
17			Average:	$77.73			
18			Best:	$102.37			
19			Worst:	$39.37			
20							

Figure 12.6: Confusing results from an analysis of the South sales region

following formula into cell A15:

= " = South"

As a result of this formula, the following entry appears in the cell itself:

= South

In response, Excel selects only the South records, not Southeast. You can see the result of this selection in Figure 12.7. The statistics table now correctly describes the sales records of the two salespeople who work in the South region.

Of course, sometimes Excel's default matching rules can be a great advantage. For example, let's say you want to select all the people whose names begin with B in a particular database. To do so you simply write a criteria range such as the following:

Name
B

	A	B	C	D	E	F	G
1	Name	Region	First	Second	Third	Fourth	Totals
2	Baker, J.	North	26.93	14.23	4.31	13.21	$58.68
3	Brown, S.	Southeast	4.32	14.74	12.70	7.61	$39.37
4	Fleming, N.	Midwest	14.73	30.12	57.63	49.79	$152.27
5	Flint, M.	West	28.96	11.43	0.25	8.89	$49.53
6	Harper., L.	West	18.29	25.65	20.14	20.82	$84.90
7	Jackson, A.	North	21.88	13.15	5.02	9.18	$49.23
8	Marlow, I.	North	36.06	35.31	42.42	29.97	$143.76
9	Smith, D.	Midwest	20.32	9.14	0.00	6.35	$35.81
10	Yern, Q.	South	15.24	27.44	27.95	20.83	$91.46
11	White, W.	South	23.12	26.67	27.18	25.40	$102.37
12							
13		Annual Regional Statistics:					
14	Region						
15	=South	Count:	2				
16		Total:	$193.83				
17		Average:	$96.92				
18		Best:	$102.37				
19		Worst:	$91.46				
20							

Figure 12.7: An exact match for the South sales region

However, to select all records that contain the single letter *B*—let's say in a hypothetical field named Code—you would have to write the criterion

Code
= B

by entering the formula = " = B".

The main point is clear: In any comparison criterion that deals with matching text values, you have to be certain that you understand the rules by which Excel selects records.

This concludes our discussion of Excel's database component. You now have some powerful tools at your disposal for working with databases on Excel worksheets: the three Data menu commands, Find, Extract, and Delete; and the built-in database functions, such as DCOUNT, DSUM, DAVERAGE, DMAX, and DMIN. The behavior of all these tools depends on the database that you enter into your worksheet, and on the criteria range that you create to select records from the database. Together these tools give you the ability to analyze and understand record-oriented sets of information.

PART V

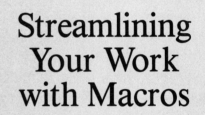

Streamlining
Your Work
with Macros

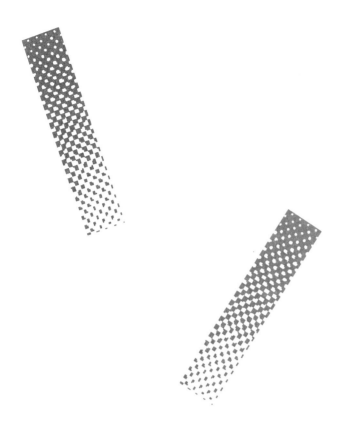

13

Recording
Macros
in Excel

Featuring:

Using the Macro
Recorder

Creating, testing, and
performing a macro

Managing macro
sheets

Using the Run
command

In the first four parts of this book you've learned to use Excel's three primary application components: worksheets, charts, and databases. Along the way, you've become adept at using the mouse and the keyboard to control the various elements of Excel's desktop environment: menus, commands, and windows.

The final chapter of this book introduces you to another Excel facility that can save you a great deal of time and effort in almost all your desktop activities: the *Macro Recorder*. A *macro* is a tool that you develop to automate the performance of a specific activity in Excel. In fact, a macro is a type of *program*—a planned sequence of steps designed to accomplish a defined task on the desktop. The Recorder is an extremely simple feature that, in effect, builds macros for you, even as you do your actual work on the desktop. These macros are then available to you as permanent tools, designed to streamline your day-to-day work in Excel.

Excel has a built-in *macro language*—a complete programming language consisting of a large set of both general and specialized functions. These functions can automate many tasks in Excel, including the performance of almost all of the menu commands that you have learned about up to now.

Excel's sophisticated macro language supports several levels of use:

- Programmers can use the macro language to develop powerful macro applications that take complete control over Excel's user environment, modifying even the elements of the desktop itself. Such an application might be designed specifically to guide users who have little or no understanding of Excel but who nonetheless need to perform complex tasks inside the Excel environment.

- On a smaller scale, programmers can create macros to help perform certain steps in specific applications. Such programs can control many kinds of activities, including input from the keyboard, window operations on the screen, output to the printer, and so on. In addition, an Excel macro can be designed to make complex decisions and to perform specified tasks repeatedly in *loops*.

- At the most practical level, Excel users who may have no programming exerience at all can build large collections of custom macro tools. The purpose of these tools is to automate the performance of Excel's menu commands and other activities usually performed via the keyboard and the mouse. While these tools are simple to create, they can be extremely useful in helping you to accomplish your daily work in Excel.

Macros reside in the third type of document window available on the Excel desktop: *macro sheets.* As shown in Figure 13.1, the last option in the New command's dialog box opens an empty macro sheet onto the desktop. A macro sheet is similar in many ways to a worksheet, but also has some special characteristics of its own. A given macro sheet can store a single macro or an entire library of macros. You can assign a unique name to each macro stored in the macro sheet. In addition, you supply a name for the sheet itself when you first save the document to disk.

There are two ways to open a macro sheet and develop a program:

- You can perform the New command from the File menu, and begin entering functions and formulas directly into the macro sheet from the keyboard.

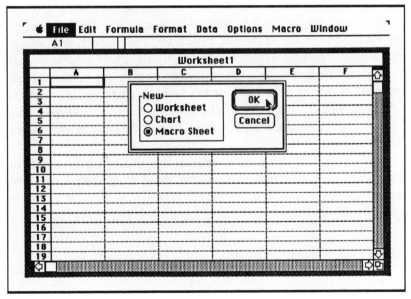

Figure 13.1: The New command's dialog box set to open a macro sheet

- You can take advantage of Excel's powerful Macro Recorder. The Recorder automatically enters the individual functions of a macro onto a macro sheet; these functions represent a sequence of activities that you have performed on the desktop during a recording session.

The Macro Recorder is the real subject of this chapter. In this chapter's exercises you'll use the Recorder to develop your own collection of macro tools. The macros you'll create perform the following familiar tasks:

- Displaying text values in specified type styles and alignments.

- Formatting numeric values.

- Entering commonly used blocks of text onto a worksheet.

You already know how to use menu commands to perform all of these tasks. Now you'll learn to automate these tasks as one-step macro tools.

This chapter will not, however, teach you very much about the macro language itself or the process of developing complex macro application programs. If you are interested in programming and you want to delve further into the macro language, you should begin by studying the book called *Arrays, Functions, and Macros*, available as part of the documentation you receive with the Excel program.

However, if you simply want to develop a collection of macro tools that will streamline your work on the desktop, this chapter will show you how. For the majority of Excel users, the most indispensable macros are the simplest ones—those created directly by the Macro Recorder.

You'll begin your work in this chapter by creating a convenient but temporary worksheet in which you can develop and test a group of macros.

Preparing a Worksheet for Developing Macros

To create macros and test their results, you may often need to prepare a temporary worksheet that simulates the kind of application in which you'll ultimately be using the macros. Figure 13.2 shows the

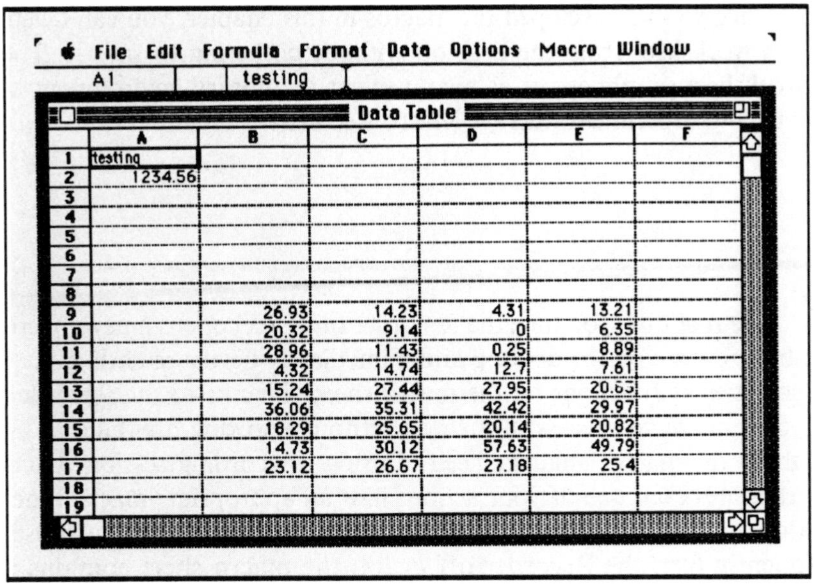

***Figure 13.2:** Preparing a worksheet for developing macros*

worksheet you'll use for this purpose in the upcoming exercises. As you can see, this worksheet contains the table of numeric values that you first created in Chapter 3. There is also room for some other information that you'll enter as you proceed in this chapter.

To prepare this worksheet, follow these steps:

1. Pull down the File menu and select the Open command. Open the Data Table worksheet from disk.

2. Use the mouse to highlight the top eight rows of the worksheet. Press ⌘-I to insert eight blank rows above the data table.

3. Select the first column of the worksheet, and press ⌘-I to insert a blank column at the left side of the data table.

4. Enter the following text value and numeric value into cells A1 and A2 of the worksheet:

   testing
   1234.56

5. Select cell A1 to prepare for the first exercise.

Once you've developed the macros in this chapter, you can delete this worksheet from the desktop without bothering to save it. The worksheet simply serves as a convenient temporary environment in which to experiment with the Macro Recorder.

Using the Recorder

The first time you turn the Recorder on, Excel opens a new macro sheet for you on the desktop and immediately begins recording your activities as functions on the macro sheet. Thanks to the Recorder, you can create successful macros without knowing anything at all about the macro language itself. During a recording session, Excel translates each one of your actions into an appropriate macro function and stores the function as part of a macro. When you subsequently turn the Recorder off again, the macro sheet contains a completed macro—a tool that you can use as often as you want to repeat the recorded activities.

To turn the Recorder on and off, and to control the characteristics of a given recording session, you use the various commands listed in the Macro menu, shown in Figure 13.3. You'll be learning to use these commands during the course of this chapter. Here is a brief preview of what they do:

- The Run command supplies you with a list of all macros currently available on the desktop, and gives you one technique for performing a macro.

- The Record command guides you through all the necessary steps to start a macro: opening a macro sheet, entering a name for the macro, and selecting a special keyboard combination that you'll later use to perform the macro. Finally, the Record command initiates the recording session.

- The Set Recorder command gives you the opportunity to specify the macro sheet location where your macro should be recorded. (This command is an alternative to the automatic process performed by the Record command.)

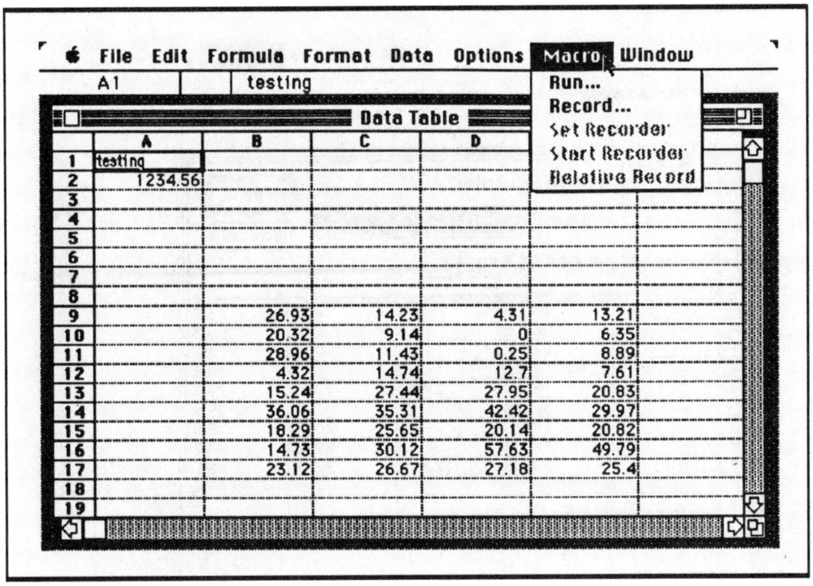

Figure 13.3: The Macro menu

- The Start Recorder command initiates a recording session. During a session, this command changes to Stop Recorder so that you can terminate the session whenever you want to.

- The Relative Record and Absolute Record commands determine how Excel generates references for your macro. (Only one of these commands appears in the Macro menu at a time.)

Performing the Record command is the easiest way to begin recording a macro.

*T*he Record Command

At this point you have not yet opened a macro sheet onto the desktop. The Record command opens a sheet for you and prepares you to begin recording a macro.

Pull down the Macro menu and select Record. The resulting dialog box is shown in Figure 13.4. As you can see, Excel requests two items of information from you: a name and an Option-⌘ key. You should supply a name that succinctly identifies the purpose of the macro you are about to create. When you subsequently get ready to perform your

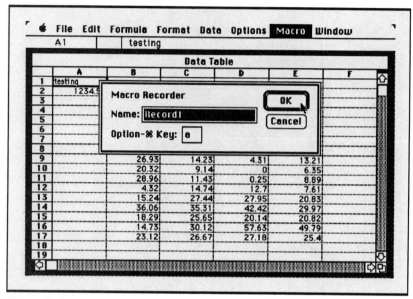

Figure 13.4: The Record command's dialog box

macro, the Option-⌘ key provides a short-cut keyboard sequence for initiating the performance. Let's discuss the purposes of these two items in more detail.

Entering a Name for the Macro

Excel has several uses for the name you supply for a macro. First of all, Excel enters the name directly onto the macro sheet, in the first cell of the macro itself. (You'll see how this looks a little later.) In addition, the name becomes the defined name on the macro sheet, as though you had performed the Define Name command (from the Formula menu) to define a name for the first cell of the macro. Finally, Excel lists each macro's name in the Run command's dialog box.

You can supply any name you like for your macro. (The legal characters for a name include letters, digits, periods, and underline characters. You may not include spaces in a name.) Of course, you should try to devise a name that indicates the purpose of the macro. As you can see in Figure 13.4, Excel's suggested name is simply Record1; this name disappears as soon as you begin typing another one.

The macro you'll create in this program's first exercise will perform some simple formatting operations on one or more text entries in a worksheet. Proceed as follows to enter a name for this macro, and to prepare for the next step in the process:

1. Enter the following name from the keyboard:

   TextFormatter

   As you type, the name appears inside the Name box. Do not press the Return key or click the OK button yet.

2. Position the mouse pointer inside the Option-⌘ Key box, and double-click the mouse to highlight the box.

You are now ready to provide an Option-⌘ key for your macro.

Entering an Option-⌘ Key for the Macro

The Option-⌘ key is a keyboard combination that you supply as a quick technique for performing your macro, similar to the ⌘ key combinations available for performing some menu commands. You can enter an uppercase or lowercase letter into the Option-⌘ Key box; when you subsequently press the Option key, the ⌘ key, and your selected key simultaneously, Excel will perform your macro. To make this key combination as easy to remember as possible, you should try to select a letter that you can readily associate with the purpose of the macro itself.

Excel distinguishes between uppercase and lowercase for the Option-⌘ key combinations. For example, let's say you enter the uppercase letter T into the box. When you subsequently want to perform your macro, you'll actually press the following four-key combination:

   Shift-Option-⌘-T

On the other hand, if you select the lowercase letter *t* as the key, you'll press the following three-key combination to perform the macro:

   Option-⌘-t

Four lowercase letters are not available as macro keys; they are e, u, i, and n. If you were to try to enter one of these keys into the Option-⌘

Key box, Excel would display an error message on the screen, as shown in Figure 13.5.

Excel's default suggestion for the first macro key is the lowercase letter *a*. You have already double-clicked the input box to highlight its contents; your next step is to enter an appropriate letter to represent the macro. Perform the following two steps to complete the Record command operation:

1. Enter the uppercase letter **T** into the box, as shown in Figure 13.6.

2. Click the OK button, or press the Return key.

Once you have completed the entries for the Record command, Excel is ready to begin recording your subsequent desktop activities. For this reason, you should be careful and deliberate about your next steps. With a few exceptions, Excel has no way of distinguishing between intentional and unintentional actions performed during a recording session; just about everything you do is recorded.

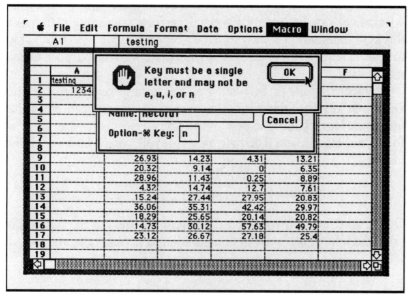

Figure 13.5: *Entering an invalid letter in the Option-⌘ Key box*

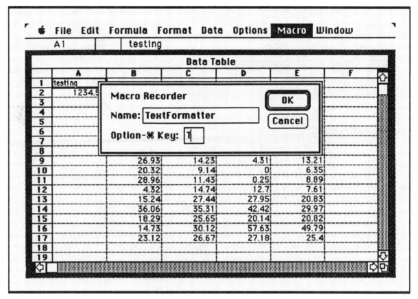

Figure 13.6: *Completing the input for the Record command*

*R*ecording Your First Macro

As a result of the Record command, Excel has now opened a new macro sheet onto the desktop and turned the Recorder on. The macro sheet is called Macro1. (Later you'll save this sheet to disk and supply a name of your own.)

You may not be able to see the macro sheet at the moment, since the Data Table worksheet is currently the active document. But the Window menu lists the macro sheet as one of the documents on the desktop, as shown in Figure 13.7. (The simple action of pulling down a menu is not recorded in your macro unless you actually select a command. You can thus safely pull down the Window menu to check the contents of the desktop.)

In the TextFormatter macro, you'll record two commands from the Format menu that change the display of a selected text entry:

- The Style command, for displaying the entry in boldface italics

- The Alignment command, for right-justifying the entry inside its cell

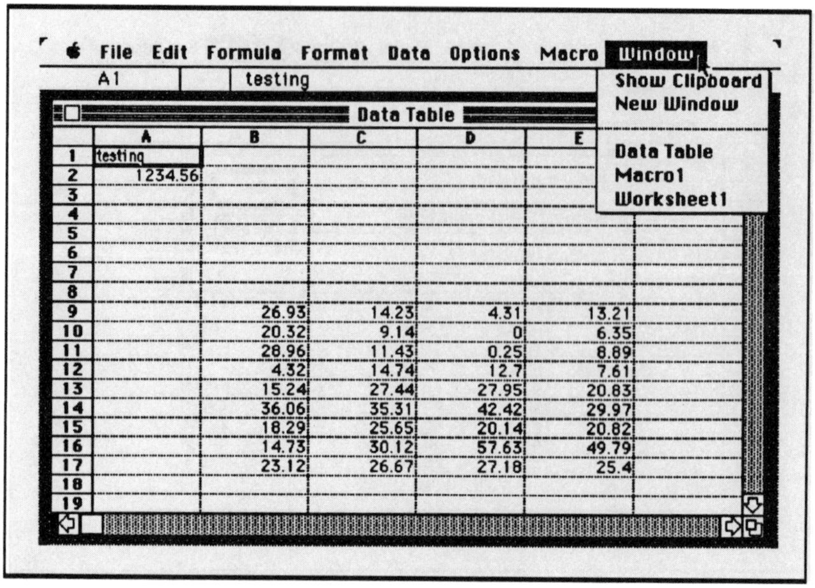

Figure 13.7: *Checking the Window menu*

The active cell on the Data Table worksheet is A1, and the Recorder is on. To record these two operations in the macro, all you have to do is perform them on the active cell. Proceed as follows:

1. Pull down the Format menu and select the Style command.

2. Click both the Bold and Italic options.

3. Click OK to complete the style operation. The word *testing* in cell A1 is redisplayed in boldface italics.

4. Pull down the Format menu and select the Alignment command.

5. Click the Right option.

6. Click OK to complete the operation. Excel right-justifies the word *testing* in its cell.

This completes your activities for this particular recording session. You are now ready to turn the Recorder off again.

The Stop and Start Recorder Commands

Pull down the Macro menu; the menu list appears as shown in Figure 13.8. Notice that the Start Recorder command has changed to Stop Recorder. Select this command now to terminate the recording session.

Interestingly enough, Excel allows you to perform start and stop operations any number of times while you are developing a macro. This feature is particularly useful when you need to perform some intermediate action on the worksheet, but you do not want the action to be recorded in the macro.

For example, you might realize in the middle of a recording session that you want to test the result of a particular command before you actually record it. To do so, simply select the Stop Recorder command. Then you can perform any menu commands you wish without recording them. When you are ready to resume the recording session, pull down the Macro menu and select Start Recorder again.

For now, you have completed the TextFormatter macro. You'll probably be curious to see what the macro looks like.

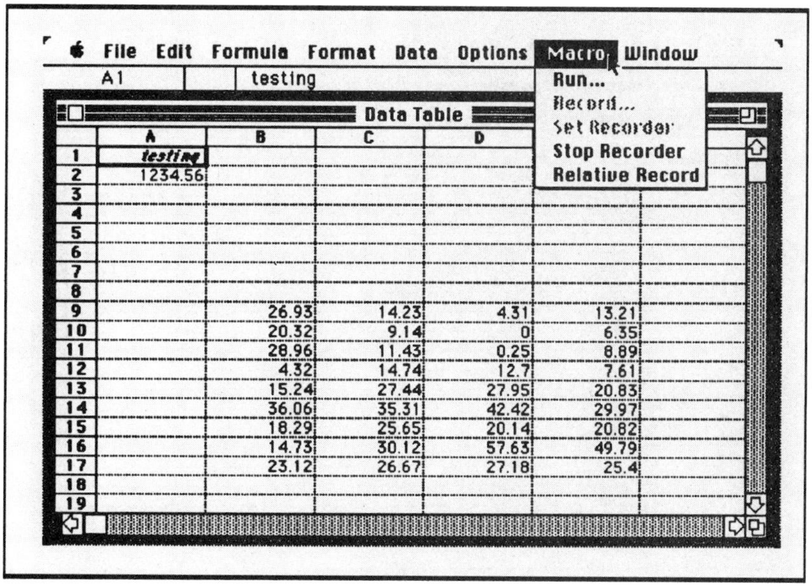

Figure 13.8: *Turning the Recorder off*

Examining the Macro Sheet

Pull down the Window command and activate the document named Macro1. Figure 13.9 shows what the macro sheet looks like at this point in your work. Since this is your first look at a macro sheet, you should take a moment now to note both the similarities and the differences between macro sheets and worksheets.

On the one hand, the macro sheet is organized as a grid of numbered rows and lettered columns, just as a worksheet is. Around the perimeter of the macro sheet you can see the same tools for scrolling, moving, and splitting the window that you have used on worksheets.

On the other hand, you'll notice that the macro sheet shows the formula that is stored in each cell, rather than displaying the values produced by the formulas. This is just the opposite of a worksheet, which normally displays the results of formulas rather than the formulas themselves. To allow more room for displaying formulas, the columns on the macro sheet are twice as wide as the columns on a worksheet.

As you can see, Excel has entered the macro down column A. The first cell of the column, A1, displays the name that you assigned to the

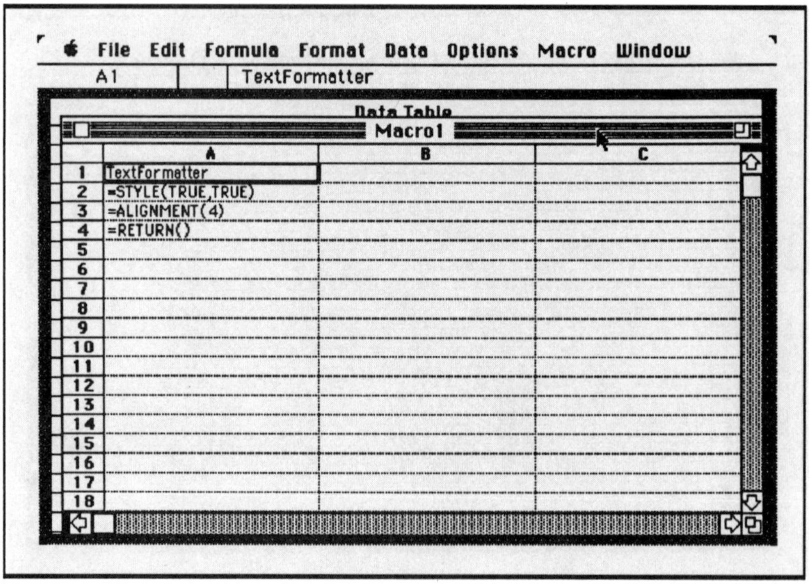

Figure 13.9: *Viewing the macro sheet*

macro. After the name, this macro contains three formulas. Let's look briefly at these formulas to see exactly how Excel has translated your desktop actions into macro functions. Keep in mind that your goal in this chapter is not to master the details of the macro language, but rather to learn how to use the Recorder. Nonetheless, you may be interested to discover how easy it is to figure out the purpose of many macro functions.

For example, you will have no problem guessing the meanings of the first two functions in the TextFormatter macro. The STYLE function performs the same operations as the Style command in the Format menu:

= STYLE(TRUE,TRUE)

The two arguments enclosed in parentheses in this function correspond to the Bold and Italic options on the Style dialog box. The values of TRUE indicate that you have activated both of these options.

The ALIGNMENT function performs the same operation as the Alignment command in the Format menu:

= ALIGNMENT(4)

The numeric argument of this function selects one of the five options in this command. The argument of 4 in this example means that you have selected Right, the fourth option in the list.

These two functions, STYLE and ALIGNMENT, are your first examples of a special group of macro functions called *command-equivalent functions*. The macro language includes command-equivalent functions corresponding to most of the menu commands that you have worked with up to now on the Excel desktop.

The final function in the TextFormatter macro is RETURN:

= RETURN( )

This function simply marks the end of the macro. During a performance of the macro, Excel moves cell by cell down the column, performing each function in turn. When the RETURN function is performed, the macro is complete and you are returned to your starting position on the desktop.

Your next step is to test the macro that you have just created. To do so, you can use the data stored on your temporary Data Table worksheet. Pull down the Window menu to select the worksheet.

Testing the Macro

Let's imagine that this temporary worksheet represents quarterly income figures (in thousands of dollars) from nine different store locations of a given retail operation. To develop this application, begin by entering the following four labels into the range B8:D8 on the worksheet:

Quarter 1   Quarter 2   Quarter 3   Quarter 4

Then enter the following row labels into the range A9:A17 of the worksheet:

Store 1
Store 2
Store 3
Store 4
Store 5
Store 6
Store 7
Store 8
Store 9

As you've seen in previous worksheet applications, column headings are easier to read if you display them in distinct type styles and right-justify them in their cells. (The right justification aligns the text headings with the numeric values below them.) It is for this purpose that you have just developed the TextFormatter macro.

While you were developing the macro you formatted the text value stored in only a single cell; nonetheless, you can now use the macro to format a whole range of cells. For example, perform the following steps to test the macro:

1. Select the range of cells that contain the column labels, B8:D8.

2. Hold down the ⌘ key while you select a second range of labels, A9:A17.

3. Press the following sequence of keys from the keyboard:

Shift-Option-⌘-T

This keyboard sequence performs the TextFormatter macro, which in turn changes the type style of the labels and right-justifies them in their cells. The result of the operation is shown in Figure 13.10.

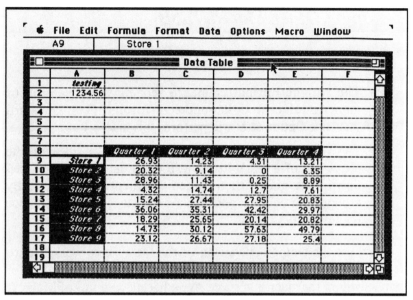

Figure 13.10: *Testing the TextFormatter macro*

In summary, here are the typical steps for creating a macro:

1. Prepare a convenient worksheet in which to develop and test the macro.

2. Use the Record command from the Macro menu to specify a name and an Option-⌘ key sequence for the macro, and to turn the Recorder on.

3. Perform the desktop activities that you want Excel to record in the macro.

4. Perform the Stop Recorder command to turn the Recorder off.

5. Perform the macro in a typical worksheet situation to make sure that the program does what you want it to do.

In the upcoming exercises you'll repeat these general steps to develop two additional macros that will prove useful to you in your work with Excel.

*D*eveloping Other Macro Tools

Here are names and descriptions of the two macros you'll create:

- The NumberFormatter macro redisplays a selection of numeric values in dollar-and-cent format. (The keyboard sequence Option-⌘-N will perform this macro.)

- The WorksheetTitle macro enters a particular title into the active cell of a worksheet and today's date in the next cell down. The macro then centers both entries horizontally around their column, and displays the entries in boldface type (Option-⌘-W).

You'll use the temporary version of the Data Table worksheet to develop and test each of these macros in turn. The Recorder will automatically store the macros in successive adjacent columns of Macro1, the macro sheet that is currently on the desktop.

*C*reating a Number Formatter

Like many macros you may ultimately want to create for your own use, the NumberFormatter macro efficiently performs one multistep menu command—in this case, the Number command from the Format menu.

Here are the steps for creating this macro:

1. Select cell A2 on the Data Table worksheet. This cell contains the numeric value 1234.56.

2. Pull down the Macro menu and select the Record command.

3. On the resulting dialog box enter **NumberFormatter** as the title of the macro and the uppercase letter **N** as the Option-⌘ key.

4. Click OK to turn the Recorder on.

5. Pull down the Format menu and select the Number command.

6. On the resulting dialog box, select the following dollar-and-cent format:

   $#,##0.00;($#,##0.00)

7. Click OK to complete the Number operation. The number in cell A2 appears as follows:

   $1,234.56

8. Pull down the Macro menu and select the Stop Recorder command.

9. Pull down the Window menu and activate the document named Macro1.

10. On the macro sheet, drag the border of column B to the right, increasing the width enough to view the entire text of the macro.

At this point your macro sheet should look like Figure 13.11. The new macro consists of two functions: FORMAT.NUMBER is the function that corresponds to the Number command in the Format menu. The function's argument is a text value representing the format you selected from the dialog box. The second function in the NumberFormatter macro is RETURN.

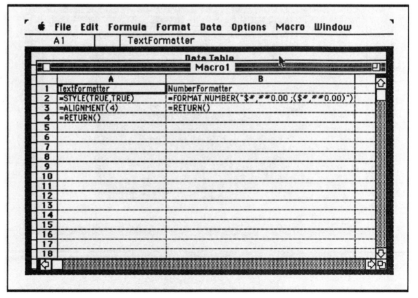

Figure 13.11: *Viewing the NumberFormatter macro*

Testing the Macro

To test the NumberFormatter macro, perform these steps:

1. Pull down the Window menu and activate the Data Table worksheet.

2. Select the numeric values in the range B9:E17 in the worksheet.

3. Press the keyboard sequence **Shift-Option-⌘-N** to perform the macro.

As you can see in Figure 13.12, the macro formats all of the numbers in the range.

Creating a Title Macro

Data entry is another common task that you can sometimes efficiently relegate to a macro. In particular, you might create any number of macros that enter specific text values into worksheet ranges. If

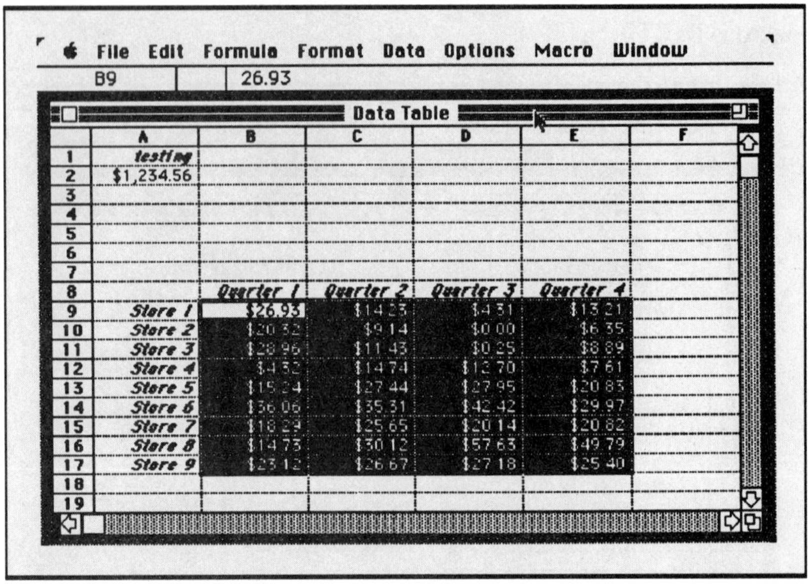

Figure 13.12: Testing the NumberFormatter macro

you find yourself frequently entering the same standard title or labels as text values in worksheet applications—and then formatting the text in a typical way—you should consider automating the data-entry process with a macro.

Here are some examples of text entries that you might want to record in a macro:

- Your name, address, and phone number

- The name of your company and your office address

- Column labels or row labels for a particular data table that you create regularly

- The title of a worksheet application that you routinely develop on a daily, weekly, or monthly basis

For example, the purpose of the WorksheetTitle macro is to enter a particular title line along with the current date at a specified location in a worksheet:

Income from Nine Stores (in Thousands of Dollars)
7–Dec–88

The title will appear in the cell that is active when you perform the macro, and the date will appear in the cell just below. The macro centers both entries horizontally in their cells and displays them in boldface type.

The WorksheetTitle macro activates cells and selects cell ranges during its performance. As you create this macro, you'll therefore have to consider the two different ways that Excel can record cell references in a macro. The two possible recording modes are represented by the Relative Record and Absolute Record commands in the Macro menu. Let's discuss these two commands.

Choosing Relative Record or Absolute Record

The last command displayed in the Macro menu is a *toggle*; this means that the command switches between two available options each time you select it. The command is always displayed either as Relative Record or Absolute Record. You can use this command either before you begin recording a macro or during an actual recording session.

The purpose of the command is to change the way Excel subsequently records references in the macro. When the default mode, Absolute Record, is in effect, Excel records cell selections as fixed worksheet addresses. You'll use this recording mode whenever you want a macro performance to select a particular cell address as the target of a subsequent operation. In contrast, when the Relative Record mode is in effect, Excel records cell selections as relative moves from the current active cell. In this case, the target of a subsequent macro performance depends on the cell that is active when the performance begins. You'll see an example of the Relative Record mode in the upcoming exercise.

Using this command can be a little confusing. The command title that you see displayed in the Macro menu indicates that the opposite mode is currently in effect:

- When the Absolute Record command is displayed in the Macro menu, Excel is prepared to record relative references in the macro. You must select the Absolute Record command to record subsequent cell selections as absolute references.

- When the Relative Record command is displayed in the Macro menu, Excel is prepared to record absolute references in the macro. (This is the default toggle status of this command.) You must select the Relative Record command to record subsequent cell selections as relative references.

You may be surprised to discover that Excel records references in macros in a different format than the one you are used to seeing. This new format uses the notations R and C to indicate the row and column locations of a particular cell. For example, R9C2 is an absolute reference to the cell at the intersection of row 9 and column 2; in other words, this reference is equivalent to $B$9.

A relative reference in a macro defines a move to a new cell, relative to the current active cell on the worksheet. Relative references appear in the RC format, but the moves are expressed as negative or positive integers enclosed in square brackets. Consider the following examples:

- R[2]C[3] identifies the worksheet location that is two cells down and three cells to the right from the current active cell.

- R[-1]C[-2] identifies the worksheet location that is one cell up and two cells to the left from the current active cell.

- R[1]C identifies the worksheet location that is one cell down from the current active cell, in the same column.

Fortunately, you do not have to create these references yourself. The Recorder automatically enters references appropriately in a macro, as long as you have chosen correctly between the Absolute Record and Relative Record commands in the Macro menu. As you develop more macros of your own, you will quickly learn to recognize the differences between absolute and relative references in a macro.

You'll see some examples in the WorksheetTitle macro.

Developing the Macro

To create the WorksheetTitle macro, perform the following steps:

1. Activate cell C4 on the Data Table worksheet.

2. Pull down the Macro menu and select the Record command.

3. In the resulting dialog box enter **WorksheetTitle** as the name of the macro and **W** as the option-⌘ key for performing the macro.

4. Click the OK button to start the recorder.

5. Pull down the Macro menu and select the Relative Record command. Excel will subsequently record cell addresses as relative references in your macro.

6. Enter the following text into the active cell on the worksheet:

   Income from Nine Stores (in Thousands of Dollars)

7. Press the Return key to activate C5, the next cell down the column.

8. Enter the following formula to store the current date in the active cell:

   = NOW( )

(You first learned about the NOW function in Chapter 5.) Press the Enter key to enter the formula into the cell without changing the cell selection.

9. Pull down the Format menu and select the Number command.

10. In the Number dialog box, select the following date format from the list of formats:

    d-mmm-yy

11. Click OK to complete the operation.

12. Back on the worksheet, use the mouse to select the range C4:C5.

13. Pull down the Format menu and select the Alignment command.

14. Select the Center option, and click the OK button to complete the operation.

15. Pull down the Format menu again, and select the Style command.

16. Click the Bold option to display the selection in boldface type, then click OK to complete the operation.

17. Pull down the Macro menu and select the Stop Recorder command. The worksheet appears as shown in Figure 13.13.

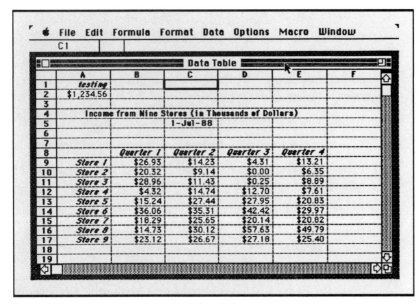

Figure 13.13: The results of the WorksheetTitle macro

18. Pull down the Window menu and activate the Macro1 document.

19. Scroll to column C, and drag the border of the column to the right, increasing the column width enough to display the entire text of the macro.

The macro sheet appears in Figure 13.14. You might want to take a moment to look at the functions that Excel has recorded in your macro. For starters, you'll find the three command-equivalent functions that you are already familiar with: FORMAT.NUMBER, ALIGNMENT, and STYLE.

In addition you can see examples of another variety of function, called *action-equivalent functions*. These functions correspond to desktop operations that you normally accomplish with the keyboard or the mouse. For example, the SELECT function selects a cell or range of cells on the worksheet. The FORMULA function enters a value or a formula into the active cell. You'll see two examples of each of these action-equivalent functions in the WorksheetTitle macro.

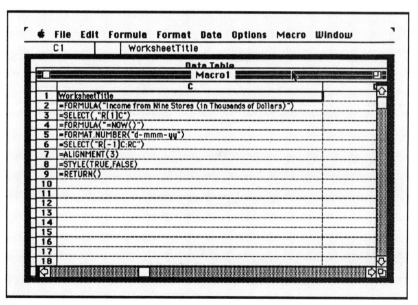

Figure 13.14: Viewing the WorksheetTitle macro

Finally, notice how Excel has recorded references in the SELECT function. You'll see that these references are in the RC format. Following your instructions, Excel has expressed the cell selections as relative references, as in this example:

= SELECT(,"R[1]C")

In the next brief exercise, you'll test the performance of this macro.

Testing the Macro

If you have another worksheet on your desktop (for example, Worksheet1), activate it now. If not, pull down the File menu and use the New command to open a new worksheet onto the desktop. Perform the following steps to test the WorksheetTitle macro:

1. Select cell D8 on the new worksheet.

2. Press **Shift-Option-⌘-W** to perform the macro.

The worksheet appears as shown in Figure 13.15. As you can see, the macro has selected cells for the two values relative to the cell that was active when you began the performance: the title appears centered in cell D8 and the date appears in cell D9.

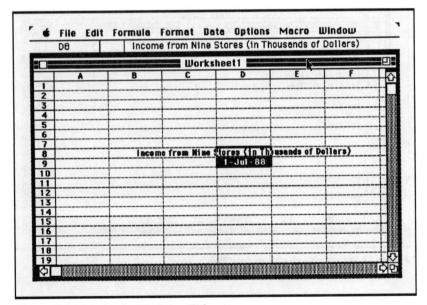

Figure 13.15: Testing the WorksheetTitle macro

*S*aving the Macro Sheet

You can, of course, use this same macro sheet for developing many more macro tools like the ones you have created in this chapter. In order to retain these tools for future use, you must save the sheet on disk. Then you only have to open the macro sheet back onto the desktop whenever you want to use your collection of macros.

Perform these steps to save the macro sheet:

1. Pull down the File menu and select the Save As command.

2. Enter the text **Macro Tools** as the name of the macro sheet.

3. Use the Drive and Disk buttons, if necessary, to activate and install the disk on which you want to save the macro sheet.

4. Click the OK button to complete the operation.

Finally, you can now use the Run command to examine a list of the macros that are available on the desktop.

*U*sing the Run Command

Pull down the Macro menu and select the Run command. The resulting dialog box appears in Figure 13.16. As you can see, Excel presents a list of the three macros stored in the Macro Tools sheet. (The names of these macros appear as external references.) At the left of each macro name you can see the Option-⌘ key that you have established for performing the macro.

You can use this list simply as a reminder of the available macro tools. Alternatively, you can actually run a macro directly from the list. To run a macro from the Run command, perform these steps:

1. Pull down the Macro menu and select the Run command.

2. Select the macro that you want to perform.

3. Click OK to initiate the macro performance.

*I*deas for Additional Macros

With this much knowledge about macros, you can create a considerable collection of valuable tools for use on the Excel desktop. Here

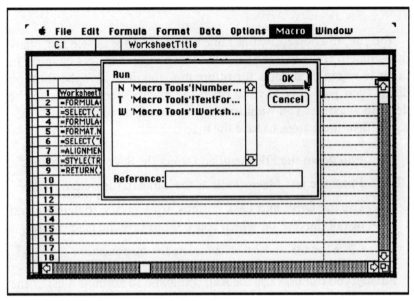

Figure 13.16: The Run command's dialog box

are a few ideas for macro projects that you might want to work on as
additional exercises:

- Create a macro that enters a series of row labels and column
  labels for a particular worksheet table and then formats
  the labels appropriately.

- Use the Recorder to build a charting macro—specifically, a
  program that creates a chart from the rows of a selected worksheet table. As you record the macro, use the Paste Special
  command (following the steps outlined in Chapter 9) to
  ensure that the chart's data series will correspond to rows of
  worksheet data, regardless of the shape of the data table.

- Develop a collection of macro tools that will help you perform the essential database operations. These operations
  include establishing a database range, establishing a range of
  criteria, and invoking commands such as Extract and Sort.

As you perform these and other experiments with macros, you will
inevitably expand your understanding and appreciation of Microsoft
Excel. You will also continue to improve your own skills in Excel's
desktop environment.

Index

!, as separator in SERIES
    function, 191
" ", for enclosing function
    arguments, 263
#, in numeric formats, 71–72
$ (dollar sign)
    for absolute cell references, 90,
    95
    for currency formats, 71
( ) (parentheses)
    for changing standard order of
        operations, 91, 127
    for function arguments, 96, 127
* operator, 74
+ operator, 74
,, as argument separator, 118, 266
− operator, 74
..., in menu options, 26
/ operator, 74
<, 241, 253
< =, 241, 253
< >, 253
=, 75, 96, 253
>, 241, 253
> =, 241, 253
^ operator, 74
⌘-., 58
⌘-?, 24
⌘-A, 175
⌘-B, 251
⌘-C, 202
⌘-D, 77–78, 94–95
⌘-E, 229, 251
⌘-F, 229, 238–240
⌘-G, 43
⌘-I, 65
⌘-L, 230
⌘-N, 52, 154

⌘-P, 105, 157
⌘-Q, 23
⌘-R, 97
⌘-S, 63
⌘-T, 90, 93, 254
⌘-V, 113
⌘-X, 113

A

About Excel command, 23
About Excel dialog box, 25
Absolute Record command,
    283, 297–299
absolute references, 78, 89–95,
    298
action-equivalent functions,
    301
active cells, 39–41, 45–46
active document, 139
Add Arrow command,
    162–165
Add Legend command,
    144–145
addition (+), 74
Alignment command, 80–81
ALIGNMENT function, 291
and condition, 240
area charts, 139
arguments, 96
arithmetic operations, 74–75
arrows, as pointers in charts,
    162–165
Attach Text command,
    145–146
AVERAGE function, 16, 128,
    262

Axes command, 171–172
Axis command, 168, 172–173

B

background patterns, 169–171,
  175–178
Backspace key, 57, 211–212
bar charts, 15, 139
boldface type style, 80–81
borders, 76, 169–171
Bottom option, 144
Built-in functions, 95–99,
  128–129, 262–272

C

calculated field, 221
calculating salaries example,
  90–99
calculations, controlling order
  of, 91
cancel box, 58
Cancel button, 65
cancelling entries, 58
categories, 188–189, 193,
  201–209
category name, 188
CategoryRange argument, 192
cells
  activating, 40–42
  active, 39–41, 45–48
  introduction to, 6
  naming ranges, 114–116,
    232–234
  referencing, 11–12
  selecting ranges, 44–45
  selecting single, 40–42
Chart menu, 144
charts
  adding arrows to, 162–165
  adding legends, 143–145

adding text, 160–161
adding titles, 145
area, 139
bar, 15, 139
building from multiple
  worksheet ranges, 151–156,
  209–211
changing preferred format
  for, 141–142
column, 139
combination, 140
creating, 134–139
creating backgrounds,
  175–178
customizing, 142–149
defined, 6
exploding, 165–167
how Excel organizes, 186–197
line, 140
modifying, 167–178
opening empty windows,
  201–202, 204
opening without supporting
  document, 213–214
orientation of, 189–190,
  201–211
with Page Setup command,
  211–212
with Paste Special command,
  202–203, 206
pie, 9–10, 140
preferred format, 141–142
printing, 156–157
producing combination,
  179–183
saving, 149–150
scatter, 140
stacked bar, 15
stacked-column, 136, 142
types of, 139–140
using unattached text,
  161–162

Clear command, 251
close box, 32
closing worksheet, 106–108
column charts, 139
Column Width command,
    68–70
columns, 220
    adding labels, 66–67
    adjusting widths, 67–70
    entering numbers, 57–60
    inserting, 65
    selecting as ranges, 46–47
combination charts, 140,
    179–183
Combination command, 180
Combination command's
    dialog box, 182
Command key, 23, 152–153
Command key combinations.
    See individual ⌘ entries
command-equivalent
    functions, 291
commas (,), 118, 266
comparison criteria, 235–237,
    240–243
computed criteria, 235,
    252–256
context-sensitive help, 24–25
Copy command, 112–113,
    201–202
copying formulas, 77–78,
    94–95
criteria, selection, 18
    changing selection, 269–270
    comparison, 235–237,
        240–243
    computed, 235, 252–256
    exact-match, 270–272
    multiple comparison, 240–243
criteria ranges, 220–221,
    234–237

cursor, 57
Cut command, 112–113

D

data
    copying, 112–113
    entering, 58–59
    extracting from database, 19
    moving, 112–113
    saving, 62–65
Data menu, 27
data points, 188–189
data series, 188–189, 193,
    201–209
database
    creating an extractable, 247,
        249–252
    defining, 18, 229–232
    defining criteria range,
        234–237
    definition of, 16
    deleting records, 256–260
    extracting data, 19
    and Find command, 237–240
    inserting records, 232–234
    introduction to database
        management, 220
    organizing, 221–223
    setting up, 246
    sorting, 223–229
database functions, built-in,
    262–272
database range, 220
DataRange argument, 192
date values
    entering from keyboard,
        122–124
    format for, 126–127
    performing arithmetic
        operations with, 127–129

and serial numbers, 124–125
DAVERAGE function, 262
DCOUNT function, 262
Define Name command, 115–116, 230–232, 238
Delete command, 229, 246, 256–260
Delete Legend command, 145
dependent documents, 150, 191, 213–214
descending sort, 11
desktop, opening chart onto, 213–214
dialog boxes, definition of, 26
division (/), 74
DMAX function, 262
DMIN function, 262
documents
  active, 139
  closing, 50–53
  dependent, 150–151, 191, 213–214
  opening, 50–53
  saving, 62–65
  supporting, 150–151, 191
dollar sign ($)
  for absolute cell references, 90, 95
  for currency formats, 71
double-clicking mouse, 21
down scroll arrow, 24
dragging mouse, 35
Drive button, 64
DSUM function, 263

E

edit box, 44
Edit menu, 26–27, 201
editing
  cancelling entries, 58
  correcting mistakes, 60–61

entering data, 58–59
  inserting columns, 65
  inserting rows, 79
  right-justifying, 59
Eject button, 64
ellipses (...), in menu options, 26
empty chart window, 201–202, 204
enlarging worksheet area, 105
enter box, 58–59
Enter key, 42, 59
equal sign (=), 75, 96, 253
exact-match criteria, 270–272
exclamation point (!), as separator in SERIES function, 191
exploding charts, 165–167
exponentiation, 74
external references, 191–192
Extract command, 229, 246–252
extract range, 247–249
extract table, 247, 249–252

F

field names, 17, 222
fields, 16–17, 220
File menu, 26
files, 62–65, 84–85
Fill Down command, 76–78, 112–113, 120
Fill Right command, 97, 112–113, 120
Find command, 229, 237–240, 246
Fit to Page option, 211
Format menu, 27, 167–178
formula bar, 57–62
FORMULA function, 301
Formula menu, 27

formulas
  copying, 77–78, 94–95
  copying two at once, 120
  creating, 74–75
  creating by pointing, 75–77
  definition of, 8–9
  entering, 89–93
functions
  AVERAGE, 16, 128, 262
  built-in, 95–99
  command-equivalent, 291
  DAVERAGE, 262
  DCOUNT, 262
  definition of, 16
  DMAX, 262
  DMIN, 262
  DSUM, 263
  FORMULA, 301
  HLOOKUP, 117–119, 128
  LOOKUP, 117–119, 128
  NOW, 127–129
  RETURN, 291
  SELECT, 301
  SERIES, 177, 190–197
  STDEV, 16
  STYLE, 291
  SUM, 16, 95–99, 128
  VAR, 16
  VLOOKUP, 117

G

Gallery menu, 139–142, 154, 180
Goto command, 43
gray text in menu options, 25–26
greater than or equal to sign ($>=$), 241, 253
greater than sign ($>$), 241, 253
gridlines, 171–175

H

help, getting, 23–25
Hidden windows, 52–54
HLOOKUP function, 117
horizontal gridlines, 173–174

I

icon, 21
inequality symbols, 241, 253
Insert command, 65, 233
inserting records, 232–234
integer value, 263
italic type style, 80–81

J

justifying text, 80–81

K

keyboard, using, 22, 42
keys, 224

L

labels
  adding, 66–67
  changing, 194–197
  fixing broken, 178
  in SERIES function, 192
Legend command, 168
legends, 143–145, 194–197
less than or equal to sign ($<=$), 241, 253
less than sign ($<$), 241, 253
line charts, 140
linked worksheets, 138
list box, 44
localized scrolling, 34, 36–37
logical value, 252

LOOKUP function, 117–119, 128
lookup table, 20, 114

M

Macro menu, 27
Macro Recorder, 278, 280, 282–286, 289
macro sheets, 6, 278–280, 290–291, 303
macros
  command equivalent function, 291
  creating, 285–293
  definition of, 278
  entering an Option ⌘ key for, 285–286
  ideas for additional, 303–304
  naming, 284–285
  preparing worksheet for, 280–282
  saving, 303
  testing, 292–293
  tools using, 278–279, 294–303
magnifying glass icon, 105
Main Chart Axis command, 180
main chart type, 179–180
Main Chart Type command, 180
Major Grid Lines option, 171, 207
marquee border, 76
menus
  Chart, 144
  Edit, 26–27, 201
  File, 26
  Format, 27, 167–178
  Formula, 27
  Gallery, 139–142, 154, 180
  Macro, 27

Options, 27
pull-down, 22
use of gray text in, 25–26, 112
viewing, 21–22
worksheet, 26–27
mistakes, correcting, 60–61
mixed references, 95
mouse, 21–22
  and activating cells, 40–42
  and command key, 152–153
  double-clicking, 21
  dragging, 35
mouse pointer, 22
multiple comparison criteria, 240–243
multiplication (*), 74

N

naming macros, 284–285
New command, 50–52, 154, 201–202, 204, 279
noncontiguous ranges, 151–153
not equal to sign (< >), 253
NOW function, 127–129
Number command, 71–72, 120, 222
number sign (#), 71–72
NumberFormatter macro, 294–296
numbers
  calculating totals, 8–9
  displaying, 14
  entering a column of, 57–60
  formatting, 70–74, 78–79
  rounding off, 14

O

on-line help, 23
Open command, 84
Open command dialog box, 85

operands, 74–75, 91
Option-⌘ key, 283–287
Option-⌘-N, 294
Options menu, 27
ordered pairs, 140
orientation of charts, 189–190,
    201–211
Overlay Chart Axis command,
    180
Overlay Chart command,
    180–182
Overlay Chart Type command,
    180

P

Page Preview option, 105
Page Setup command,
    102–104, 211–212
panes, dividing desktop
    window into, 121–122
parentheses ( )
  for changing standard order
    of operations, 91, 127
  for function arguments, 96,
    127
Paste command, 112–113
Paste Function command,
    96–98, 265
Paste Name command, 116,
    265
Paste Special command,
    201–209
Patterns command, 168,
    169–171, 177
personal finances example,
    8–14
pie charts, 9–10, 140, 165–167
Pie command, 154–156
preferred chart format,
    141–142

Print command, 82, 104–105,
    157
printing charts, 156–157
printing sideways, 211–212
printing worksheets, 81–82,
    104–106
pull-down menus, 22

Q

Quit command, 23
quotation marks (" "), for
    enclosing function
    arguments, 263

R

ranges, naming, 114–116, 232
Record command, 282–284
records
  definition of, 17, 220
  finding, 237–243
  inserting, 232–234
  sorting, 223–227
Reference command, 90, 93,
    254
references to cells, 11–12. *See
    also* absolute references;
    relative references
relational operators, 241, 253
Relative Record command,
    283, 297–299
relative references, 78, 89–95,
    298–299
RETURN function, 291
Return key, 59
right-justifying records, 59
rows, 220
  adding labels, 66–67, 79
  inserting, 79
  selecting as ranges, 46–47
Run command, 282, 303–304

S

Save As command, 64,
  149–150
Save button, 65
Save command, 63
saving charts, 149–150
saving worksheets, 62–65
scalar dates, 125
scatter charts, 140
scientific worksheet example,
  14–15
Screen Size option, 211
scroll arrows, 33
scroll bars, 33
scroll boxes, 24, 33, 34–37
scrolling, 24, 34–39
Select Chart command, 175
SELECT function, 301
selection criteria, 234–237,
  269–270
serial numbers, 124–125
SERIES function, 177,
  190–197
series name, 188, 190, 194–197
Set Criteria command, 221,
  229–230
Set Database command, 220,
  229–232
Set Recorder command, 282
Shadow option, 175
Shift-Enter command, 42
Shift-Return command, 59
Shift-Tab command, 42, 59
Shift-⌘-F command, 238–240
Show Active Cell command,
  39–41
size box, 33
Sort command, 27, 221,
  224–229
sorting, 10–12, 223–229
split bars, 122–123

spreadsheet, definition of, 7
stacked bar chart, 15
stacked-column chart, 136, 142
Start Recorder command, 283,
  289
starting Excel, 20–23
statistical tables, building,
  264–269
STDEV function, 16
Stop Recorder command, 283,
  289
Style command, 80
STYLE function, 291
subtraction (−), 74
SUM function, 16, 128, 95–99
supporting documents, 150,
  191
supporting worksheets,
  178–179

T

Tab key, 42, 59
text
  adding to charts, 143–149,
    160–161
  attached, 145
  changing alignment of, 80–81
  changing background of,
    169–171
  changing style of, 80–81
  in light gray, 25–26, 112
  unattached, 145, 161–162
Text command, 148–149, 168,
  174
text value, 263
TextFormatter macro, 292–293
tick labels, 168
title bar, 32
Title macro, 294, 296–297,
  299-302

titles, for charts, 145–149
toggle, defined, 297

U

unattached text, 145, 161–162
Undo command, 27

V

VAR function, 16
vertical gridlines, 207
vertical line, blinking, 57
VLOOKUP function, 117

W

what-if operations, 12, 99–101
Window menu, 27, 52–53
windows
  closing, 50–53
  dividing with panes, 121–122
  elements of, 32–34
  expanding, 50–53
  hidden, 52–54
  moving, 48–50
  opening, 50–53
  selecting as ranges, 46–48
  sizing, 48–50
worksheet menus, 26–27
worksheets

basic skills, 85–88
building charts from multiple
  ranges in, 151–156, 209–211
cancelling entries, 58
closing, 106–108
defining database, 18
definition of, 6–7
developing macros for use
  with, 280–282
dividing into panes, 121–122
enlarging area of, 105
entering data, 58–59
expanding, 10–12
inserting data into, 65
linked, 138
naming ranges in, 114–116
opening additional, 50–52
opening from disk, 84–85
previewing, 105
printing, 81–82, 104–106
saving, 62–65
scrolling, 34–39
sorting, 10–12
supporting, 178–179
WorksheetTitle macro, 294,
  296–297, 299–302

Z

zoom box, 33, 50

SYBEX Computer Books
are different.

Here is why . . .

At SYBEX, each book is designed with you in mind. Every manuscript is carefully selected and supervised by our editors, who are themselves computer experts. We publish the best authors, whose technical expertise is matched by an ability to write clearly and to communicate effectively. Programs are thoroughly tested for accuracy by our technical staff. Our computerized production department goes to great lengths to make sure that each book is well-designed.

In the pursuit of timeliness, SYBEX has achieved many publishing firsts. SYBEX was among the first to integrate personal computers used by authors and staff into the publishing process. SYBEX was the first to publish books on the CP/M operating system, microprocessor interfacing techniques, word processing, and many more topics.

Expertise in computers and dedication to the highest quality product have made SYBEX a world leader in computer book publishing. Translated into fourteen languages, SYBEX books have helped millions of people around the world to get the most from their computers. We hope we have helped you, too.

For a complete catalog of our publications:

SYBEX, Inc. 2021 Challenger Drive, #100, Alameda, CA 94501
Tel: (415) 523-8233/(800) 227-2346   Telex: 336311
Fax: (415) 523-2373

Worksheets: Major Skills and Tools

Skill	Tool	Page
Activating a cell	Mouse, keyboard	40
Built-in functions	Paste Function command	95
Changing column widths	Mouse, Column Width command	67
Closing a worksheet	Mouse	53
Controlling the order of operations	Formula bar	91
Copying formulas	Fill Right, Fill Down commands	77
Copying two formulas at once	Fill Right, Fill Down commands	120
Cutting and pasting	Cut and Paste commands	112
Date arithmetic	NOW function	127
Dividing a window into panes	Mouse	121
Editing data or formulas	Formula bar	60
Entering date values	Keyboard, NOW function	122
Entering formulas	Formula bar	75
Entering numeric data	Formula bar	57
Entering text data	Formula bar	66
Formatting numbers	Number command	70
Formatting text	Style, Alignment commands	80
Formatting the printed page	Page Setup command	102
Inserting a column	Insert command	65
Inserting rows	Insert command	79
Lookup operations	LOOKUP function	117
Moving to a selected cell	Goto command	43
Naming a worksheet range	Define Name command	114
Opening a new worksheet	New command	52
Opening a worksheet file from disk	Open command	84
Printing a worksheet	Print command	81
Saving a worksheet	Save command	62
Scrolling, entire worksheet	Mouse, keyboard	37
Scrolling, localized	Mouse	34
Scrolling to the active cell	Show Active Cell command	39
Selecting a range of cells	Mouse	44
Selecting rows or columns	Mouse	46
Sizing a window	Mouse	49
Specifying relative or absolute references	Reference command	89
What-if experiments	Worksheet organization	99

Charts: Major Skills and Tools

Skill	Tool	Page
Adding a legend	Add Legend command	143
Adding a title	Attach Text command	145
Adding an arrow	Add Arrow command	162
Adding unattached text	Formula bar	161